E N G

CHILDREN

ENGAGING CHILDREN

Community and Chaos in the Lives of Young Literacy Learners

JoBeth Allen
Barbara Michalove
Betty Shockley

Heinemann
Portsmouth, NH

Heinemann
A division of Reed Publishing (USA) Inc.
361 Hanover Street
Portsmouth, NH 03801-3912
Offices and agents throughout the world

The authors and publisher wish to thank the following for permission to reprint previously published material appearing in this book:

Figures 26-3 and 26-4: "My Dinosaur's Day at the Park" by Elizabeth Winthrop. Copyright © 1979 by Elizabeth Winthrop. Reprinted by permission of the author.

Every effort has been made to contact the copyright holders and the children and their parents for permission to reprint borrowed material. We regret any oversights that may have occurred and would be happy to rectify them in future printings of this work.

Library of Congress Cataloging-in-Publication Data
Allen, JoBeth.
Engaging children : Community and chaos in the lives of young literacy learners / JoBeth Allen, Barbara Michalove, Betty Shockley,
p. cm.
Includes bibliographical references (p.).
ISBN 0-435-08767-3
1. Socially handicapped children—Education—Language arts. 2. Language experience approach in education—Georgia. 3. Reading (Elementary)—Georgia—Language experience approach. 4. Socially handicapped children—Georgia—Biography. I. Michalove, Barbara. II. Shockley, Betty. III. Title.
LC4085.A45 1993 93-14853
371.96'7'09758—dc20 CIP

Front-cover art: "Discovering Choices" by Brenda Joysmith.
Copyright © Joysmith Studios, Emeryville, California.
Cover design by Jenny Jensen Greenleaf.
Printed on acid-free paper in the United States of America.
93 94 95 96 97 10 9 8 7 6 5 4 3 2 1

CONTENTS

SECTION FOUR
Shannon

SECTION FIVE
Reggie

SECTION SIX
Ricky

SECTION SEVEN
Lee

SECTION EIGHT

Engagement, Community, and Stability

ACKNOWLEDGMENTS

We thank the children who taught us. We learned more from Joseph, Jeremiah, Shannon, Ricky, Reggie, and Lee than they did from us; they were patient and helpful throughout the study in talking with us, sharing their reading and writing and at times their very lives. In addition to our school children, we thank our home children: Carly and Jamie Shockley, Jenny Anglin, and Rachel, Luke, and Paul Allen. Our insights and emotions as their mothers many times illuminated our understanding of other children, other parents.

We thank the families who shared their children with us. They trusted us to tell their children's stories. We thank our own families, especially our husbands Skip Shockley, Clyde Anglin, and Lew Allen, for believing that these stories were important enough for us to devote several years to the telling, and for supporting us with their time and genuine interest.

We thank our Walnut Street School family. Many educators supported our inquiry through various forms of collaboration. Special gratitude goes to the following teaching aides, administrators, secretary, and resource and homeroom teachers: Sandy Balistieri, Sharon Denero, Alice Eaves, Martha Elder, Sherrie Gibney, Kay Hales, Mary Lynn Lane, Felicia McHargue, Patricia Brown, Robin Osborne, Adaline Royce, Peggy Thaxton, Frances Ward, Margie Weiderhold, and Susan Willis. Michelle Garrett not only helped color-code the data, she substituted in Betty's and Barbara's rooms, allowing them a half hour weekly to meet with JoBeth to analyze data.

We thank our colleagues who reviewed the book. Yahaya Bello provided the critical perspectives of race and class that we requested to examine these issues from afar, to help us stand back from the people and relationships we knew intimately, to "make the familiar strange." Teacher Jane Holland provided local perspective, reading carefully for accurate representation of district and community issues. At Heinemann, both Philippa Stratton and Nancy Sheridan provided thoughtful insights. The comments of all these readers were invaluable in revising the manuscript, and our thinking.

We thank other professional colleagues. Joel Taxel, editor of *The New Advocate*, donated countless books to our classrooms. Judith Preissle Goetz and Lee Galda offered valuable methodological advice. Emilie Paille, a colleague at Georgia State University, offered us her condo on Florida's beautiful Emerald Coast; we drafted nine chapters during that peaceful week. Anita Peck and Mandy Howard provided outstanding secretarial support. JoBeth's department of Language Education, and the College of Education as a whole, value both collaboration and naturalistic inquiry. Various aspects of the study were supported by grants from The University of Georgia Research Foundation, the Spencer Foundation, and the International Reading Association's Elva Knight Grant program.

We thank the many restaurants that literally sustained our inquiry. This is a heartfelt thank you and a recommendation to other researchers. Find places that you really look forward to going to at the end of long teaching days, that offer an ambiance of comfort and hospitality away from the work world. We were nurtured by Athens' cooks and waitresses (especially when they refilled tea and coffee for hours on end) at the Lumpkin Cafe, T-Bones, Trumps, the Grill, the Bluebird, the Last Resort, to name a few. We also have fond memories of several Florida spots, most especially the Lake Place. We recommend the crab cakes most highly!

Finally, we thank the authors of fine contemporary literature who nurtured our minds and hearts. You will find the names of many of them among the pseudonyms we selected for adults in the book. Many research meetings began or ended at favorite bookstores, including The Old Black Dog, Book Warehouse, Oxford Books, and Isis and Osiris. Nearly every research meeting included book talk (and often exchange), food, and children—both our own and the engaging children on the pages that follow. We found it to be a wonderful combination, so wonderful that we have begun a new study together.

INTRODUCTION

Engaging Children has three levels of meaning: how teachers are engaging children in genuine literacy, how the process of engaging in a literate community increases learning, and how truly engaging we found each child as we got to know him/her. In the fall of 1988 we began a longitudinal research project,[1] hoping to examine the effects of whole language instruction on the students teachers worry about the most. The six children we chose were not identified because of race or gender (five are African American males, one an African American female) but because as students they were experiencing extreme hardship. They were, we feared, being failed by the educational system. These were the students we worried about the most, the kids all teachers talk about at recess with a colleague, or at the dinner table with a spouse, saying, "I'm really worried about . . . " We share their stories out of true respect for them as learners and as people, a respect that grew as we came to know the children better.

This book is the story of what we learned. When the study began, our six focal children were in Betty's first-grade and Barbara's second-grade rooms; JoBeth was an invited co-researcher in both rooms. We followed the children closely through two years of school, and followed them from a distance their third year by interviewing their teachers. We collected information by observing each of our six focal children on a regular basis, interviewing them regularly about how they were becoming readers and writers, collecting their writing (including weekly pen pal letters with university students), and recording their reading. We met regularly to analyze our various data sources and to begin putting together portraits of these *Engaging Children*: children who are engaged by teachers in literacy learning, children who engage with texts and each other, and children who are themselves engaging.

The most compelling stories are the children's. You may wish to start by reading the six profiles, beginning with "Joseph in His Own Voice" (Chapter 2). You could then go back and read the classroom and research contexts in Chapters 1, 2, and 3. You may wish to know more about how the profiles were developed; in this case, be sure to read the appendices as they are referenced in Chapter 1. After reading the profiles you may want to ask yourself, "What important decisions were made that affected the success of these students?" Then compare your conclusions with the ones we draw in the final chapter, where we discuss decisions of teachers, policy makers, and the children themselves and the impact of these decisions.

Lucy Calkins (1991) has written: "The challenge we've taken on in establishing reading-writing workshops is not only to help children write well, but also to help them live well. The challenge of helping children write well—and live well—

1. Portions of this study were supported by the International Reading Association Elva Knight Research Grant, a Spencer Foundation Small Grant, and a University of Georgia Faculty Research Grant.

is bigger than any of us and bigger than any of our theories. It's a challenge that's big enough to live for" (pp. 3–4). That is our challenge as teachers. As researchers our challenge has been to document, reflect on, analyze, and share with you how these six children go about writing, reading, learning, and living.

Robert Coles wrote in his introduction to teacher/researcher Vivian Paley's (1990) *The Boy Who Would Be a Helicopter*:

> I hope that all of us who . . . meet [Paley], an inspired teacher, and her lively young students will remember how she chose to present this book to us, with the emphasis on faithfully rendered experience, so that generalizations and abstraction follow modestly. In an age when ambitious theorists strut across any stage they can find, assaulting us with pronouncements meant to advance careers, here is a teacher who lets life's complexities have their full dignity, who moves ever so gently and thoughtfully from observed life to carefully qualified comment. . . . (p. ix)

Our goal as researchers and writers is to approach the level of Vivian Paley. We leave it to our readers to decide if we have shared the complexities of these students' lives with full dignity and if our commentary is careful and qualified. If so, we think you will learn, as we have, from and about engaging children.

CONTEXTS FOR LEARNING

ONE

Studying the Students We Worry About

A Collaborative Investigation of Literacy Learning

The birth of the study

Nine elementary teachers (including Betty and Barbara) and one college teacher (JoBeth) sat in wickers and rockers on Barbara's screened porch. Children's books, basal teacher's manuals, state-mandated curriculum objectives, and books by teachers we admired, like Vivian Paley (1981) and Andrea Butler and Jan Turbill (1984), surrounded us. The piles were eclectic, even dissonant. Over the hum of the oscillating fan, each teacher shared plans for developing whole language learning environments when school resumed the next month. We had talked throughout the course about personal, curricular, and social implications of whole language instruction: How will the kids react? How can I teach the state objectives? How might I combine reading workshop and basal instruction? How will the other teachers feel if I'm doing something different? There was a building sense of excitement, with a palpable edge of anxiety.

First-grade teacher Helen Gillespie cut to the core issue: "How will we *know* that what we're doing is actually any better than what we've always done?" she asked.

Forming a research team

This was exactly the kind of question teachers at Walnut Street Elementary School had been asking of themselves for several years, as they concentrated their staff development efforts on reducing the risks of failure for their high-risk population. Through their school-based staff development process (Gibney, 1988), they had identified areas that they felt would enhance the chances of success for all students. They had worked with students on improving their self-concepts by encouraging positive self-talk; they had radically lowered their retention rates, and had participated in peer coaching sessions to help each other reach self-determined teaching goals. Now they felt it was time to tackle the curriculum.

Teachers felt that in spite of efforts to help all children be successful in the school's curriculum, many children were not succeeding to their fullest potential.

If they could not make the child fit the curriculum, maybe they could work from the other direction and make the curriculum more appropriate for the child. They felt the prime culprit was the inflexibility and inappropriateness of the reading and language arts textbook curriculum, especially as commonly practiced in the district: early ability grouping, basal-determined promotional guidelines, sequenced skills instruction, and little opportunity for reading and writing for meaningful purposes.

Walnut Street School, through their partnership with The University of Georgia's Program for School Improvement (Allen & Glickman, 1992), asked JoBeth to work with them to explore ways to develop language arts curricula appropriate for all students, especially those who had not been successful in the textbook-dominated curriculum. The school made a commitment to learn about whole language instruction in a variety of ways, and to research any innovations that might occur. As negotiations continued in establishing a long-term working relationship, it became clear that we shared some beliefs about how the changes should be studied:

1. Comparative studies (i.e., basal versus whole language) were divisive as well as nearly impossible to do meaningfully and accurately (Bond & Dykstra, 1967; McGee & Lomax, 1990).
2. We didn't need more tests, nor did we feel that currently mandated standardized tests (Iowa Test of Basic Skills, Cogat, Georgia Criterion Referenced Test) told a very complete story.
3. Our focus should be students who were locally and nationally labeled "at risk," although we rejected the label.

As we explored our beliefs, needs, and expectations, it became evident that a qualitative study would be most appropriate. JoBeth preferred a collaborative study (Allen & Carr, 1989; Carr & Allen, 1988), hoping that one or more teachers would invite her as a fellow researcher to study questions of mutual interest. Helen's question led to the initial research agenda: What are the effects of whole language instruction on the children we worry about most? The group on the porch, teachers from Walnut Street who had taken a summer course to explore a whole language philosophy, began talking about how they might study changes they planned to make in their classrooms the following year. Clearly, teachers would need to become researchers in their own classrooms.

When teachers from the summer course shared their philosophies and their plans with interested faculty during the first weekly meeting in a year-long whole language seminar, JoBeth issued an invitation. Teachers were encouraged to observe and document the literacy development of one or more students that they were particularly worried about. We would use these profiles of learners to share information about literacy learning with other teachers within the school. Anyone who was interested in extending this observation into a research project was invited to be a member of a research team. JoBeth also asked if anyone would be interested in collaborative research with her.

Seven teachers and JoBeth formed the Walnut Street Research Team, which met once or twice a month throughout the first year of the study. Betty Shockley (first grade) and Barbara Michalove (second grade) invited JoBeth to study with them in their classrooms.[2] The research team worked together all year, not because we were paid (we were not), or because someone was doing doctoral research (no one was at that point), or because we just liked each other (although we did). We worked together as a community of learners (Allen, Combs, Hendricks, Nash, & Wilson, 1988) because we had very important questions driving our teaching and thinking, and this seemed like one way of investigating those questions with other experts interested in the same issues.

The research process

We spent the first month determining which children we would study. We did not approve of the popular "at-risk" jargon (see Allen, 1989). We felt that labeling children was detrimental and an ineffective way to meet their needs. Yet we were acutely aware that there were multiple factors in the lives of some of our children that mitigated against school success. We decided to use a term from the practical knowledge of teachers, and study the children we were *particularly* "worried about." (Teachers, like parents, worry about *all* of their kids.)

After a few days of school each teacher made a list of students she was worried about, for whatever reason. Many of the children had repeated one or more grades, received special services, had recognizable social or emotional problems, or had troubled family situations. The lists were quite long in both classrooms. From this pool Betty, Barbara, and JoBeth began taking notes on various aspects of each child, observing both academic and social behaviors and talking with previous teachers. By the end of the month, we had identified three focal children in each class that we were most worried about.

We continued by observing and interacting with our focal children. We began data analysis immediately, which prompted us to include additional sources of information, based on our weekly discussions of what we were learning. We interviewed the children quarterly, collected writing and reading samples, and observed and interviewed in resource (special education and Chapter 1) classrooms. Appendix A contains an extended explanation of both data gathering and data analysis.

The study was designed to be longitudinal. The school made a commitment to place our three first-grade and three second-grade focal children in whole language classrooms throughout their elementary school years. There was at least one teacher moving toward whole language instruction at each grade level, and some of these teachers indicated an interest in pursuing the collaborative research. We were enthusiastic about documenting the long-term effects of whole language instruction, of a stable instructional philosophy and familiar learning structures, on children whose early school experiences had been less than successful.

The study was simple in design, but the real world of schooling is not always stable. A beloved teacher became seriously ill and had to resign midyear. The community expanded, built new elementary schools, and redrew the school attendance boundaries. Four of our children left the security of an old school for

2. Marsha West, fifth-grade teacher, also collaborated on the first year of the study; then she became a media specialist at another school. Her research is included in *The Reading Teacher* article "I'm Really Worried About Joseph," March 1991.

the unsettling promise of a new one. One parent moved every three months. The state tried to ensure a quality education by testing that forced third graders who didn't meet criteria to repeat third grade. Therefore, our simple research design of following the children in whole language classrooms throughout elementary school became impossible. Instead, we followed the children through various communities and unforeseen chaos to document what really happens in children's lives, not just what we as educators would wish or design for them. To help the reader follow the unpredictable paths of the children's lives we have included the chart shown in Figure 1-1 (see also Appendix B).

Researcher beliefs

We did not begin our research as blank slates. We believed, from everything we had read and from our collective teaching experiences, in the principles of whole language instruction. We believed, with Erickson (1984), that research such as ours "should be considered a deliberate inquiry process guided by a point of view, rather than a reporting process guided by a standard technique or . . . a totally intuitive process that does not involve reflection" (p. 51).

Why would we expect whole language instruction to be particularly effective for the students we worry about? Why did we think that the dependable structures of daily reading and writing workshops (Hansen, 1987), multiple daily teacher read alouds, big book shared readings, and extensive opportunities for meaningful reading and writing would improve the chances for literacy learning? We made explicit our shared assumptions, based both on our readings and on our own observations and analyses; many of them grow out of the Vygotskian theory of knowledge as socially constructed. Betty, Barbara, and JoBeth believed:

1. During the critical period of emergent literacy, most children learn best by going from whole to part. We assumed that many of the children at Walnut Street School had extensive verbal and experiential interactions at home, but not around such literacy events as bedtime stories, repeated storybook readings, interactive writing times, etc. Providing the whole of these experiences before digging into the parts of sound, letter, and word analysis is essential.
2. Children who observe literate others develop a desire to be members of this "literacy club" (Smith, 1988a), just as children who observe language users want to learn to talk. Children who have had limited positive associations with literacy need to be around adults who "model joyous literacy" (Holdaway, 1979).
3. All real learning must make sense and be purposeful. The literacy opportunities at the core of our curriculum were designed to engage students in real reasons for reading and writing: reading self-selected books, reading to learn about a research topic, writing to share information, writing to express personal experiences and feelings, corresponding with university pen pals, and reading and writing just for the fun of it.
4. Children who "fail" in school have also been failed by the school. We wanted to create literate environments where students could take risks without risking failure. In such classrooms, all children would be equal, not

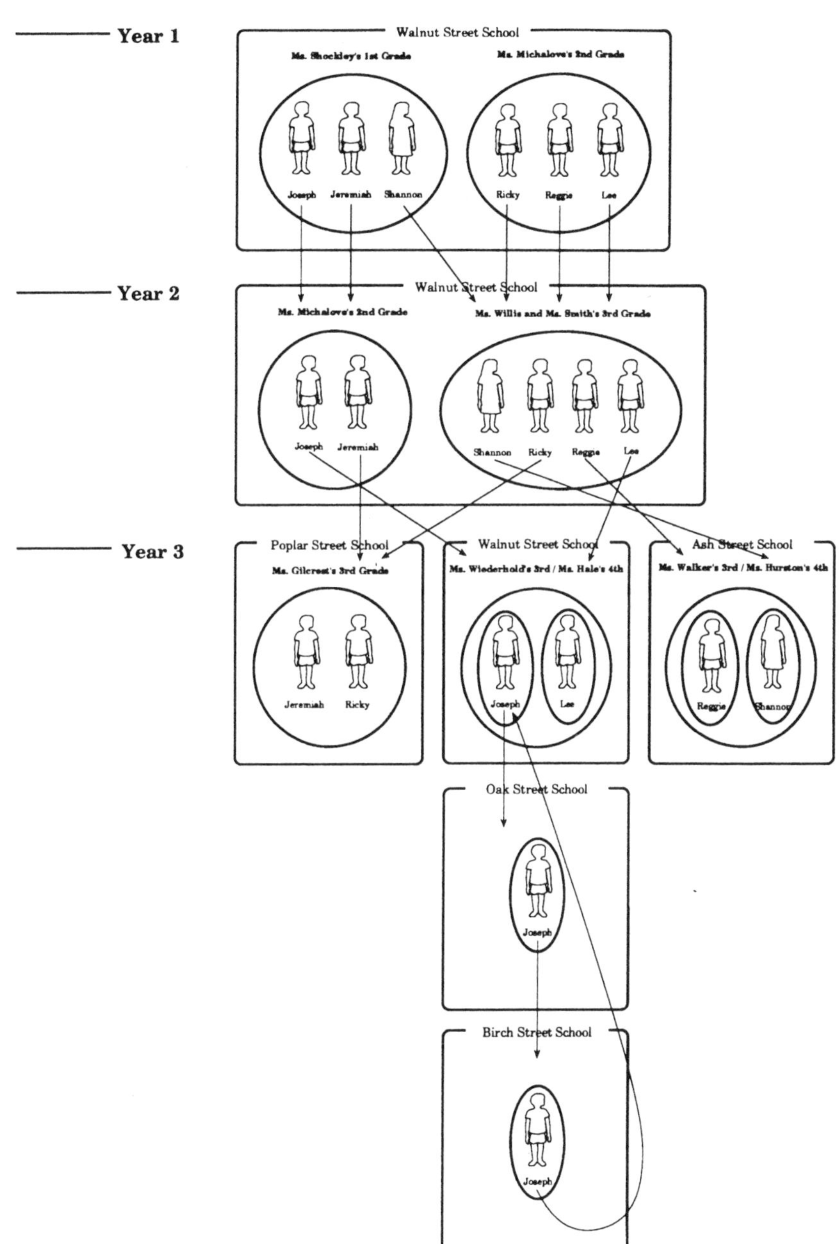

FIG. 1–1 *Six Focal Children, Three School Years*

in what they already knew, but in what they could learn. We suspected that some of our children would have to relearn risk taking because of the failure they had already experienced as learners. All six of our focal children had been retained at least once.

5. Every child should have time to read, to write, to interact with peers, and to extend a learning activity to its natural, rather than a preordained, conclusion. We had studied developmental stages and the "gift of time," a phrase often synonymous with retention. We had also studied the statistics on retention and dropout rates: about half of all students who have been retained once don't graduate from high school; nearly 90 percent of students who have been retained more than once drop out of school. We felt that the gift of time should be given every day, not with extra years in school.
6. Developing responsibility for one's own learning is especially important for children who view themselves as failures. We emphasized real choices—what books will you read, how will you figure out unfamiliar words, what part will you share, what will you write about today, who will help you, which words might be spelled incorrectly, which story will you publish, what will you do when you get frustrated? We thought if children really took responsibility for their own learning and classroom behaviors, they would have fewer reasons to exhibit negative behavior, to rebel against a teacher's authority.
7. Students who do not view school as a positive, successful experience often do not feel they really belong in a particular class or even in the school as a whole. We believed that through our development of communities of readers and writers, everyone would experience that sense of belonging. Everyone would know s/he had something important to contribute; everyone would be both a teacher and a learner.

These beliefs, articulated one day during the first summer's extended data analysis sessions, fit solidly with the literature on whole language teaching. Our beliefs echoed or harmonized with Cambourne's (1988) seven conditions for literacy learning and Holdaway's (1984) elements of effective literacy environments, to name only two esteemed theorists. As widespread as these beliefs have become in the current literature, few studies have addressed the learners we were concerned with. We felt that we were asking important questions of ourselves, questions that whole language educators have been urged to address by Lisa Delpit (1986) and Maria de la Luz Reyes (1991) concerning the appropriateness of this instruction for all learners.

What we are learning

Each child had issues that seemed to almost define him or her as a person and a literacy learner that first year. For some children, these central issues remained the same, or became heightened in ensuing years; for others, the core issues changed subtly or substantially. These are the stories you will read in the rest of the book. We defined an *issue* as a recurring quality, behavior pattern, stated value, or concern that characterized a child in his/her own concept of self, as best we could ascertain that, and/or in our concept of that child. The following are the major issues we identified initially for each child.

Initial first graders

Joseph

- He was in charge, of himself and of others; he exhibited a strong sense of responsibility.
- He demanded justice and fairness.
- His school world and home world were in conflict with each other at times.

Jeremiah

- He had a passion for creating.
- He seemed to put himself at risk with both children and adults by his dependent, irritating behavior.

Shannon

- She was out of place, both at home and at school.
- She wavered constantly between confidence and self-doubt.
- She developed a strong sense of herself as an author.

Initial second graders

Reggie

- His friends were the most important thing to him.
- He was a tough guy.

Ricky

- He was withdrawn from everyone.
- He was not a risk taker.

Lee

- He persevered against discouraging odds.
- He was retarded—or was he?
- He was a member of the community.

We have puzzled about what to call the stories of these children's lives—is *stories* too informal, indicative of author invention; is *case studies* too formal, indicative of psychological inquiry? Perhaps we should avoid jargon again and simply describe what we did. We studied children; these are child studies. We have written them as portraits, which Sara Lawrence Lightfoot (1983) says are "defined by aesthetic, as well as empirical and analytic, dimensions" (p. 369). Each section begins with a self-portrait, the child in his or her own words. The next portrait is done by the child's first teacher, the next by the following year's teacher, and the final through the words of the third year's teacher. We see the same child from many perspectives, making it easier to note the uniformities as well as the divergences of their lives.

The portraits go beyond a mere record of literacy development. We examine the elements in each child's life that caused us to worry about these children the most in classes where we worried about many of the children. They were one or two years behind in school already; they were receiving services for mental retardation, remedial reading, and/or behavior problems; they had problematic lives outside of school; and/or they seemed unengaged by school literacy events. But we do not focus on these risk makers; rather, we focus on the students and their teachers as risk takers (Allen, 1989).

In addition to the individual portraits, we examined important themes that were common to these children's lives. These themes, which will be discussed more fully in the final chapter, include the following:

- *Engagement*, involving the paths to, and effects of, sustained and meaningful engagement with literacy; several of the children were not engaging with books and/or writing when we began our inquiry.
- *Community*, involving the impact of membership in a literate community, with its rights, roles, and responsibilities; several of the children initially were not seen by the class, or did not see themselves, as contributing members of the community.
- *Stability*, involving the classroom, school, home, school district, and state practices and policies that led either to stability or upheaval.

Organization of the book

The book is divided into eight sections. The first section which includes this first chapter, is a discussion of key elements that were studied and why we did the study. Chapters 2 and 3 include a description of Betty's and Barbara's classroom contexts and researcher perspectives. We describe our development as whole language teachers, our instructional decisions, and how the decisions affected our students. The next six sections include a thick description of the transactions observed. The final section develops themes and recommendations.

The sections profiling our six children are written in the following format:

- First, the child in his/her own voice, a profile of the child as a reader, writer, and learner developed entirely from the quarterly interviews (see Seidman, 1991, on this technique).
- Second, the child from Betty's (Joseph, Jeremiah, and Shannon) or Barbara's (Reggie, Ricky, and Lee) perspective, based on all data sources for the first year (see Appendix A).
- Third, the child from Barbara's or Susan's/Judy's perspective (Susan Willis, September–January; Judy Smith, January–June), based on all data sources for the second year of study.
- Fourth, the child from the third year's teacher's perspective, based on interviews with each child's teacher plus other available data sources (see Figure 1-1 and Appendix B).

We have learned a great deal, perhaps as much about the simplicity of our initial questions as about the children. We feel a tremendous responsibility to the children to share their lives with you in an honest and sympathetic way, in a way that gives you an understanding of them as members of their communities, as children buffeted by the upheaval of home and school, and above all, as truly engaging children.

TWO

Finding My Way with First-Grade Learners

Jeremiah claimed his best ideas just "slipped up in my mind." Nora decided to use the phrase "As the days went on" in her first-grade story because her "brain just went right to work!" I (Betty) can understand and appreciate both these insights because that's what it feels like for me as a teacher and now a classroom researcher. Some of my best ideas just seemed to "slip up in my mind," while some of my best decisions came from hard brain work. To implement a whole language philosophy in a basal-led district also required a combination of increased sensitivity and serious study. Learning to be a good "kid watcher" (Y. Goodman, 1988), understanding myself as a reader and writer, and risking new ways to do old things all came together and formed some wonderful surprises for me and my students. I've learned to design inquiry so that knowledge is constructed while the windows are left open to appreciate new views. Learning becomes a union of systematic analysis and surprise. At least that's what Jeremiah, Nora, and I think.

Sondra Perl and Nancy Wilson (1986) discovered in their study of six teachers that "how teachers teach writing, or probably anything else for that matter, is a function of who they are, what matters to them, what they bring with them into the classroom, and whom they met there." I would like to borrow their findings here for use as amended headings: "Who Am I," "What Matters," and "Decisions I Made." The children will tell their own stories for "Whom They Met There."

Who am I

First of all, I am not the best or most experienced whole language teacher in the world, but I don't apologize for that. In fact I'm really proud of the risks I've taken in order to grow and learn professionally. I recently read an interview of southern publishers in which Chuck Perry, publisher of Longstreet Press, stated: "I feel that to grow you need to walk near the edge, and if you walk near the edge you are going to fall sometimes. That's more fun to me than staying back. You don't get as good a view from there" (Griffith-Roberts, 1991). I wonder if that's what a fellow teacher had in mind when she found out I was going to teach first grade this new whole language way. She let me know that she would be there to pick me up when I fell on my face. Yes, broadening my views and walking near the edge were going to be risky, but I anticipated real joy in the process.

I really thought that being a whole language teacher would be fairly easy. My personal biography and my philosophy of learning supported such a move, and I was emotionally charged by the prospect of doing something I really believed in. Lucy Calkins (1991) expressed my biggest concern when she wrote, "All too often when we revise our classrooms, we do so in a piecemeal and timid fashion, adding a little of this and a little of that without asking whether the ideas fit together into an organic whole" (p. 128). I wanted to do it all—all at once. I soon found out that it's one thing to have a philosophy; it's another thing to bring those beliefs to life in a classroom setting. Such organic wholeness takes time to grow; you have to recognize the weeds before you can turn them into mulch.

After I graduated from the University of North Carolina at Chapel Hill in 1973, I became a social worker in Raleigh. I was in awe of the families I worked with who faced enormous daily challenges. Their strength and spirit continue to nourish and instruct me. A few years later, when I was working at home as a personal "social worker" to my own two children, I learned firsthand the power of parenting. I was the kindergarten mom who couldn't just walk her son to the door and say one goodbye. I hugged him, kissed him, gave him more unnecessary words of encouragement, finally walked away, and then returned for a few more quick checks. Soon I realized that schooling provided the truest form of social work possible. So I decided to become a teacher.

When I was preparing for teacher certification, I was fortunate to have a four-year-old daughter at home. I would go to the university and listen to an instructor tell me things like how many zillions of times children had to see a word before they could remember it, and then I'd return home to welcoming invented messages written by a preschooled hand. By her natural attempts to become literate, Carly kept me questioning. Lee Galda, through her teaching and sharing of books like *What Did I Write?* by Marie Clay, offered me some much needed instructional balance.

When my daughter entered kindergarten the next fall, she was already reading. Because of this she was marched through the basal series double time. I'll never forget the night I found her crying in bed saying, "If kindergarten is this hard, I'll never make it to college!" A quick check into her classroom routines gave me a reason for her trauma. She was officially working in the third preprimer because there was an unwritten rule in her school that kindergartners could not go on to the primer until first grade. She was, however, being taught isolated skills from higher level books. Carly was particularly upset that evening because she couldn't remember when to change the "y" to "i" before adding "es"!

I have learned from many children, not just my own. You have to be open to their kind of teaching, however, or it gets by you. Children don't stand in front of you and say, "This is what you must learn from me now and I will test you on it tomorrow." They bring you their lives and ask you to learn who they really are. Remember the song from the TV show "Cheers"? "Sometimes you want to go where everybody knows your name." I want to know my young learners as people in order to reduce as much as possible the assumptions I make as an interpreter of their learning. Again, Lucy Calkins (1991) gets to the real heart of the matter: "When we know the particulars of a human being's story we are called out of ourselves to care" (p. 16).

I taught kindergarten for five years, and I know I learned more from those youngsters than they did from me. One of the most important things I learned was that children could indeed be trusted to take responsibility for their own learning. When the adult logic of teaching was transposed with the logic by which children learn, "blessed moments" happened (Bissex, 1980). I learned that children could "read" without reading like grown-ups, and they certainly could represent their feelings on paper before they mastered sound-symbol relationships.

Then I moved to first grade. I should have known such a change wasn't going to be as simple as turning left and continuing to the end of the hall. The other first-grade teachers seemed to know how you "did" first grade. My goal to create a first-grade classroom that was more of a natural step from kindergarten required a giant leap of faith. I'd entertained the idea of moving to first grade for some time. Honestly, I was tired of people saying, "You can do that kind of thing in kindergarten but not in first grade. In first grade you *have* to work in the basals every day or you'll never cover it all. The students won't be where they need to be in order to do well on the standardized tests and they won't meet promotion guidelines if you don't." In this approach time meant pages, and pages meant progress.

What matters

What matters is that the students and I get to decide what matters in our classroom. But can we really do that? The school board says it knows what's most important for us to be doing. The central office people have their objectives. Each school administrator has his or her approach. Individual schools have developed their translations of acceptable practices. Each grade level has its goals. Finally, individual classrooms filled with individual needs emerge, if they can, out of all the clutter. And this has been only a local scenario. It's hard to even conceptualize the limits of a national agenda.

So what to do? All of the above expect you to deliver, and deliverance has most traditionally come in the form of test scores. I was pleased that my students' test scores were good at the end of that first year of whole language instruction.

Understanding what I see children do matters to me. I knew I didn't know enough about the language of literacy. I felt I was finally seeing real learning, but I didn't know how to explain it, how to make it real for others. I saw children writing letter-like configurations, letters of the alphabet listed in no apparent order and with no phonemic correlation to what they said they were trying to communicate. I was intrigued by the child who wrote a four-page retelling of "Little Red Riding Hood" using only the letters in his first name. How could I tell others who spoke the language of readiness skills or "basaleze" what I was seeing and expect any credibility? I really felt handicapped. By reading and rereading the works of Elizabeth Sulzby, Susan Sowers, Lucy Calkins, Nancie Atwell, Don Graves, Jerome Harste, Regie Routman, Ken and Yetta Goodman, Vivian Paley, Frank Smith, Marie Clay and others, I was able to get some answers. I learned to record my observations of children in the language of emergent literacy. Now my documentations reflect a shared professional vocabulary. I know how to communicate with others about what I'm seeing and I have a frame of reference for decision making.

Learning about children's literature was not only important but fun. Of course I had read trade books to my classes in the past, but never to the degree I intended to with this new focus. I had never even had a children's literature course. The children and I learned together. I learned the most by doing author studies. We started with Donald Crews and other favorites, and at times included authors from our basal series. James Marshall was our first basal-connected author study. We learned about him as a writer and a person. Each day I would read aloud or we would read together one of his "real" books or a story he had written for the basals; there were several in the many basal levels we kept in our room. In this way we learned the breadth of an author's work and we could make comparisons and associations between trade book and basal stories. We did not limit our studies to one author each week; we pursued our friendship with an author as long as it remained interesting and there were more stories.

Getting books in my classroom and keeping them there was very important. I went to yard sales on Saturday mornings and bought children's books for nickels and dimes. I borrowed from the bookshelves in my own children's rooms and spent way too much of my own money. The school also periodically funded some of my efforts. Now I'm on a self-imposed book diet. I'm always tempted by new publications and I still succumb too often for my teacher's budget, but I try to rely mostly on the additions gained from book club bonus points. Our school media specialist is very helpful, but it is not fair for me to check out books and keep them in my room all year.

Having my own classroom library—a ready resource—has really mattered to all of us. It was critical that the children be able to return to their books over and over again. They needed to be able to reread the books they could read fluently, and they needed the time to work on reading new and not-so-familiar texts. The books, like the time to read them, had to be a dependable component of the classroom. I can now turn my students over to authors with real confidence.

It was important to me that books and the enjoyment of reading become a focus at school and at home. I wanted my students and their families to have expanded access to the books at school. Our class library books became home books as well as school books, with children freely checking them out each day.

Parents wanted their children to have homework. The presence of homework in first grade seemed to carry some sort of coming-of-age message for the students also. On the first day of school they wanted to know what their homework was going to be. It took some trial and error to design a homework plan that was in line with our daily classroom practices. The year Joseph and Shannon and Jeremiah were in my classroom we had what we called "Trade a Book" time. After reading workshop each day, the children would return to their seats with the book they had enjoyed reading the most. In turn, they would each do a brief book talk about their book and ask if anyone would like to have it to take home for home reading that night. I would write down their choices so I would have a record of their reading preferences.

Over the last couple of years we have improved on this plan. Reading is now joined to its complements—writing, speaking, and listening—and the response has been amazing. At the end of reading workshop each day, the students bring their take-home book to our reading circle and tell me the title of their choice. I write the student's name and his book choice in our record log, and then the student puts the book and his reading journal in a large ziplock bag to take home. Parents know to plan for a reading time with their child each night, and the response journal provides an opportunity for them to talk together about the book they've shared.

These dialogic journals have given me a special opportunity to share information about reading. Parents tell me about things they've noticed about their children as readers and I can offer advice about how to support their young readers. During our first open house and in a letter, I explain that reading with their children should be a relaxed and comfortable time. I suggest that they ask the child if she wants to read the book by herself or if she'd rather the parent do the reading. An invitation is also offered to the parents to talk about the books with their children and to compose a written response together or support the children in their efforts to respond on their own. This simple but dependable and meaningful homework plan makes real and personal connections between home and school. Every family has responded, and several excerpts from these journals are included in Figure 2–1.

Being a professional teacher matters to me. I have pride in my profession. I believe excellent teachers are the key to excellent educations. I also believe that teachers are most effective when they have a choice about what and how they teach.

Everything I do at school with children matters. It matters a lot. If I'm well prepared by understanding the changing needs of each child, it matters. If I'm not, it matters. What we might think of as the little things matter too. I'm sure that given all the opportunities to learn in my classroom, what really mattered most to my students today was that the rabbit came to visit from our fifth-grade buddy class and pooped on the rug!

Decisions I made

What about reading and writing?

Reading and writing workshops have been a part of every day since I started teaching first grade. We usually begin our workshops with a shared reading experience that is followed by a mini-lesson, and then the students choose their topics or their books and work independently until we stop for a sharing or response period.

The children amaze me with the depth of their engagement. It is not uncommon for students to write or read for thirty or forty minutes at a time and complain when it is time to stop. When I scheduled reading workshop just before lunch, the children solved the dilemma of such an interruption by taking their books with them. Some children propped larger books up in front of them while they ate, others waited until they were through eating to look at theirs, but books were central to much lunch table talk.

Writing has become such an integral part of our lives that children tell of putting paper and pencil beside their bed so they can write down "their good ideas." When I apologized to a parent for not communicating with her as well as I had hoped to, she quickly put me at ease: "You don't need to write me notes; success is written all over the children's faces. Delia wants to read and write all the time."

What I decided was, there's really not much difference between what adult readers and writers need and what child readers and writers need. We need uninterrupted time, ready access to a wide variety of quality literature, the right to choose what we read, and friends to share their interpretations and to challenge ours. How do I get uninterrupted time to read and write? I have to make it. As an adult I can structure such times in my own life, but often children can't unless we help them. Part of my role as a teacher is to guarantee them such times. I've

Mrs Shockly 9-19-91
choose Old MacDonald
as her reading for last night.
She started out singing the song
Old MacDonald until I sit
down with and pointed it out
word for word but she did good.
Thank you.

9-20-91
You may want to let
do the book "her way" first
then together you could
get her to point with you
to the words as you
reread the story

9-25-91
In the book the House,
read the story to her father
and he was very pleased at
the fact that she is in the
1st grade and reading books.
and doing so well.
Thank you.

I'm very pleased with her
progress too. I know it makes
her feel good about her reading
when you celebrate her
accomplishments with her.

9-30-91
In the story I Can Fly
did very good. Her
reading was very good and
Maybe she's ready to move on
to a few more words. I mean a book
with a few more words. If you think
so also.
Thank you

I agree. She can read
more difficult books but
like everybody, young readers
enjoy reading things that
are easy for them too.

10-2-91
Mrs Shockly,
In the story of the Balloon
Performance. seem to
have some problems with many of
the words. Maybe she got a story
with to many difficult words
for her right now. But still I
enjoyed her Thank you
reading.

This is probably an example of
one of those times
chose a book that it would
be best for you just to
read to her. When you get
ready to read together

continued next page

FIG. 2–1 *Home-School Journal Excerpts*

each night, you might
begin by asking —
Do you want to read your
book to me or do you
want me to read to you?
Sometimes after you read
even a more difficult book
she may ask to read it
after you. Let her be
the leader. One of the
most important things
about sharing books
together is talking about
them together. Thanks

10-3-91
— Was very excited
about the books she chose to
read to me, so excited she
read them over and over
again. And I was so
Pleased. Maybe last night
she did want me to read the
story to her I don't know but I
will ask her from now on. Because she was a little upset
that she didn't know a lot of
the words And I don't ever want
her to feel pressured.
Thanks.

FIG. 2–1 *Home-School Journal Excerpts (continued)*

learned that "the spirit and intimacy of the workshop are much more important than the structures: the mini-lessons, workshops, and share meetings we put together like so many legos. And that spirit, that intimacy comes from sharing bits of life" (Calkins, 1991, p. 20), including my own.

I decided to make my literacy explicit for my students. From the beginning of this study I've kept a writing tablet in my purse—what Lucy Calkins now calls a "writer's notebook." I make a point to use it in front of my students, even if it means stopping in the middle of a discussion to write something. I also keep a book in my purse (just how big is this purse?) and I tell my students that even though I make time to read every night before bed, there are also other times that often present themselves quite unexpectedly, and I want to be prepared. Reading and writing are an everyday part of my life, and I think it's important that my students know it. Many times I've used examples from my own reading as mini-lessons for reading or writing workshops. I've summarized suspense novels, shared lead sentences, and talked about reasons for abandoning choices.

I am a "joyfully literate" (Holdaway, 1979) adult. The students will catch me reading when they come into school in the mornings or when they come back from a specialist's class. They know what I'm reading and notice when I get a new book. They also know I get new books for the class as well as for myself from The Old Black Dog, my favorite bookstore. (In my attempts to make my reading come to life for my students, I probably left a few with the mistaken notion that there is this old black dog who brings Ms. Shockley books, wagging his tail behind him!)

What about the basal?

As a teacher in this district I was required to do the magazine tests for each basal level. Each child had a reading card that supposedly documented his performance on these end-of-level tests. At the time this was *the* only acceptable way for teachers to account for student learning. In first grade there were five levels of basals—three preprimers, a primer, and the first-grade reader. In order to be promoted a student had to pass the magazine tests through the primer with 80 percent mastery.

When I was beginning first grade with Joseph, Shannon, and Jeremiah, the mass of material scared me more than anything else. The burden of student texts, teacher's editions, student workbooks, teacher's annotated workbooks, teacher's resource notebooks, and testing materials for each of the five levels was visually and physically overwhelming. I've always wanted to stack all of it on an industrial scale somewhere to see how much it really weighs. It was clear to me the materials outweighed many six-year-olds!

Thinking this would be obvious to everyone, I decided to take all this stuff with me to a presentation at a local civic organization. I dramatically heaved it all onto the head table and waited for the gasp of amazement. To my surprise the audience thought it was just wonderful that our students learned so much in just one year—surely we teachers were doing a good job! The "it's good for them" philosophy probably supports many of the false assumptions about education in this country today.

Believing that I could help my students learn to read in a more natural way, I reduced my anxiety by deciding to find a complementary way to do both what the district said I had to do and what I wanted to do. I made a list of skills that were actually tested at each basal level (most were editing skills), added several that I thought were essential, and created an outline of what writers do. This practice has served me well from the beginning. I had now captured five basal magazine tests in two pages—I could even carry that around with me! I used this outline as a guide for my mini-lessons in reading and writing workshops and for setting goals in our editing conferences (see Figure 2–2).

Initially, I decided that instead of going through the tests sequentially, I could teach the skills in mini-lessons and conferences and then directly test those skills in the magazine tests. I soon had to abandon this strategy because even though a child might understand the skill and even be able to apply it in her own writing or reading, she often couldn't read the passages as presented on the test. Finally, I've learned to be patient. I just wait until after Christmas when most all the children are independent readers. By then, the first preprimer test seems much less threatening. This plan was not at all in agreement with our county pacing guidelines; my principal, however, encouraged me to continue, since the children's progress was well documented in other ways.

I essentially went through the same learning process in deciding how to make peace with the reading workbooks that the county provided. The first two years, I'd pull them out periodically for the students to practice in cooperatively. They did the pages they could understand—the ones that were truly practice for them. To understand the level tests, they needed to have some prior experience with that kind of testing format. Last year I offered the children the *Bells* workbook (Houghton Mifflin's first preprimer, 1986) for practice in the same cooperative

Things I Can Do in Writing

I can be an author.

I can choose my own topic.

I can be an illustrator.

I can draw.

I can be an editor.

I can write letters.
a b c d e f g h i j k l m n o p q r s t u v w x y z

I can write beginning sounds.
a b c d e f g h i j k l m n o p q r s t u v w x y z

I can write ending sounds.
a b c d e f g h i j k l m n o p q r s t u v w x y z

I can write vowels.
a (long, short) i (long, short) u (long, short)
e (long, short) o (long, short) y (as i and e)

I can write words.

I can write clusters.
fl fr br tr pl st sc bl sl gl

I can write digraphs(initial and final).
th ch sh ck

I can write plurals (s).

I can write punctuation marks.

I can reference pronouns.
I we it this she he they her them us

I can write events in order (sequencing).

I can write contractions.
n't 's 'll 'm

I can write compound words.

I can write possessive words ('s).

I can write details.

I can write commas in a series.

I can write new words from base words (add endings).

I can be a publisher.

I can write a book.

I can write for the newspaper.

I can write a report.

I can write a letter.

I can write directions or instructions.

I can write a sign.

FIG. 2–2 *Outline of Writing Skills*

way after Christmas vacation, and then began the testing in February. For organizational purposes I tested the levels in order, one per month, February to June. If I knew in advance that a child would be moving, I did the necessary testing so I could complete the transfer form. If we were surprised by a move, I stated that this child had not been tested but read books that might be similar in difficulty to basal level _______ .

I experimented with self-selected reading groups to give the students opportunities to read together in the basal readers. Several times during that first year I invited the children to choose one of the three preprimers at the beginning of independent reading time. Our classroom aide, Ms. Elder, and I each led a group; the third group was usually student led. It was amazing the way the children moved easily and freely among the level choices—treating their contents more as anthologies than graded story remnants. For instance, Shannon might choose to read in *Bells* (PP1) for two days and then skip to *Trumpets* (PP3) the next day. Each self-selected group would decide on a story to read together, and then they would move on to reading other books they chose from our classroom library for the rest of the independent reading period.

I wanted my students to fit in with the traditional school culture too. If their friends were talking about Boo Bear, I wanted them to be able to contribute to the discussion. I helped make the stories in the primer *Parades* accessible for all the children by offering them as plays. Different teams would choose a story to read together and then act it out for the rest of the class. And again, these books were always available to be read independently or to be checked out for home reading.

Even though the basals were on the shelves equally with the trade books, they had a different significance to the children at first. Early in the first year Darnell and Jonathan decided to read together, and Darnell questioned Jonathan, "You still in *Bells*? Me in *Trumpets*!" They both got *Trumpets* books. Darnell said, "You got to learn to read—you got to read these books!" Eventually, we all weaned ourselves from these formulaic staples.

At the end of my first year in first grade, everyone except Joseph met the promotion guideline of 80 percent mastery on the first primer. However, I knew from listening to them read every day that there were a few children in the class who were still emergent readers. This has also been the case every year since. What does that say about those kinds of isolated skills tests and about how readily schools seem to accept that definition of reading ability?

I'm now deciding if it's appropriate to connect skills mini-lessons with the literature I share each day. I try to make more natural connections with the craft of authorship in our shared discussions instead of redirecting their interest to focus on skill development. I'm now feeling like I understand how to be a good demonstrator of the things good readers do (Clay, 1985) and to let the "authors take over" (Smith, 1992). I am still learning and loving it.

What about the rest of the day?

Over the years there has been more evolution in this area than anything else for me. That first year in first grade I tried to hear individual voices. I wanted to respect them as unique learners contributing to our class community as a whole but we never quite got there. My way of doing this was to have the children choose an area of interest they wanted to learn more about while they were in first grade. I chose whales, Jeremiah chose parrots, Joseph chose "airplanes at night," Shannon selected monkeys; others studied owls, volcanoes, vehicles, and a host of interesting topics.

Lists of our research topics were posted in the office, in the media center, and at JoBeth's university office, and each family was sent a copy. The children were supported in their investigations by the contributions of books and other materials from many sources. The greatest thing for the children was having JoBeth arrive with her bags full of books from friends at the university who had sent particular books to particular children. Everyone loved these gifts for learning. This was, I think, a valid beginning to let children's personal interests influence curriculum, but it fell short of my expectations. We never produced a product that we could be proud of accomplishing together. We heard the individual voices, but they never came together into a song we could all sing.

The next year, we took another step toward a more integrated approach. We moved from "me" to "we." Instead of a focus on individual investigations, we worked on small-group involvements. That year, all Walnut Street teachers worked together on integrating instruction around quarterly school-wide themes. For example, while investigating patterns and cycles in nature, our class also studied patterns and structures of stories. One significant connection we made was a comparison of the layers of the earth with the layers of ideas in cumulative tales. We connected all our learning in this area more concretely when we read Joanna Cole's (1987) book, *The Magic Schoolbus: Inside the Earth* and constructed a duct taped cardboard box tunnel that encircled the room. Each small group was responsible for adding on one section, complete with its significant features. Each group made a real contribution to the total product, but they were still separate sections held together by tape, not vested inquiry.

It was one thing to be engaged as a reader and a writer, but by last year my students were additionally engaged by ideas. Although books could take us into the world of ideas, it was physically creating our own learning environment within our classroom that allowed for a day-long connectedness of ideas that had not been possible before. Zora Neale Hurston (1937) said it better when she wrote, "And furthermo' everything is got tuh have uh center and uh heart tuh it, and uh town [classroom] ain't no different from nowhere else" (p. 38). By constructing a medieval castle environment together within the walls of our classroom, and later the dark world of outer space, we gave our learning a heart, a center. We situated ourselves in a kind of inquiry that built on itself in a way everyone participating was aware of and contributed to. The thing that changed the most was extending the choices during reading and writing workshops to include the whole day. We were a literate community, learning to read and reading to learn.

Joseph, Shannon, Jeremiah, and I, along with the rest of the class, shared something really special. It was a first for us all. None of us had lived in a whole language classroom before. It felt new. It felt good. It felt scary at times. We exposed ourselves as real learners to real learning. Individually and collectively we grew. Doing it ourselves mattered to all of us. Creating authorship together helped create the supportive community we needed.

Early in that first year of first grade, Darnell responded to a friend's writing by saying, "I liked the first part all the way to the end." Well, I don't know where the end of my educational journey will be, nor that of Joseph's, Shannon's, or Jeremiah's. But like Caleb later added to Darnell's commentary, "I like the whole thing!"

THREE

Creating a Community of Learners in Second Grade

I (Barbara) came to teach second grade after seven years of teaching kindergarten. I loved teaching kindergarten! All of my years as a kindergarten teacher were during a time when I had freedom to create the curriculum in my classroom in response to the needs of the class. There were some basic skills that I was responsible for exposing the students to, but the push to teach kids to read in kindergarten had not yet arrived. There were no workbooks that the students had to complete; dittos were not a part of the program.

The classroom was rich in experiences for the children. We took many field trips, cooked weekly, acted out stories, took hikes in the woods, built and labeled buildings in the block area, and had numerous visitors come to share a part of their lives with us. It was an alive and changing environment. As a teacher, I felt I knew the best way to help my children really learn.

At the heart of creating this type of classroom was the belief that children want to learn, and will if provided with a stimulating environment and time to proceed at their individual pace. My role as a teacher was to create the environment, to supply the tools to keep it running smoothly, and to observe and respond to the students' interests and needs, all the time helping them to continue learning. It was (and is) very important to me that every child feel valued and successful in my classroom. When I was assigned to teach second grade, I carried these basic beliefs about learning with me.

There I faced the seemingly impossible task of creating a living, changing, and exciting classroom as well as covering the stack of textbooks that the children had to complete to go on to third grade. Math, science, social studies, spelling, language, and two reading books all had to be completed by the first of June. I panicked. Here I was, alone with twenty-nine students and this huge stack of books. So I watched and listened closely to what the other second-grade teachers were doing, and copied them.

We started at the beginning of the books and carried on until we reached the end. There were reading groups, seatwork, strictly scheduled times for each subject, and very little time to do the things that had made my kindergarten classroom so alive. I was frustrated; the students were frustrated. Many of them weren't able to keep up; many already were far ahead. I knew I had to come up with a different approach for the following year.

Over the summer I participated in JoBeth's class on the whole language philosophy of teaching reading and writing. It sounded so familiar. I kept saying to myself, "Oh, yes, I did that in kindergarten." The philosophy seemed to encompass my own beliefs concerning the role of the teacher. It also provided a way to help each student continue learning at her own level and develop feelings of self-worth. By the end of the class I had decided it was certainly worth a try in solving the dilemma I had faced the previous year. So I made a plan. I would ease into it slowly, dividing time between textbook-driven and whole language instruction. I would be covering myself in case whole language didn't really work.

Creating a learning environment

I tried to design the classroom to stimulate the types of interaction I wanted to take place. My plan included writing, reading, listening, math, and art centers, an open space to gather on the floor, and lots of wall space to display the children's work. After about ten minutes in the small portable classroom where I would spend the year with twenty-four students, I had to change these plans. I settled on a book display area with a cozy sofa, a shelf for writing and math materials, an open space on the floor, and two small tables for the students to work together and do small-group work. The students' desks took up the remaining space in the trailer. Wall space was limited.

The first two weeks of school we had reading and writing workshop every day. I hoped to establish the routines that are so important in creating a learning environment (Graves, 1983; Hansen, 1987). We didn't begin work in the basal readers or the language book because I wanted the students to know what I valued, that for me these real reading and writing experiences *were* the curriculum, not adjustments to it. This delay served two purposes. It provided the time to establish comfortable routines within the reading and writing workshops. More importantly, it gave me an opportunity to include all students in these instructional times, which took the majority of our morning.

There were three students in special education programs who were barely into first-grade level reading in the basal series. If we had begun the year working in reading groups that excluded these children, I'm certain they would never have become contributing members of the reading and writing community. The importance of those first two weeks became clear in retrospect.

At the beginning of the year I had pictured reading workshop as students choosing books, my teaching a mini-lesson, then the students reading quietly at their desks for fifteen minutes. After reading we would have a sharing time. By the third day of school I began to wonder where I had gotten the picture of seven- and eight-year-olds reading quietly at their desks. It just wasn't happening. So I changed my expectations about reading time and gave children the option to read anywhere in the room with whomever they chose. Reading workshop began to be a time when everyone was involved with books.

I saw the students helping each other and sharing the excitement of reading. They read all over the room, usually with a friend. The small sofa next to the bookshelf was the favorite spot. Next was the very small space under my desk. The kids pulled chairs next to each other, and read on the floor and under tables. I rarely saw children reading at their own desks, unless I had restricted them for inappropriate behavior. The major problem with reading workshop was getting enough books into the classroom.

I didn't have such a clear picture of writing workshop, but it went well from the start. The students were eager to write about their experiences and to share their writing. Again, I observed that second graders' ideas of working do not include any quiet time. There was a lot of exchanging ideas and information but no silent time to work on one's own. I was observing much enthusiasm, but not as much writing as I knew the children were capable of producing. I decided to split the writing time into two sections. There would be ten to fifteen minutes of silent writing time, and ten to fifteen minutes of conference time. During the silent period students had to work on their own; the conference period allowed them to continue writing alone, to write with friends, or to share their writing with other students. During the silent time I wrote; during the conference time I went around and talked with students. I soon saw that the silent time was essential for writing so I enforced it strictly, using a timer to indicate the end of the period.

For the rest of the year our daily writing workshop consisted of a mini-lesson, five minutes to talk with friends about what they planned to write, ten to fifteen minutes of silent writing, ten to fifteen minutes to write or conference, and time to share.

I strived to encourage the growth of a community of learners helping and supporting each other. One way I did this was through reading aloud. I read stories to the class two or three times each day throughout the year. These sessions allowed me to introduce new books, reread class favorites, and provide the whole group with a large number of familiar books. This proved to be very important, especially for the students who were not fluent readers. I observed this group of children seeking out the books I had read aloud; their familiarity with the story allowed them to read independently. I used these sessions to introduce and compare books by the same author. (However, these sessions compounded the problem of getting enough books into the classroom.)

I also modeled many responses that would help our classroom become a supportive community of learners. I made sure I reinforced interactions I saw that would add to this effort. I frowned upon interactions that detracted. I made it very clear that certain ways of behaving were not acceptable in our room, and I began the year with rules gleaned from readings about other whole language classrooms. These rules changed as I observed them in action, sometimes according to my ideas of how our classroom would function better. At other times I got student input about rules and changed them accordingly.

By the third week of school I changed our reading schedule to include basal reading groups two days a week and reading workshop three days a week. We had two reading groups, each based on the book the children were placed in from the previous year. We used the title of the book for the names of the reading groups. When students were not working with me in a reading group they were responsible for completing boardwork. The boardwork consisted of completing pages from the language and the spelling text. I encouraged the students to work quietly together to complete their assignments.

With the inclusion of reading groups I began to see an entirely different side of my students. Kids who were attentive and eager to participate in reading workshop were inattentive and disruptive during basal reading group. They had an "I can't do it" attitude, or in some cases an "I won't do it" attitude toward the basal. It troubled me to see the same children reacting so negatively to basal reading instruction, but I knew they had to complete the second-grade basals to be promoted. So we plugged away. At the time I couldn't see any alternatives.

We continued with this schedule throughout the fall; however, the skills began to merge. At the beginning of November I began to integrate the skills taught in the language text into our writing workshop sessions. By the end of the month we had stopped using the language text altogether. I also began to integrate some of the reading workshop activities into the basal program. When the children needed to read a certain story, I assigned them a partner. By assigning partners I was able to pair students who needed some extra help with students who were able to supply help. I kept extra copies of the basals we were using on the bookshelf and included the three special education students in these sessions.

Snags in the plan

Getting enough books into the classroom was an ongoing problem; I became increasingly aware of the importance of books staying there all year. I tried several different ways during the year to solve this problem. I used the libraries in our community, both the public and the university library. I ordered paperbacks from the book club the students ordered from, many times getting free books from bonus points. JoBeth brought in many books that had been donated by Joel Taxel, editor of *The New Advocate*, a children's literature journal. I swiped my daughter's books for months at a time. Our principal gave the second-grade teachers money to purchase three hundred books to share among us. This helped, but the boxes of books rotated among seven classrooms. I found the children searching for familiar books, which were no longer in our room. As I built up my classroom library from all these sources, I worked on including multicultural books. Some titles my students particularly enjoyed were *The Stories Julian Tells*, by Ann Cameron; *The Hundred Penny Box*, by Sharon Bell Mathis; and *Mirandy and Brother Wind*, by Patricia McKissack.

Sharing was another major problem. Many children wanted to share their writing every day. We didn't have time, and the attention span of the listeners didn't allow everyone to have a turn. Children often chose their best friends to share next, so everyone did not have an equal opportunity. I tried sign-up sheets, but that didn't seem to be the answer. They solved the problem of students just picking their best friends, but did nothing to help with the main problem of time limitations. We tried small groups, but the students had so much trouble managing their own behavior that these didn't function very well.

We continued to have problems with sharing the remainder of the year. I chose large-group sharing the majority of the time, mainly to avoid behavior problems. At times I let the children vote on how we would share. Sometimes I would stay with the group who wanted to share in a large group and send the small groups to different corners of the room. Looking back, I believe small sharing groups could have been successful. If I had spent more time modeling and teaching appropriate behavior in the groups, and having the students role-play ways to act, I think the children would have learned how to interact.

Even though we never found a solution to the sharing problem in writing workshop, most of the children continued to be productive and interested. I can't say the same for our basal reading sessions. There were numerous students who lost interest in their books, especially students who were not fluent readers.

I had noticed that many of the kids were merely decoding words while they read basal stories, often missing the plot of the story. I wondered why they did this in their basal readers but not with trade books. I soon realized that in reading workshop they were free to choose their own books, they often chose books they had heard, and they were able to work with a friend. The basal reading program didn't allow for these options. I began to read the stories from the basals aloud while the students followed along in their books. This activity was a whole-group lesson. The children shared books, following text and listening to the stories in both of the basals. We continued this practice throughout the rest of the year. The children began to view the stories more like other literature in our classroom. Everyone was included in discussing the stories. It was a small change that brought a portion of the basal curriculum into the community we were trying to create.

Even with these changes, basal days continued to be problematic. I wrote in my journal, "Basal days are driving me nuts. I feel like I'm pulling teeth." A large number of students did feel as if their teeth were being pulled. The students who were struggling with reading suffered the most. They could be successful with books they chose, but had a very difficult time dissecting language into the small parts that the basal workbooks demanded. As frustration levels grew, I knew I had to come up with some alternatives to teaching the skills tested in the basal series. I felt there must be some way to help the students meet promotion guidelines and keep their self-esteem.

I asked myself, "What are the components of the reading workshop that help children feel successful?" The parts they seemed to like the best were the freedom to choose their own literature and the spirit of everyone working together to help each other learn. I decided to experiment with teaching the skills tested in the basals in ways that included these particular components of reading workshop.

I began cautiously, choosing skills that were easy to transfer to any written text. One of the first I tried was sequence. I taught a mini-lesson on sequence using examples from the children's lives. Next I read a short story, and the class discussed the sequence of events in the story. Then the children read for fifteen minutes. When they came to share I encouraged them to tell us the sequence of their book. After sharing they completed the test from the basal series on sequence. Students who weren't involved in the testing read or wrote at their desks while the others completed the test pages. Every child passed the test. We were all happier and we had more reading workshop time.

Between the first of January and the end of February I attempted more of these types of lessons. I began to realize many skills were covered in several levels of the basals. Some days it was possible to teach a skills lesson, then test everyone in their basals on that skill. We completed fewer and fewer workbook pages. I started using the workbook only to reteach individual students who needed additional instruction. Integrating the basal into the reading and writing workshops became easier as time passed. By the beginning of March our reading groups, as we had known them at the beginning of the year, ceased to exist. I taught whole-group lessons, then pulled together small groups that needed extra help.

We all felt better about the basal. Students who had struggled so hard within that program didn't seem quite so overwhelmed. There was some concern from the students about not completing every page in the workbook. One child asked, "Can we go to third grade if we don't do all these pages?" Others were upset because we skipped pages. I explained to the class that we were studying the same things taught in the basal, just in a different way. I also reassured them by explaining thatthey have to pass the basal tests to be promoted, not complete every page in the workbook. I gave them the option of taking the workbook home and completing any pages they wanted; no one ever chose to take it home.

Reflecting on the year, I see that my flexibility and commitment were major ingredients in making it work. My years in a kindergarten classroom had trained me to respond to the students' needs, and that training helped me in teaching second grade. From the start, I told myself I would try to let my whole language philosophy guide my teaching throughout the entire year. I knew there would be times when I would be discouraged and tempted to return to a basal-driven approach, but I hoped I could keep my commitment alive through the periods of doubt that I knew would be part of the process.

Teaching as research

When JoBeth asked for teachers to participate in conducting research, I jumped at the chance. I figured if I agreed to study how my students were responding to whole language instruction, I would have to follow through with the commitment to whole language teaching that I was making at the start of the year. Also I wanted to take advantage of her expertise. I thought, "Here's this person who knows how it is supposed to be done. Just what I'll need to get me over the rough spots." So I leaped into the role of researcher, having very little idea what that would mean for me and the students in my classroom.

Once I had agreed to be a researcher I began to wonder what that meant. I had a vague idea, but nothing specific. I looked up "research" in the dictionary. It said, "to study thoroughly." This sounded like what we were going to try, but when I thought about how we would go about studying thoroughly, my images became unclear.

The first week of school I held JoBeth at bay while establishing some basic rules and routines. The sixth day of school I succumbed to her impatience and she came to observe reading workshop. JoBeth stayed for one hour, writing notes constantly. I couldn't wait to see what she had written. When we got a chance to talk she shared her detailed record of who said what, to whom, when, and where. I was dismayed. I thought, "How in the world can I take those kinds of notes and still teach?"

The following week I tried jotting down similar kinds of notes during reading and writing workshop. After a few days I accepted the fact that it wasn't possible. I had to come up with a system that would work for me. Many things happened throughout the day that helped me learn about the students, and I began to spend time in the afternoon or evening writing my reflections on the day. These weren't the same type of notes that JoBeth recorded. They were a mixture of insights and events that seemed important and what I thought about them. This approach was comfortable. I had kept teaching journals other years and this was very similar. I continued to take reflective notes throughout the year. I didn't write every day, but I was constantly reflecting on events in the classroom.

After observing the class for three weeks, we began to compile a list of students we were worried about. My definition of what type of students were "at risk" was influenced by the staff development work I had participated in the preceding year. I had a list of factors that seemed to be instrumental in children failing in school. It included children who had repeated grades, children who were functioning below grade level, children with severe behavior problems, and children who lived in extreme poverty. As I observed the students in my classroom I kept this list in mind.

When I first volunteered to conduct research in my classroom I very firmly stated, "Just one child. I know that's all I'll have time to study." Choosing that one child wasn't easy. There were seventeen boys and seven girls in the class. Just going by the factors I felt created difficulties for children in school, the possibilities were numerous.

The children I worried about

All of the children I was concerned about were reading on a first-grade or kindergarten level. Nancy was an insecure, frightened child. She told many stories that were untrue and talked and wrote incessantly about how much her mother loved her. She had difficulty getting along with the other children and displayed a lot of helpless behavior toward adults. Mary also seemed unsure of herself. She was very reserved around adults and seemed distrustful. She had recently returned to her mother's home after a year in foster care. Mary had repeated first grade, yet continued to struggle with reading most texts. Nathan's reluctance to relate to adults also aroused my concern. He had moved from another state, and was one to two years younger than the rest of the students in the class. He hadn't said a word since school began. He copied text during writing workshop and kept to himself during reading workshop.

Bonita had difficulty completing any task. She was constantly talking and had a hard time staying in her seat during whole-class sessions. Being unable to live with her parents because of their drug abuse, she lived with her grandmother. This seemed to bother her, as she talked about her mother and her brother frequently. Van also had trouble engaging. He had been physically abused in first grade; I wasn't sure if the abuse was continuing. His mother was concerned about his progress in school and hovered over him trying to help. Fredrick wandered in and out of the present reality. He appeared to have numerous petit mal seizures throughout the day.

Vanessa's lack of progress in reading was puzzling. Her first-grade teacher had placed her in Chapter 1 reading. I was aware of her unsettled family life, yet she interacted well with the other children and seemed to have confidence in herself. Kent's reading was still picture governed. He was placed into the program for learning disabled students, where he worked in a basal preprimer. Kent had no confidence in himself as a reader and writer, yet displayed good interpersonal skills with adults and children. He wouldn't attempt to write in writing workshop. Wendy spent the afternoon with a special education teacher. Her severe speech problems made it almost impossible to understand her language. Chad's mother was concerned about his progress, and she passed this concern on to Chad. She reported he whined and cried at home that he couldn't do his work. At school he had difficulty with reading, but seemed quite confident and wrote great stories. He took many risks and didn't hesitate to become involved.

Reggie and his siblings appeared to be raising themselves with little adult supervision. He often came to school tired and inappropriately dressed. His lack of self-control and his physical aggression created problems throughout the day. He had repeated first grade, yet seemed to be making little progress. Ricky was just the opposite. He rarely spoke to adults and seemed to mistrust everyone. He had also repeated first grade and had been placed into the behavior disorders program for his explosive outbursts of temper. I didn't observe these outbursts; however, his extremely withdrawn behavior alerted me. He seemed to be making a conscious effort to be uninvolved. Lee had spent most of his life in various foster homes. Lee's emergent literacy reminded me more of my own three-year-old than the other children in our classroom. Lee was placed into the mentally handicapped program and spent half of the school day with a special education teacher.

It was hard to choose one student out of this group. JoBeth and I watched and talked about the individual students. By the end of September I had targeted Reggie as the one student I would study. Reggie seemed to be a prime candidate for school failure. His lack of progress the preceding years in first grade had created a lot of frustration for him. This frustration fueled his behavior problems, which were constant and disruptive to all of us.

Even though I had decided to study Reggie, we continued to discuss the other students we were worried about. Ricky got added to the list as my concern for his lack of involvement grew. He seemed to be holding in so much anger and mistrust. He flitted through the day, never staying long with any activity or person. He took no risks in learning situations and interacted infrequently with the other students.

JoBeth just kept on and on about Lee. "He's so interesting," she said. I was skeptical of studying a mentally handicapped child, not sure that he would make any progress. Would I be setting myself up for failure as a whole language teacher by choosing to study a mentally handicapped child? As I reflected I realized he had already shown a great deal of self-confidence and real risk taking in writing workshop. His handicap certainly hadn't stopped him from assuming a place in the writing community. I had to admit Lee really was interesting. Lee also became part of the study.

Throughout the year my observations, reflections, and attempts to understand these three students' development extended to everyone in the class. I noticed more and was able to respond to students on an individual basis. I learned a lot about them through their writings. I became aware of milestones in their growth and what influenced their growth.

I realized how very important it is for children this age to talk about what they are doing and to work together. I saw students helping each other learn, many times teaching something to another child that I had been struggling to teach. As the students' confidence grew they took it outside the classroom. My students began to ask other teachers to let them read to their classes, even reading to classrooms of fourth and fifth graders. They were so proud of themselves!

I was adamant at the start of the year; I would study just one child. In retrospect I can see that studying one child, or even three children, was just a beginning. Like tossing a pebble into a pond, the ripples affect the whole pond. I saw that happen through my research of these three students. My study of Ricky, Reggie, and Lee changed my teaching for the entire class, how I thought about each student as a learner, the link between my observational assessment and instruction, and how I came to view the students I worried about most.

We concentrated on the three focal students, yet continued to discuss any child we were worried about throughout the year. As the year drew to a close we again compiled a list of students we were worried about. This time I wasn't so influenced by my list of factors that contribute to failure. It grew from knowing the students.

Nancy, Bonita, Mary, and Chad remained in the group of students I was concerned about. They all continued to need extra help in reading. Fredrick continued to have his seizures, but had made a lot of progress. He became a competent reader and a more responsible member of the class. Kent moved to another school. Van continued to be easily distracted, but was on his way to becoming a reader. Vanessa proved to be the most literate person in the classroom. She read constantly and was sought out by other children to help them with reading and writing. Wendy appeared to make little progress during the year. Nathan finally opened up and began to talk toward the end of the school year. His participation in a student-organized production of Jack and the Beanstalk (he was the Beanstalk) seemed to be the turning point. He became a fluent reader and his self-confidence seemed to have grown.

The following boys were added to my list of students I was concerned about: Drew was in the gifted program, and very bright, but he seldom took risks and was reluctant to become involved. Norris was also in the gifted program. He was able to use language wonderfully, but seldom followed through with what he began. His behavior problems made it difficult for him to relate to the other students. Thomas, another bright student, just didn't seem to care about anything we did in school. He took no risks and didn't dare to become involved.

Year two: Learning new steps

Joseph and Jeremiah moved from Betty's first grade to my second grade. Things were different the second year. For one, I wasn't in a trailer but in a large, bright classroom with tables instead of desks. An old cherry tree grew directly outside our plate glass window, providing us with a whole world in miniature to observe all year long. And I knew I was at a different stage of development this year, because I invited JoBeth to join us on the first day of school.

In some ways I was now a better researcher, though not as thorough as I had been the previous year. Not choosing the students I was studying influenced my mixed feelings about my involvement. I'm not sure I would have picked Jeremiah and Joseph as the children I was most worried about. When I had observed in Betty's room the previous May during my planning period, both boys seemed to be involved. At first, Jeremiah didn't seem to have any problems working well in our second grade. Joseph had difficulty the first day, but after that seemed quite self-assured and willing to work hard. As time passed and I got to know these two students better, I did begin to have substantial concerns about them.

Experience continues to be the best teacher. I was a good student and was able to avoid some of the problems that I had encountered, or perhaps created, the previous year. The first year I had a hard time getting the kids to date their work, so I bought a date stamp. I loved it. Toward the end of writing workshop, before we shared, I walked around and stamped every student's paper. Not only did I make sure all work was dated, I made sure that I saw everyone's work every day.

I began to use modeling more often as a strategy in my teaching. I verbalized my own thought processes to the children. My expectations were clearer. Instead of waiting for the type of behavior I wanted to see occur, and then praising it, I used mini-lessons to teach the kids specific ways that they could help each other in reading and writing. These appropriate ways of behaving in a community of learners extended to everything we did in our classroom.

Many of the children that were in my class had been in Betty's room the previous year and were familiar with the routines in reading and writing workshop. Early in the year I was able to add to these basic routines. We practiced sharing in small groups and with partners. When everyone became competent we were able to use a variety of group sizes for sharing and avoided the problems we had had the previous year. When we had whole-class share sessions I always ended by saying, "If you didn't get to share today, find someone who hasn't heard your story and read it." One way or another, everyone had the opportunity to share every day.

I had been concerned about the amount of progress that some of the students had made in my classroom the previous year. I wanted the kids to work at their own pace, but I meant for them to work and to grow. I was more explicit about my expectations and developed consequences for the children who were not using their time wisely.

I was more trusting of myself and the students. I didn't use the basals as much as I had the previous year. I had collected more books that could stay in our classroom all year, and I taught a broad range of skills through these trade books and the children's writing. I used all of our textbooks as resources, using the parts of them that were helpful. There was no seatwork when I pulled together skill groups; the rest of the class read alone or with friends.

There were also schoolwide changes that affected what we did in our classroom. In response to overall concern about the size of the school (over 900 students) and the instability many of the children experienced in their out-of-school lives, we created "family" groupings. These were three kindergarten-through-fifth grade groups with two classrooms at each grade level. Within each family we had nuclear (K–2 and 3–5) and extended (K–5) clusters. We worked with other grade levels in our families. Our second grade met with a fifth grade class for thirty minutes every Friday for a buddy reading time, keeping the same fifth grade buddy throughout the year. We presented plays to each other and planned special "book picnics" when we took baskets of books and snacks to enjoy under a shady tree.

Our nuclear family also created some shared times so that the students would become familiar with the teachers in our family and we could get to know the students. Once a week we had a sing-along, which each class took a turn leading. We also traded classes for a thirty-minute story share once a month. In this way we developed a sense of family that we hoped would ease the transition each year. Another schoolwide change involved working to create thematic units for all grade levels that incorporated science and social studies; literature was included in these units. I found that the children read more widely in both of these content areas.

Year three

The third year I came closer to creating the vibrant, alive classroom that I had enjoyed so much during the years I taught kindergarten. State funding supported a wonderful full-time paraprofessional, Ms. Morrison. Together, we continued to provide time and choice to the children through reading and writing workshop. We made many more opportunities for active learning available to the children. For example, when we studied maps, we took imaginary trips to countries on the different continents of the world. The children used their knowledge to plan our itinerary. We simulated cross-Atlantic flights and ocean voyages. When we arrived at our destination we opened a restaurant serving food from that country. We studied their language, folk tales, music, and customs. We did art projects using techniques that were common in the country we were visiting.

Even in this learning environment I had students I worried about. But becoming a researcher in my classroom helped me to change the narrow idea I had initially of which students I should be worried about. Now it wasn't so clear. I worried about students who weren't living up to their potential, who weren't as successful as they could be.

I realize all teachers have the opportunity to be reflective researchers. When you teach a lesson and half the class gives you a blank look, you ask yourself, "How else can I teach this concept?" That's research. You observe, and respond to what you have observed. You begin to be aware of the intricate teaching and learning dance with your students. Researching took me a step further into my students' lives. The more I tune in the better I become at knowing when to lead, when to follow, or when to play a sedate waltz or a lively rap. And each year I become better at helping them learn, as I learn to listen and hear their inner music.

JOSEPH

FOUR
Joseph in His Own Voice

First grade with Ms. Shockley, Walnut Street School

September

I don't know. I make a killer shark, a killer cat, too, and killer people. I get help. From people. I don't know, they help me make killers. I want to have fun. Everyone helps. When I grow up, I'll read stuff I like. Bye. [He has been edging toward the door; he leaves, ending the interview on his own terms.]

December

Joseph does not want to be interviewed.

February

Mmm—I'm learning to write, write, "r"-"e"-write "r-e-t." I'm learning how to read just like I can read this book. It's about animals, and I like to play with friends, my brothers and cousins. My baby cousin died and my big cousin died, because the fire blowed them up and bust the window. Tomorrow we going to see them at the funeral.

First time I had a book, I used to play with all kinds of animals in this book. You see this shark, it getting ready to bite, and this [lots more commentary on animals]. I know about it if I read it. It's easy to read, you get you a book. One day I might learn how to read this book [*Arthur's Valentine*, by Marc Brown]. And this book—see this lion? My grandmother used to have a pet just like this, it kill people who mess with her. If I know how to read a book, I know how to read one that's different.

See that bee? My brother die from a bee sting him. That goat got horns—they kill people with them things. I love this book [*Arthur's Valentine*], I get it every time. I'm going to read it. [He reads silently, then throws in a textual invention: "I love you Shockley." He kisses the page.] Listen, I'll read it to you.

I told you, I read about planes and bears and big wheels. I'm writing about friends. Nobody but myself helps me. Next, I'm going to write "Happy Valentine's Day." My cousin and friend and brother are going to help me. Thank you. [Again, he leaves before the interview is completed.]

June

I'm learning how to read *real* good. What grade is that book [he picks up *Discoveries*, a 2.2 basal]? My mama teaches me how to read. She used to be reading every time and I used to listen. Next I want to read the red book [*Parades*, the basal primer all students in the district are supposed to complete before being promoted to second grade]. I learn it easy—my daddy teach me that. When I grow up I read *Trumpets*—everything—all the books in the whole world—Hulk Hogan books, wrestling books.

In writing, I'm learning talking and writing. Mrs. Shockley help me. Nope, not the other kids. I'm going to write everything I know how to write. When I grow up, I can go to school, I can go to work.

Second grade with Ms. Michalove, Walnut Street School

October

I'm learning how to draw pictures and write stories. I like writing stories. Nope, nobody helps me. What I'll learn next, hmm, I don't know about that. [He is watching JoBeth record his responses; suddenly he issues a directive.] Stop writing cursive. *Stop* writing cursive. [She does.] I want to write stories and draw pictures—wait, scratch out "write stories"; I ain't going to do that. [Joseph takes the pencil away from JoBeth, politely but firmly, and writes the responses to the rest of the questions. JoBeth has just asked him what he is learning to do as a reader.] TAK ACATS [talk a sentence]. I learn it by reading stories, like PEIRS PEIPEIRS. [He has taken the interview sheet and reads aloud, "What would you like to learn next as a reader?" with a little help. Then he writes.] I LIKE TO DER [draw]. How do you think you'll learn it? MY DAD LEAN ME What do you think you'll read when you're a grown-up? WEW THE PER Winnie the Pooh, Winnie the Pooh . . . [Joseph returns to his room singing.]

January

I don't know, I be reading *Each Peach Pear Plum* [Ahlberg & Ahlberg, 1978], Christmas stories. I pick, my mother taught me how. She read me some books, ordered some books and read them to me. My favorite at home is Christmas stories and Halloween and Easter and Valentine's Day; I like all the stuff be coming up. I learn by my mama, my daddy, um yep, people at school—I forgot. When I'm grown up, I read grown-up stuff.

I just been writing stuff, like cats, dogs, pigs, friends, in stories with me and stuff like that. I write *My Friends* because I love to be writing with my friends—Carter—and my cousins—Delia [in his class]. Nope, nobody help me—yep, Ms. Michalove and Teena and Benson. They just told me. I write about apples, oranges, all kinds of fruit. My mama help me, she tells me, I don't know what she going to tell me.

February

I'm learning how to write a long story, how to talk about school in my story. The idea come from real life but the story is fiction; it ain't real. Vickie help with spelling,

Carter too, and Caleb, Weston, Benson, Kenny, and Colin. I write about—I don't know, till I get to the other story. I might start one about cars.

March

I'm learning how to write stories about animals, Big Foot, friends. I wrote more talking in the stories. My mama learned me how to write about cars—how to spell the names of cars. And my big brothers—they write some stuff and tell me to look at it. Latonya help with spelling. Carter, we take turns writing with each other; first he write a sentence, then I write a sentence. Vickie help with spelling. Caleb, he be writing stuff and sometime I copy him and sometime he copy me. Benson help me read sometimes, and Colin, sometime I help him, then he help me. My father, I visit him, and he teach me how to write in cursive. And my mother, Ms. Michalove, and Ms. Gibbons. I want to write about mean bad animals, write about bears, and spell better. My mama and daddy, and the teacher next year will help me. And my grandmama, she reads the Bible all the time, she know how to tell stories.

June

I'm learning to read better, to read *Curious George* [Rey, 1941], and hard words, long books, and to skip words I don't know and keep going. My cousins, Nate, he's seventeen, and Redbone, he's twenty, he died, and Carter, we read together. Latonya, she helps me with words I don't know, she'll tell me words. Delia, when we be at home she reads books to me and my sister. Ms. Michalove, and Ms. Gibbons and Ms. Bradley—she help me pass my test—and at home mama and daddy help me. I want to learn how to read hard words; my mama and daddy teach me how. When I grow up, I'm going to read some mail and stuff.

Third grade with Ms. Weiderhold, Walnut Street School

May

You want to hear me read? Here, this one's "Jasper and the Hero Business." [He summarizes the story from *Adventures*, the 2.1 basal.] Okay, I got ten minutes. [Joseph reads with high accuracy, including several self-corrections. He watches the clock carefully, and at exactly 9:00 says he has to leave to see the school play. The interview continues after the play.]

I don't know; I'm learning to read gooder. I been going slowly, but I'm going—I don't know how to answer these questions—I can't think right now—how about 10:30?

[JoBeth asks carefully, "Is there anything you want to tell me about writing?"] I ain't hardly write that much—but my dog died, though. How come you didn't bring my writing folder? My dog used to run after cars all the time, finally he got hit. His eye came out, he had blood in his throat . . . No, I can't write about it, see my sister loved him real bad, and my brother loved him, but I didn't hardly like him—is five minutes almost up?

No, we didn't have writing in the other schools I went to. I liked Birch Street School. Why didn't you visit me there? My friends I used to stay with came to that school. It's time for me to go. I don't want to miss anything—see at 10:30 we have math, then at 11:00 . . . [He recites the day's schedule. JoBeth asks, "Next year, do you think you'll want to read with me and talk like we've been doing?" There is a *very* long pause, maybe two minutes. Finally he smiles and says, "I'll *read* to you."]

FIVE

Sing a Song of Joseph

Joseph in First Grade at Walnut Street School

Sing a song of Joseph
A pocket full of woe,
Four and twenty wishes
With no place to go.
When the books were opened,
He began to sing.
Now isn't that a dandy dish
To set before the king?

Joseph joins the first-grade community

I didn't know a smile could grow. It did on Joseph's face. It was not an automatic response to pleasure; it was more like a creeping sense of security. It was easy at first to see Joseph as a snake in our class garden. He slid in every morning without acknowledging anyone else's presence and took his place to wait for the world to warm up enough for him. Sometimes you'd think he just came out from under a rock. He'd yawn. He'd stretch. He'd dangle from his chair. He could also seem quite threatening. So what was it that made this child so endearing? Why did I (Betty) work so hard to catch a glimpse of that smile?

A first inspection provided no hint of an extra school year in a special needs kindergarten. His size seemed just right for first grade. He was neat and clean except for the sleeves of the red and black jacket that he wore all day, every day, which were stained from his habit of wiping his constantly runny nose. I was aware of his special education status of both mildly mentally handicapped and behavior disordered. His aggressive and disruptive behavior had just contributed to his removal from another first-grade classroom across the hall from ours. After I learned he would be moved to our class, I remembered seeing him fighting on the playground. I recalled his kindergarten teacher having to physically remove him from the area on more than one occasion.

I felt a need to prepare the class for Joseph's coming. I told them a new boy would be joining us who didn't yet know how to behave as well as they did. It would therefore be our responsibility to help him learn not only to read and write but also to behave appropriately. The children responded to my less than subtle plea for assistance with a sense of concern and maturity that was heartwarming. I then had a private conversation with Joseph before he entered the room. I wanted to welcome him, and at the same time clearly state my expectations for his academic and personal success. I felt somewhat like an overprotective parent. This child's reputation certainly had preceded him. His first few days with us were spent rather uneventfully. He leaned back and fell out of his chair too much, but he didn't strike out at anyone. The class was marvelously helpful and accepting. I was concerned both with his aggression and with his lethargy during instructional periods of the day. The only thing he showed any real enthusiasm for was playing "war" with a deck of cards.

Instructional transitions, walking in lines, and recess seemed to be the most difficult times of the day in terms of his behavior. One day in November we watched Joseph on the playground in his typical playground mode. He was chasing people, hitting one child, trying to throw another to the ground. He wouldn't come when I called and had a very defiant look on his face, his mouth open and his eyes hard. On a similar day our principal observed in our classroom one morning and joined us for recess immediately afterward. That afternoon at a faculty meeting, she told the story of "Joseph the hoodlum." She was concerned about how much of an impact we as teachers could truly have on the lives of our "at risk" students if they could maintain acceptable behavior within the more structured setting of the classroom, only to revert to hoodlum status during the freedom of recess.

In my dealings with Joseph I was anxious about losing control myself, in effect showing him that I could not be a dependable personality in his life. It would have been so easy to take him to the office or to his special education teacher when he misbehaved, but I felt by doing that I would be sending him the message that I was weak and could not effectively deal with him myself. I knew his admiration was reserved for the tough guys. If I could not be his kind of tough, at least I could be consistently in control of myself.

I made a conscious effort to let Joseph show me the way to help him. I worked to be aware of what he showed an interest in doing and what seemed to cause him distress. I wanted to build on his strengths and minimize time spent in situations that were difficult for him to handle. On occasion I supported his choice to leave an instructional setting to do what he chose, as long as his actions did not disturb the rest of the class. His engagement or disengagement, clearly registered on his face, signaled when such options would be appropriate. For instance, he always wanted to participate in writing workshop but could not always write for as long as the rest of the class, so he would build with LEGGOS or play a math game or look at a book when his time clock signaled enough. He would sometimes become disruptive and have to sit by himself. This removal from the group and loss of opportunity to participate did not happen often, because initially his primary interest in writing workshop was getting to share. He could not share if he had not participated well up to that time.

I was surprised by the consistency of Joseph's eagerness to share. In this arena he was a real risk taker and a model for other classmates who might not be as confident about sharing such early print attempts. It was quite a shift from his earliest days, when he was aloof and alone, engaged only in "war." Although he shared his unconventional writing early on, he worked increasingly to standardize his writing. He often used patterned sentences and was reluctant for a long time to spell anything "wrong." One day in December he was trying to write a sentence that looked right. He left out the word "a," so he erased the whole sentence to insert that one letter. When I suggested he squeeze it in, he protested, "But *they* can't see it there!"

I also began to see Joseph becoming engaged by books, after an initial period of seemingly total disinterest even for books on video and my read alouds. As with writing, the community seemed to be influential in drawing him in. If he was examining a book with a small group of friends, his interest was high for as long as the group stayed together. A second element, again parallel with his writing, was experiencing success as a reader. If he chose to read independently, his engagement was complete unless for some reason he felt unsuccessful with his interpretation of the text. Joseph also seemed to enjoy the listening center, where all readers were successful. He would often start the day by going there. It did not seem to matter whether he listened alone or with a group; he quickly got caught up in the story or song on the tape.

Cautiously but surely, Joseph was becoming a member of the reading and writing community.

The judge, the jury, and the convict

Joseph's intense sense of justice evolved as his most pressing issue. His personal justice system seemed to guide his actions and reactions during the "hoodlum" moments as well as his academic life, sometimes reducing his effectiveness as a learner. Not being "messed with" was always more important than learning or pleasing a teacher. He was the only meaningful evaluator of any given situation; my interpretations had little relevance to his social schema until after he had delivered his complete verbal and sometimes physical account. Expressions of his fairness doctrine were varied in their intensity but were ever present. In October he criticized Ashley's drawings indignantly: "You got her (Ms. Shockley), and her (Dr. Allen), but not Ms. Elder." In February a classmate asked about his writing: "Why'd you put Cory on all the pages?" Joseph answered, "Because he was asking me too many questions and I had to pay him back." He even applied his standards to literature. He responded very strongly to Arnold Lobel's book, *Frog and Toad All Year*. His emphatic review included: "They made this book good because that's the rule. When he knocked him off the sled—because people hurt somebody, they got to hurt them back, as long as they be by themselves—unless they got a teacher or a mother. Then tell the teacher or the mother—got to get their lick back if the mother or teacher don't do nothing."

Joseph was a real study in contrasts. He seemed ready to fight to the death to avenge himself in any altercation with a peer, but when he was disciplined and asked to sit by himself at lunch one day, he cried uncontrollably in front of the whole class. He did the same thing another afternoon when he thought he wasn't going to get any popcorn. Beyond the tough guy image he presented most of the time, there was a sensitive and caring Joseph who walked his younger sister to kindergarten and readily responded with compassion to any classmate who appeared to be upset. And again, he spent each day in and out of control.

Joseph was also among the students I was most worried about because I felt him to be on a "path to prison" (Walker & Sylvester, 1991) if he didn't begin to value something culturally positive as fiercely as he defended his honor. Several family members had already followed that path. If not diffused, his explosive personality could at an early age decide his fate. Joseph needed options. The school system had to provide them, and I was next in line at the literacy ticket window, passing out tickets to his future.

I attempted to make learning personally meaningful and purposeful for Joseph. I didn't tell him he couldn't write about killer cats and draw pictures of people killing people. I offered him choice of writing topics daily and valued those choices privately and publicly. I supported his steps to share more and more of his personal self with us as he slowly let down his guard and began to risk being more than a sideline member of our community. I followed his lead, and through consistent reflections in my teaching journal, tried to sensitize myself to the changes he was willing to make. I paced and paralleled my teaching agenda for Joseph with who he was.

I knew being equal was very important to Joseph, as it is with all children. I believe if he had been placed in a bottom reading group he would have been a failure from day one. As it was, with self-selected reading groups and daily reading workshops, Joseph was never in a down situation where other kids were above him. He had a fair and equal chance in this classroom where there was always respect for individual rights and needs. By the end of the year, Cory issued Joseph's most valuable report card by saying, "He got smart fast!"

The king of the universe

Another major issue for Joseph that year seemed to be a strong sense of responsibility. He never forgot his coat like most first graders were prone to do now and again, and he seemed to know the limits of what he could reasonably take care of. He rarely took books home; on one of the few occasions he did ask to take a sample of his work home, he apologized the next day because someone at his house had torn it up. He was always concerned about the welfare of his younger sister.

Joseph was not just in charge of the things he felt belonged to him, however; he wanted to be in charge of everything! He had a sense of self that was not comfortably conforming. He did not automatically do what was asked of him, but seemed to think about the rule or request, to evaluate its reasonableness, its appropriateness for him. He did not like being interviewed by JoBeth; perhaps the questions were too hard, perhaps too private. It was important to me that he maintain this sense of self and still survive in a system that was not designed for kids like him. He began his educational career as a "mentally retarded, behaviorally disordered" African-American male—what were his odds for success?

Joseph went to his special education class every day for 90 minutes until January, when he started resisting my reminders that it was time to go to Ms. Gibbons. On January 31, Ms. Gibbons told me that the other kids in Joseph's group were still working on controlling their behavior, but that Joseph was usually "in control." By February he tried to stop going altogether. Ms. Gibbons told me, "That's probably alright. He's changing so much." In his reevaluation, Joseph, Ms. Gibbons, and I decided that he should reduce his time and only go on Tuesdays and Thursdays. When he was retested, he was found no longer to be mentally handicapped! When he was first tested, his IQ was 64 and his adaptive score was

77. Two years later, testing revealed an IQ of 67 overall and an adaptive score of 86. He still qualified for special services for behavior disorders as he had a maximum score on hostility. Interestingly, Joseph's choice to be a steadier member of our classroom coincided with his increasing membership in our class "literacy club" (Smith, 1988a).

Joseph accepted, in fact demanded, responsibility for his learning. Joseph had his own literacy agenda, one that seemed to become more urgent as he grew in proficiency. Relevance and utility were the primary energizing factors in Joseph's awakening to the powerful potential of print. As mentioned, in the early days especially, I rarely felt like Joseph was engaged in any of the literacy events I tried to create. As the community wrapped itself around him, he slowly trusted its warmth and dependability and used it to find a less resistant voice. The first time I was aware of his attention really being redirected by a writing event was when a fellow student used the name of another student in his story. Many times after that, whenever someone would include another student in his writing, Joseph would quickly try to check out the named person's reaction. He was being drawn into the action by the students and their developing uses of print.

Over time he protected himself with a select circle of friends that he chose to write with or about almost daily (see Figure 5-1). These were fellow writers he could depend on to respect him as still tough but talented as well. When he wrote with these boys, he would venture into new territory—risking and growing. He often granted shared authorship to these buddies. Several of his books began without a title but boldly printed on the front were the credits: By Cory, By Joseph, By Jonathan, By Darnell. He would allow this group to help him with spellings and they would welcome his ideas for their stories. Figure 5-2 is an example from April of this kind of writing that Joseph engaged in so intently with his peers. The many erasures are evidence of this group work.

The first reading event that gained a voiced response from Joseph was a request that I reread Shel Silverstein's poem, "Rock 'n Roll Band" because as Joseph told us, he "played band with his cousins sometimes." I had obviously found a piece he could make some personal connection with.

His first sharing opportunities were shocking for me, but for Joseph they seemed to be supported translations of his childhood images: killer cats and killer people. Later in September Joseph continued his early theme, but expanded both his involvement and his text. He read to JoBeth, "This is a book. A killer cat. That one going to get killed, that one die. That boy. The end." (He had four folded construction paper books; he read from the next one.) "The cat—that the good cat." JoBeth asked what "PNAN" said. "I don't know," Joseph replied, going on to the next book. "This cat, no, I didn't tell you (looks back). Oh, this another cat, it growed. He doesn't know a killer cat after him. The boy walked out of the house. He didn't see the killer cat. Oh. I read you this, but I didn't read you the words on this one. The boy want to be nice to the mean cat."

Joseph sometimes used his writing as a form of accountability of his actions, and the actions of others. He wrote about his friend Cory in February, letting Cory and the class know that he could use the power of literacy to record social events and name the participants. Joseph was sharing his book with the class. He looked up in the middle with a big grin and read much more fluently than the previous day. He stopped and laughed with Cory about one part and then stopped at several other points to explain and add information. After some of his written dialogue, he

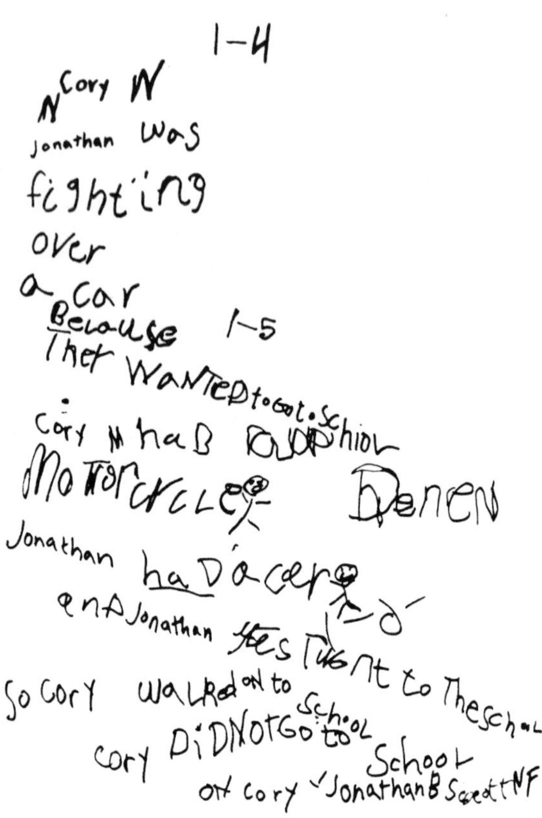

FIG. 5-1 *Joseph's Circle of Friends*

said: "That was me!" [or] "Cory said that. I paid you back, didn't I Cory!" Then he chose Cory to share next. Later after Darnell shared, Joseph pronounced his evaluation of the day's writing by saying, "Your story and Cory story and my story the best stories—and Jonathan."

Some teachers see developing responsibility as an enforcement procedure—kids learning to do what they're told to do when they're told to do it. But allowing Joseph to engage in decision making about his own learning as often as possible increased his options for success. Instead of developing on-going power struggles, we stretched his already developed sense of responsibility. I recently read Tracy Kidder's book *Among Schoolchildren* and regrettably had a hard time feeling close to the teacher, Ms. Zajac. As I read the book, I worried about why my reactions to this book were so flat, why I couldn't identify with this teacher. After all, I was honored that someone would write about my profession and schoolchildren. I think my lack of empathy stemmed from the fact that Ms. Zajac was one of those teachers who focused on product at the exclusion of process and enforced her restrictive standards in a very hard-line way. The only events that truly aroused my emotions were when Clarence was sent away to the Alpha class, a self-contained class for children with behavior problems, and when Robert attempted to complete his

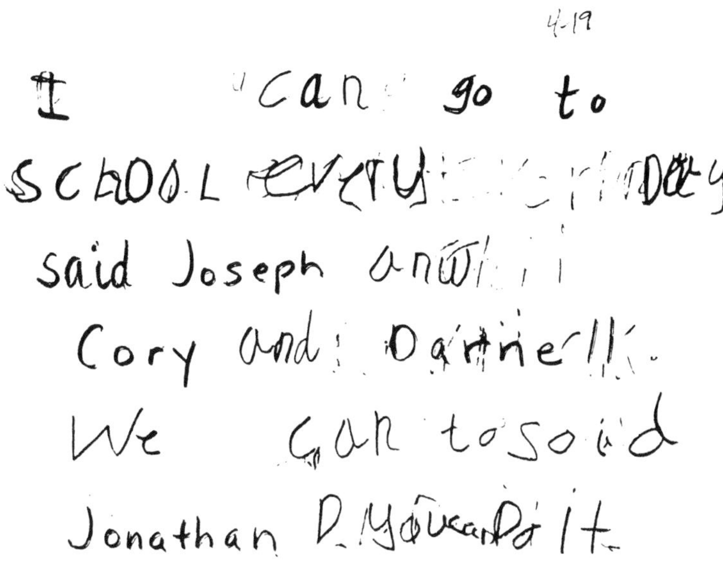

FIG. 5-2 *Joseph's Writing (April)*

science project without the kind of home support most of the students received. Both of these things could happen to Joseph. What would have happened to Clarence if he had been allowed to explore his options in a more supportive way when he first entered school? Why couldn't a public risk event like the science fair where student efforts and knowledge were displayed and compared have been a supported choice rather than a requirement for Robert?

I worked to support Joseph as he learned to apply his strong sense of responsibility to his school life. So did his friends. One morning in March, Joseph asked to read *The King of the Mountain* (Martin, 1970) to the class. As he moved to take his place in the author's chair, Delia announced, "Presenting the Great Joseph!" After he read the final line of the book, "I am the king of the universe!" he grinned at his audience and triumphantly declared, "That's me!"

Was this the silent, hostile child who dangled from his chair those first days of school, the child who fought and threatened? How did he develop this voice, this sense of self-confidence? Had the hoodlum indeed become a king?

The author-ity

For Joseph, genuine responsibility for his own learning was essential; "do-what-I-say" responsibility was neither possible nor desirable. He demanded control, and rose to the challenge of leadership. One of his paths was authorship.

Writing provided a legitimate use of power for Joseph. We had seen that authoring his own life was very important to him, and now through the writing workshop forum, he could be center stage and be in control.

As I grew in my understanding and acceptance of his personal characteristics, Joseph was growing as a reader and a writer. At first the only word he could write was his name, and he participated in writing workshop simply by writing letters, drawing pictures, and telling his picture story. In September he often wrote random letters that he referred to as words. Through his telling of a picture story, it was evident that directionality was a problem. He retold his stories by turning pages back to front to middle and reading bottom to top. On one occasion he kept turning his book around and around as he tried to explain the contents.

By October the letters he chose to convey meaning were mostly variations on his name. On October 14 he drew a "mean cat," and I asked him to try to label the picture by writing the word "cat." He said he couldn't but then he wrote "cu." I asked what the word cat ended with and he answered "t" and added the letter. By October 17 he had used a speaking bubble in his writing, and the next day he insisted on writing the letters himself in a cardboard blank book. He wrote "D" and "N" to stand for "the end" on October 20, and by the next day was calling his publishing company "the boy press." On the 25th he wanted to know how to spell the "real word sun." By December 13 he was very proud of writing five pages in one day about "a car can take you to a house," etc. And on the first day back after Christmas vacation he began a story about Cory and Jonathan fighting over a car, which he continued to work on for several days. During this time he was primarily asking teachers and friends how to spell words, risking little to invention.

Joseph was absent for six or seven days later in the month and we were thrilled when he returned and asked for the story he had been working on before his absence. In an attempt to reread what he had written, he started pointing to sequential lines, reading at least some of the words. Toward the end he tracked word for word and self-corrected at several places. He asked me to spell "did" but got the rest by himself: "Cory did not go to school." Joseph asked, "Cory, you remember that time you weren't at school? I wrote it right here—'Cory did not go to school' because that's when you was gone." He continued monitoring his writing by saying, "Now, I got 'Cory and Jerald were fighting over a car because. . . . '" He reread it all fluently with one self-correction, reading aloud but to himself as he carefully traced his path with his pencil. "Now let me see. . . . " He was totally engrossed in the reading/writing fabric he was weaving, studying the patterns and structures thoughtfully before adding another strand.

Then the day came when Joseph initiated writing himself. It was February. He had finished making a book poster for "Reading Day at the Mall," and he independently went and got paper and started writing. He filled one side of a sheet of lined paper (his choice) with a patterned dialogue between animal characters (cat, dog, pig), which were words he knew how to spell, in a "Little Red Hen" kind of story structure.

I can can you yes dog pig cat

He read this as, "I can. Can you?" "Yes," said dog. "Yes," said pig. "Yes," said cat.

can you pig help
can you dog help
can you cat help
I can cat dog pig
I cat dog pig
I can can you cat yes

Then after lunch he independently began again.

> I can can you yes
> I will you hats
> I will will you yes
> yes I will do it can you do it
> no I can not yes you can

The next day he sat by himself and went right to work continuing his writing from the past two days. He didn't ask for help but wanted to share immediately. By March he had stretched a little past his dependable word patterns but still did not experiment much with invented spellings. He used words he knew how to spell or asked members of his writing community for correct spellings. Getting it "right" was important to him.

From Joseph's initial writing concerns of killer sharks, killer cats, and killer people, he had come a long way to end with stories about friendship.

His progress in reading was equally unique, and again, he was the authority. Getting it "right" in reading was also important. To Joseph, "getting it right" meant being able to read the basals.

In September I rarely felt like he was attending to the stories I read to the class. These were the times when he was most likely to curl up on the floor with his back to me. By October, however, even though he still didn't seem involved during story time, he was showing signs of a developing interest in books. When Ms. Hood, our student teacher, first joined our class, Joseph entertained her by reading a dinosaur book he had been hoarding in his cubby. Joseph pointed to words, moving along with each syllable, until Caleb interrupted and Joseph whirled around and deftly grabbed him by the throat. Just a few days later I observed him reading *Spot Goes to the Circus* (Hill, 1986) to Cameron. When he finished his first invented reading of the story he said, "You want me to read this again to you? You can look that way and still listen." Is it possible that Joseph had in fact been listening all those times he was turned the other way? Later in the day he cried because he noticed Gavin could really read a whole book. There was a new dimension developing, a willingness to be engaged by books, and even to risk reading them. But his standards for himself and others of what constituted a successful reading event remained high.

I was very anxious about how much if any reading interest this supposedly retarded boy would maintain over the Christmas break. I had real fears about essentially having to start over with Joseph. Fortunately, the new year seemed to bring with it a heightened interest in reading and literature and an accelerated learning pace.

At the end of January, I decided to make Joseph my reading buddy during our morning reading time with our fifth-grade buddy class. I was feeling unsettled about Joseph's progress, especially since testing season was getting closer and closer. I decided to check on his reading in basal terms, the terms our district used to define progress. I brought *Bells* (PP1) with me for our first session and was surprised by how quickly he recognized new words. He read the first two stories. I wondered if I needed to teach him more sight words using word cards or if just reading would provide enough support. On February 1 I tried using word cards (old habits do die hard). It wasn't helpful. In fact it seemed harmful. He struggled with these decontextualized words. He must have felt, once again, like he didn't know so much. When we read together I could feel his confidence growing. When we named sight words I could sense a growing concern. We laid the cards aside (forever) and resumed reading *Bells*. By the next day Joseph had finished reading that first preprimer. He said, "My mama, she be real proud when she know I can read. I be in *Drums* (PP2) tomorrow when I come to school in the morning? I didn't practice it (*Bells*). I just read it!"

During reading buddy time the next day, Joseph picked out *Drums* to read, the first time he'd initiated the activity. We read the first story together, alternating character parts. He did quite well and he knew it. He leaned back and stretched in his chair with pride every time he completed his part. On February 8 I noted in my journal: Supporting Joseph as a reader (not doing word cards or workbook pages) seems to be building his confidence at a quicker pace. He seems so much more self-assured.

By February 10 he had finished *Drums,* and by the last day of school he was able to participate in a class reading of the last story in *Carousels* (the 1.2 basal) by reading a page aloud to the class.

Joseph associated reading success with the basals. He knew the levels even though we did not use the basals in the classroom in a strictly ordered fashion (we had no ability groups). He had his own literacy agenda, and I tried to be sensitive to it. Doing "school reading" matched his view of a successful reader. As Lucy Calkins (1991) points out, "[Children] may not want a prescribed curriculum, but they do want a course to run, one that is largely of their own making, and they want to feel as if they're going somewhere. It's not only teachers and parents, but youngsters also, who want clearly delineated goals, systems for frequent feedback, and records of growth" (p. 253). Perhaps basals provided these necessary markers for Joseph and were so tolerated because he had not had to spend day after day in a low-ability group with other struggling readers, doing skills tasks that only loosely related to reading. In a traditional basal-led setting, Joseph could have spent that first half of the year (or longer) in the first preprimer instead of learning to understand himself as a learner while he developed understandings of what reading was all about. He experienced success in the basal because (1) he had already learned how to read; (2) he was asked to read in it, not just "do" it; and (3) because reading successively higher levels of the basal was important to his image of himself as a successful student.

As we read the basal series in a tutorial fashion, Joseph was also actively involved with the class trade books. One afternoon in April he chose to stay in the room while the rest of the class went to P.E. He was reading our big book version of *Teeny Tiny* (Bennett, 1989), and I was pleased by how respectfully he was handling the book. He tenderly called it "pitiful" where the binding had started to separate from one of the pages. In fact, there seemed to be a gradual blending of the two kinds of texts as Joseph would ask, "Who's it by?" when we'd begin a new basal story.

While the basal was his yardstick for success, he knew that he had learned from the sum total of his reading experiences during the year. On the playground one day, I had some of the class books with me and Joseph's sister was outside with her kindergarten class. Joseph ran over to the book pile and grabbed *Night of the Twisters* (Ruckman, 1984), our class read-aloud chapter book. He excitedly showed it to his sister saying, "Here goes that book!" I never knew he was listening when I was reading! Some of the kindergarten children started bringing me books to read from our stack. Joseph ran by and said, "Yea, you keep going over it like that and you'll learn to read. That's how you learn to read."

Joseph claimed full credit for his skill development. When JoBeth asked him on March 17 how he got to be such a good reader, Joseph readily responded, "I started reading and then me and Ms. Shockley read with each other, and then I started reading." JoBeth asked, "How did she help you?" Joseph said, "She didn't help me. I started reading to her and then I learned."

Joseph's emergent literacy is an example to me of every young child's natural desire to learn to read and write. Perhaps they all don't go about the process in quite the same way, but the need is evident. As Joseph became literate, his options for acceptability were increased. He no longer had to solely rely on his tough guy image to gain respect but could legitimately participate in academic endeavors, and the more he participated, the more he seemed to value the process. He was an authority figure in our community as both a reader and a writer.

Joseph still lives in two different worlds. Even though he made impressive literacy leaps, it is not clear that such skills will be enough support for life outside of Walnut Street School. Socially and emotionally he grew to risk being the good guy and even began to smile and laugh at appropriate times instead of mostly when someone else was in trouble. He still had erratic days academically and behaviorally, but the frequency, duration, and intensity of inappropriate choices lessened. But how could this be enough when he was confronted by contradictory input from those in his other world—brothers and cousins, people he really cared about? As he learned he reduced his risks, but he did not erase them.

Complex worlds

Joseph's most explosive episode happened on March 13. Significantly, it was a Monday, always his most difficult school day, a day of transition between worlds. This was the first Monday after a week of standardized testing. The excerpt that follows is from my teaching journal.

> He entered the classroom without speaking to anyone—kind of stood near his chair for awhile—sat down—refused to do morning work that Ms. Hood took over to him—didn't stand up for the pledge of allegiance or the national anthem.
>
> I asked him to come read in the hall with me. He chose three books: *George and Martha* [Marshall, 1972], *King on the Mountain*, and *Pinnochio* [a controlled vocabulary book by Margaret Hillert]. When I saw he had the *Pinnochio* book, I said, "Oh you can read this book!" and he did—the whole book. He didn't offer me a part and about half way through he stopped in amazement and said, "I read that all by myself!" I said, "You certainly did." So he read that whole page over just to prove it to himself.
>
> During morning recess, Andrew had a bag of Bugle snacks that Marcell had given him. The bag was practically empty and Joseph came up and asked if he could have some. Andrew told him to get some but Joseph said, "I take them all if I reach in. You give me some." Andrew did and Joseph ran off saying "Thank you, man!"
>
> After recess, he went in the bathroom and pulled his own tooth—a molar. When he came out I asked him where his tooth was. He pointed back in the bathroom and I suggested he go and get it for the tooth fairy. He looked up at me

with a puzzled expression and asked, "How you get the tooth fairy to come?" (His tooth had gone down the drain.)

He dropped his tray at the end of the lunch counter. After he picked up his tray, I showed him where to wash his hands and I took his fork and got him a new one. He was annoyed with me for doing that because he hadn't "wasted his fork." Then he went to sit down and discovered that someone was sitting where he wanted to sit. I explained that I was sorry but the other children were there first. I walked off to get my lunch but noticed that Joseph had put his tray down and was walking around—deciding what to do. When I looked up again, he had found himself a place at a table away from our class!

He was very outgoing and seemed comfortable while the pen pals were visiting.

By afternoon recess time, all seemed normal. We'd been outside about 10 minutes when Ryan came and told me that Joseph had thrown him down. "Joseph! Come talk with me please." He came hesitantly at first, stopping to hang by his hands on the monkey bars on his way. When he finally got to me, I asked him if he had thrown Ryan down. Joseph quickly reacted by saying "Marcell told me to!" I reminded him that he didn't have to act on instructions from other children, that he could make his own decisions. Marcell said he didn't tell him to do it and that he was play-wrestling with Ryan and Joseph came over and got rough. Ryan agreed, then Darnell tried to interject a comment, and Joseph rushed at him and pushed at him with great force. I quickly took Joseph by the arms as I stood behind him pulling him away from Darnell and the enlarging group. Darnell's twin brother Darneal called Joseph a peanut.

Joseph was furious! I can't describe the tension and power I felt in his arms. He tried to struggle free to go after Darneal but I had a firm hold. If Joseph had gotten loose, I really think he would have seriously hurt Darneal. I've never seen Joseph so powerfully out of control. Another first-grade teacher offered to watch my class while I escorted Joseph inside. As we distanced ourselves from the playscape, I could feel his resistance lessening to the point where I was able just to keep my arm around his shoulders. He didn't struggle at all as we entered the building or the classroom.

Once inside the room, I told Ms. Hood (the student teacher) that Joseph could not go to P.E. He had been talking and complaining but suddenly started to cry and loudly comment on how he hated this school, etc. I asked Ms. Hood to return to the students outside and assist Ms. Clifton. She closed the door behind her. Joseph continued to cry and complain while I stated calmly and firmly that I would always care about him and try to help him and be his friend no matter what, but that he could not react so violently to others or he would end up in jail one day (interestingly at one point in his arguing he said, "You wouldn't come visit me if I was in jail!").

Anyway, I repeated my support for him while at the same time he continued to "badmouth" Walnut Street School and me. As he talked, I noticed he was moving to turn his back on me until finally he ended up standing at one end of the table with his back to me while I sat down and recorded the episode. He never turned around to see what I was doing. He continued his distressing commentary for twenty minutes. At one point he yelled, "I'll kill him—shoot the brains out of that boy!" And also, "I believe what my cousins say—this school start trouble—I didn't believe him—now I do. I ain't supposed to come to this school no way—I get on that little bus with my brother—go to Poplar Street School—I ain't coming to this school no more!" He talked about schools and said, "Walnut Street ain't no better than Pine Street School, when I go to kindergarten. One thing I hate about this school—it ain't got no swings!" Then he compared playscapes and talked about a

FIG. 5–3 *Killer People*

> big slide at one school. "I'm going to stop school—live back in the apartments—tomorrow I be in Poplar School. I ain't got no friends at this school, just Jonathan and Cory. . . . "
>
> He talked some more about past teachers, then said, "Ask my big cousin do I hit unless somebody hit me—nobody better not hit me!" He continued talking but his voice got softer and quieter. He ended by talking about how much fun he'd have after school playing with his cousins when he gets off the bus. I have said nothing. We are interrupted by a voice on the intercom asking for Jonathan. Joseph offers to go to the playscape and get him. I ask if he can do that without bothering anybody else. He nods yes and goes. I watch without him knowing. Jonathan is agreeably retrieved and I ask Joseph if he would mind helping by straightening up around the room. I leave the room. Joseph does an excellent job. Not only does he do the tasks I asked of him but he also reads the names on the writing folders and places each one in the owner's cubby. The room looked great and so did Joseph.

We included this whole vignette so readers could see that the issue of justice, and the fine line between king and hoodlum, permeated much of Joseph's daily life. It was as if he was in his own therapy session. I was just there to make sure he didn't hurt himself or anyone else. As some incidents in this revealing day demonstrate, Joseph was developing some strategies for monitoring his own behavior, but not being "messed with" was still a driving force.

The incident also showed me how near the surface physical violence was for Joseph. I had a shock of recognition when I heard him say, "I'll shoot the brains out of that boy." He had used the same phrase in one of his September writings, a picture of a male shooting another male in the head (see Figure 5–3). And earlier that year, there had been a newspaper story about a relative of Joseph's who had allegedly robbed a store. "Kill me, blow my brains out," he had told the arresting officer as the officer secured leg irons and handcuffs. No matter how safe and dependable I tried to make Joseph's world at school, he contended with a very different world when he walked out of our room.

Once Joseph was looking through our science textbook and noticed a picture of a hamster. He announced to his friends that his brother used to have one of them. I overheard and asked what happened to the hamster and Joseph proceeded with a grim account of how "his brother had put glue all in its eyes and mouth" and "how the hamster would walk a little bit and then fall down dead." On more than one occasion, Joseph shared major family concerns with us. The police had to come to his house at least twice because his older brother had been caught stealing from the neighborhood convenience store, for which he had spent a weekend in the Youth Detention Center. Joseph was very protective of his family and noticeably disturbed by such events. Another time, his chin quivered as he recounted how his step-brothers had to move in with them because their father had hit them. And one night a faulty space heater caused the death of two of his cousins. Joseph said, "All they needed was some air and they wouldn't have died." When he was angry one afternoon he threatened, "I'll scratch a teacher just like my brother do if she make me mad!" This brother had been suspended for not obeying a teacher, and had moved to a separate school for children with severe behavior problems. When I drove him to the university one Saturday morning to meet Bill Martin, during the Children's Literature Conference, Joseph informed me that his cousins told him that the university was "a white people's place." Time after time he was reminded by people and events on both fronts that his school world and home world were quite different.

But perhaps most telling of all were the times when his innocence about "usual" childhood experiences became apparent. For instance, during our trip to the university one of the students put a coin in the fountain and made a wish. A few days later in class Joseph asked, "Those wishes come true at that place?" He held up a quarter for me! And of course, "How you get the tooth fairy to come?"

I can't leave my story of Joseph without sharing how honored I was to be part of his life. I had a well-established relationship with his mother, a woman adept at doing for her children by whatever means necessary. One parent conference I visited them in their third home of the year, and she and I listened to Joseph read for over fifteen minutes. She calmly and competently helped him on a few difficult words and took obvious pride and interest in both his reading and his writing. I had his sister in my class the next year and he often stopped by to visit with both of us. One day when I asked her if their mother read to them at home, she said, "She read to me but she don't read to Joseph anymore—he can already read lots of books." When I saw him in the halls as a big third grader and he called out my name and grinned from ear to ear, I knew a smile could grow and that I had made a difference. One teacher may not be able to offer more than a glimpse into life's possibilities, but collectively we hold the world in our hands.

SIX

"I Love to Be Learning with My Friends"

Joseph in Second Grade at Walnut Street School

It was the first day of school. The bell had just rung and all the students were settled quietly at tables. I (Barbara) heard a child wailing in the hall and thought to myself, "Ah, that must be a kindergartner. That's one advantage of teaching second grade, no criers." A moment later an irritated secretary stuck her head in my room and said, "Ms. Michalove, this child is one of yours."

I hurried into the hall and there was Joseph: King of the Universe. He was pitiful. I put my arm around him and gently led him into the classroom, pointing out his friends from first grade. He calmed down immediately. He looked especially relieved to see JoBeth. An hour later his mother peeked her head in the door to see if he had arrived at school.

I'd heard about Joseph from first grade: Joseph the bully, Joseph the leader, Joseph the mildly mentally handicapped (MiMH) *and* behaviorally disordered (BD) student. I hadn't heard about Joseph the wailer. It was not a side of Joseph that he revealed often during his year in my classroom. But the image of Joseph frightened to tears the first day of school stayed with me as I got to know him.

"If you had two you'd give me some"

Fairness was important to Joseph. He wasn't concerned only for himself, but for everyone. As early as his first day in my classroom he was calling our attention to the issue. When Jeremiah, Colin, and Caleb shared a book with the class, Joseph noticed that Caleb wasn't reading. He pointed this fact out three times to everyone, then finally said, "Say something, Caleb."

One morning Joseph was sitting on the sofa reading an oversized book, *Teeny Tiny*, with Jeff. Joseph said, "I'll read the first page, then you read the next page." They began reading and were joined by Jonathan. "Jonathan, hold this book so we can read it," instructed Joseph. After two pages Joseph said, "Let Jonathan read this page." Jonathan moved around to join them on the sofa. Joseph kept track of whose turn it was to read until they finished the book.

Joseph's friends often shared their snacks with him. One day in December he asked Caleb for some of his snack. When Caleb refused to share Joseph said, "If you had two, you'd give me some." He then shared his orange with Caleb. This was the first time that Joseph had brought a snack to school.

Joseph was quick to point out when he observed or experienced something that he considered unfair. In January he told me, "I don't never get to type." Most of his classmates had already had a turn to type, and he had waited patiently for a long time.

When I was helping kids edit their writing to prepare it for publication, I worked from a list on which they signed their names. They checked their names off after we finished working together. The list stayed on the wall in the classroom. One day I called Jeremiah to come work with me, and Joseph called out, "Nora is first." He was right; Nora was first on the list, but she wasn't quite ready to edit her paper.

When a teacher at school gave Joseph some clothes he was very excited, especially about a Bulldog sweatshirt that was included. He told me that he would wear it to school the next day. When he didn't wear it I asked him why. He said "My brother cried and cried, so I let him wear it." He also gave one of the shirts to his friend Carter "because he didn't get any."

Joseph's sense of equality and fairness pervaded everything he did. As he wrote a letter to his pen pal he said "I'm going to say 'How old are you?' She should have told me. I'm fixing to get her back; she asked me how old I am. There, I got her back."

Joseph had all of us under constant surveillance. It seemed as if he were policing our actions for breaches of fairness. He had high standards for himself and others, and when these standards were violated, Joseph had a hard time handling himself. In a stressful situation Joseph's vulnerability came to the surface. In December a substitute bus driver unjustly accused Joseph of misbehaving on the bus. Joseph began running around the bus circle, where ten buses were preparing to leave school, wailing and crying. A teacher finally grabbed him and helped him talk with the bus driver.

One day I removed Joseph from our classroom for threatening to "kill" Chris if he told on him for calling people names. Joseph began crying loudly. He was upset because he would miss a party we had planned for the afternoon. He was even more concerned that Carter, who had also been involved, be removed too. Once I reassured him that Carter would not be allowed to stay in our room either, he calmly went to stay in another classroom for the afternoon.

Once when Joseph got into a fight in the bathroom, he already had his name and a check on the board for various infractions of our class-generated rules. I took him to time out for fifteen minutes in another classroom. On the way he cried and wailed, saying he wished that he were moving to another school. He didn't argue that it wasn't fair, as he had helped to write the rules and the consequences with his classmates at the beginning of the year. After fifteen minutes he returned to our room and worked happily for the rest of the day.

Responsibility and high expectations

Along with Joseph's well-developed ideas about fairness, his sense of responsibility guided his behavior. He generally kept track of everyone, and what should be going on at school. If someone missed a chance to do something because they were absent or we ran out of time, Joseph always reminded me that they still needed a turn.

When we straightened the room he took care to put things away properly, even when his friends were encouraging him to "just put them anywhere."

When Joseph broke our class rules he accepted the consequences without arguing. He didn't lay blame on others when he made a choice that got him into trouble. His feelings of responsibility towards his family were also apparent. He watched out for his younger sister on the bus and made sure that she got to her classroom. He told me, "Sometimes she don't talk to nobody, but she talk to me."

In January Joseph began the day telling Teena that he and his brother were going to beat up her and her sister. After listening to him hurl threats at Teena for fifteen minutes, JoBeth asked him why he was mad at Teena. He said, "I'm not mad at her. She always like to get her brother on people, and he got on my brother. Then I feel like beating her up, but I didn't want to fight. I'm going to move on Friday because we tired of the people living over there. I hate that place, it bad. The kids are bad." These feelings of responsibility towards family also came out in dramatic play. When Joseph was the biggest billy goat in "The Three Billy Goats Gruff" he ad libbed at the end of the play. "I told you I save my two brothers!" Joseph also talked about his brothers in his writing (see Figures 6-1 and 6-2).

Joseph had high expectations for himself and worked hard in school. When writing he would erase and rewrite as he composed. He liked working in the basal workbook, which we did occasionally, where the right answer was so clear. He took a teaching role when he worked in his reading workbook with Colin. He told us that *Carousels*, the basal reader, was his favorite book. Joseph knew that the basal series was an important measure of school success. He worried that Colin and Nate wouldn't "make their grade" because they couldn't read the second-grade level basal. He proudly showed that he could read it.

Joseph had high standards for himself as a writer. As Joseph became a better speller, he would get upset when he couldn't spell words correctly. He wrote a letter to his pen pal and struggled over spelling "want." JoBeth assured him that she could read it. He responded, "But she (the pen pal) won't be able to read it," and demanded that JoBeth give him the correct spelling.

As he became a better writer he changed his expectations of himself and began to take more risks. At the beginning of the year his pieces were short and often influenced by preprimer basal writing. At the end of the year he was writing books with tables of contents, more complex plots, and interesting characters. He began to plan orally what he would write next and to work on one piece over a long period (see Figure 6-3).

Joseph still went to Ms. Gibbons' room twice a week for forty-five minutes. He was concerned when he had to leave the classroom at a time that took him away from his work. He said, "I might not get done like the rest." He praised his own efforts and set goals for himself. During writing one day he said, "I'm going to make a book and get up there and share." When we practiced for a standardized test he raised his fist in a cheer and announced, "I got mine all right—yea!" During sharing time in writing he responded to another child's question for clarification and said, "I know it, I paid attention."

Joseph did pay attention, to every detail. He needed the structure of our classroom to stay the same. If there was a change he immediately pointed it out. I always wrote our schedule on the chalkboard. If I didn't get a chance to do this before Joseph arrived he would tell me, "Ms. Michalove, you didn't write the schedule." One day after a substitute teacher had been there, Joseph told me,

The little red cat scratched my brother
and my brother went out of the house and
throwed him in the woods.

FIG. 6–1 *"The Little Red Cat"*

"She writes too big on the board." He also complained that Ms. Bradley, our hour-a-day aide, wouldn't let him help Colin with his reading.

He seemed to have a script in his head of how things should be at school. He didn't like when reality varied from his script. When Jeremiah asked JoBeth how to spell "much," Joseph said, "She going to say 'm-m-m-uch, sound it out.' Just like Ms. Michalove." That was my standard response to the numerous requests I received for spelling help during writing workshop. Later in the year Benson asked JoBeth how to spell "yea." She spelled it for him. Joseph was shocked; he said accusingly, "You told him!"

My brother went to
the movies
in clean clothes.

FIG. 6–2 *"My Brother"*

"I'll read it first, y'all"

Joseph liked to be in charge. Reading and writing workshop gave him a way to be in charge that was acceptable in school. He often took a leadership role during these times. Early in September Joseph was reading *Each Peach Pear Plum* with Caleb and Jonathan. He asked them if they wanted to share. Later when they shared with the class, Joseph held the book, sat in the author's chair, and answered the questions. Jonathan and Caleb stood behind him and joined in when he read a page to the class. Another day he read with Colin and Kenny, directing the whole time. "I'll read it first ya'll," he told them.

Joseph naturally slipped into the self-appointed role of Indian Chief when we acted out the story of Christopher Columbus' voyage to America. He yelled vehemently at the intruders, "Go back to your own country!" The other students in the classroom accepted Joseph's leadership role, in this and other situations. He often directed small-group sharing sessions. He told Vickie, "You got to pick me, I was here first." She picked him. After he shared his writing he asked if anyone else wanted to share, but he told the small group, "I want to see a long story."

Joseph stayed in charge when he wrote with friends. One day he told Carter, "It's about time you started writing real good." Another day he tried to influence Carter's decision about sharing alone or with him. He told Carter, "I thought we always write together, now you different." Carter responded, "I got to share by myself sometimes." Joseph wasn't real happy with this response, but accepted it.

Joseph's power issue extended to adults also. He needed to be able to choose his position. On various occasions during the year he came into our room with a belligerent attitude. He would tell me he "wasn't going to do anything." I refused to accept the responsibility of making him do "anything." Instead of demanding that he do his work, I made his choices clear to him. He could stay in our room and work with us (I'd list what we had planned for the day) or he could go to time out in another classroom. It was up to him. I would give him some time to think about his choice. He always chose to stay with us and learn.

JoBeth encountered Joseph's desire to control things when she interviewed him. In October he gradually took over the interview. He started by telling her to

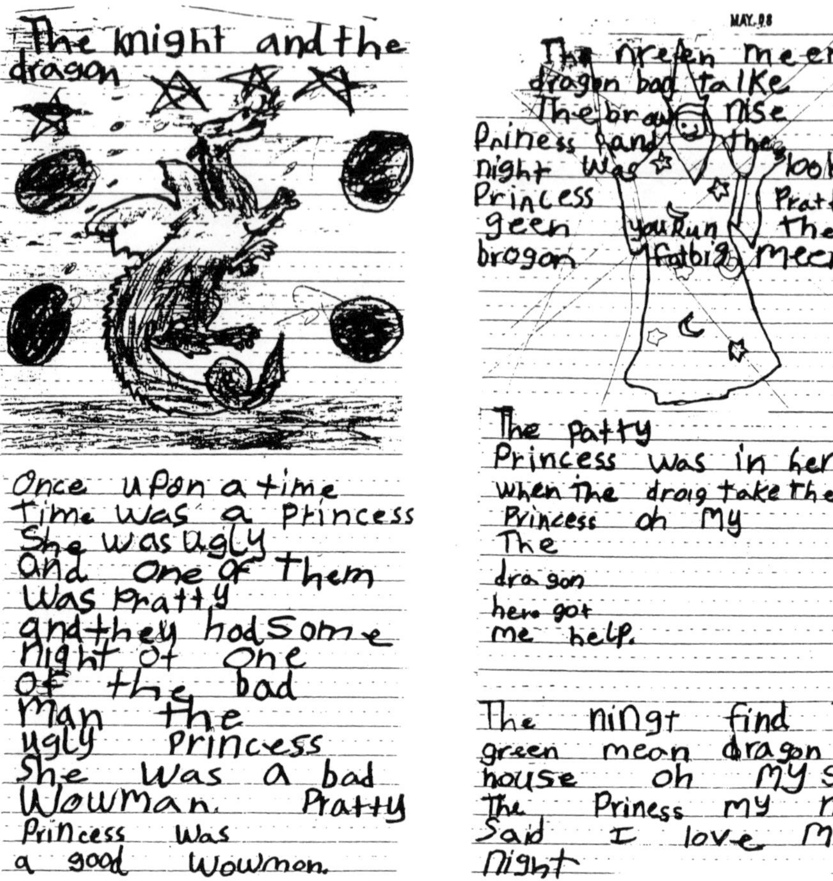
The knight and the
dragon
Once upon a time
Time was a Princess
She was ugly
and one of them
Was Pratty
and they had Some
night of one
of the bad
man the
ugly Princess
She Was a bad
Wowman. Pratty
Princess Was
a good Wowmon.

MAY. 98
The green meen
dragon bad talke
The brawn nise
Priness and the
night Was looking
Princess Pratty
geen you Run the
brogon fatbig meen

The Patty
Princess Was in her room
When The draig take the
Princess oh My
The
dragon
here got
me help.

The ningt find The
green mean dragon
house oh My Said
The Priness my night
Said I love My
Night

The knight and the dragon

Once upon a time [there] was a princess. She was ugly and one of them was pretty and they had some knight. One of [them was] the bad man. The ugly princess, she was a bad woman. [The] pretty princess was a good woman. The pretty princess was in her room when the dragon take the princess. "Oh my, the dragon have got me. Help!" The green mean dragon had taken the brown nice princess and the knight was looking [for the] pretty princess. "You run [from] the fat, big, mean, green dragon." The knight found the green mean dragon's house. "Oh my," said the princess. "My knight," [she] said. "I love my knight."

FIG. 6–3 *Joseph's Knight and Dragon Story*

"stop writing in cursive." Then he began reading the interview questions for himself. Finally, he took the pen out of her hand and wrote his own responses to the questions.

What was important for Joseph was being the one who decided. Often I felt as if he wanted to involve me in a power struggle. But a struggle never materialized, partly due to the way I handled the issue and partly, I think, because Joseph really wanted to be good at school.

School was important to Joseph. His older brothers had many difficulties in school, but Joseph genuinely seemed to like school. Joseph's sister told her teacher, "Joseph plays nice teacher, my other brothers play mean teacher." School was a theme he used frequently in his writing, and he often had one character convincing another that school was a good place to be, as in the following story he wrote on October 23:

thes story	This story
is aboyt	is about
the green withe	the green witch
in a old hvme	in a old home.
she gat a good cat	She got a good cat.
One apon a	Once upon a [time]
there was a	there was a
withe who said	witch who said
I can go to scool	"I can go to school,
scool is good?	school is good?"
You like scool	"You like school,
scool vab Fun	school is fun"
said the withe	said the witch.

Being a friend was important to Joseph. It was a newly acquired skill for him, one he had begun developing the previous year. The importance of being a friend developed concurrently in his writing. He used various characters acting out friendships in his stories throughout the year, a theme that had also permeated his writing toward the end of the previous year in Betty's room. Figures 6–4 and 6–5 are typical of his many friendship stories. Figure 6–5 about the little puppy is also an example of what Joseph talked about in his February interview of how he got "ideas from real life, but the story is fiction."

Joseph's desire to control what happened in his environment also had its negative side. He often teased other children. Many times it was in fun, but sometimes he couched threats in his banter. He told his good friend Carter, "You a big man, but you got a little butt." Carter laughingly responded, "Well at least I got a butt." He teased Chris about his drawing, then told him, "Make sure you don't get near me, I might hurt you." When Chris was asked to sit alone, Joseph said, "He just a little baby, have to sit by himself." While such verbal interactions are common among African-American males (Irvine, 1990), there was often an edge of anger in Joseph's voice that seemed to make the other children take him seriously.

Joseph did fine handling himself as long as the day progressed in a predictable manner. On days when things were out of the ordinary he had a hard time. He was one of two children who didn't bring valentine cards for his classmates. The other child spent the morning making cards for everyone. Joseph spent the morning terrorizing everyone.

When things were bad for Joseph he either totally fell apart or began to act like a gang leader. At times he tried to get gang-type groups going on the playground. I kept a sharp eye on this type of behavior and stopped it before it gained momentum. Joseph was a leader and perfectly capable of creating some real social problems in our classroom. This type of behavior became more frequent the last month of school. Was he "practicing" behavior that he would need in his neighborhood over the summer?

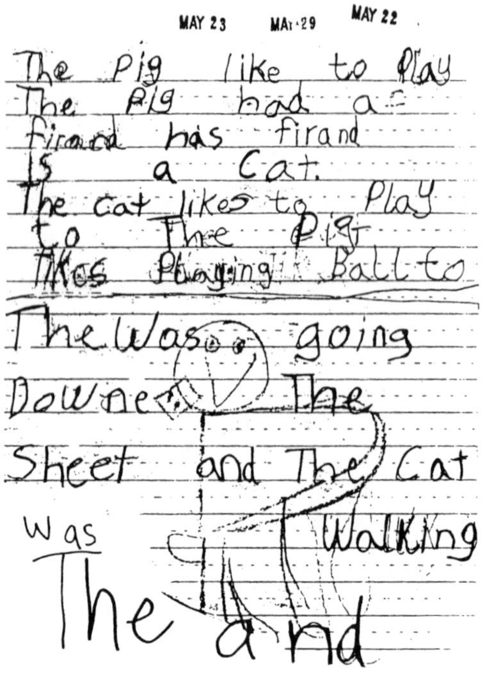

MAY 23 MAY 29 MAY 22

The Pig like to Play
The Pig had a
firand has firand
is a Cat.
The cat likes to Play
to The Pig
Was Playing Ball to
The Was going
Downe The
Sheet and The Cat
Was Walking
The and

FIG. 6–4 *Joseph's Pig Story*

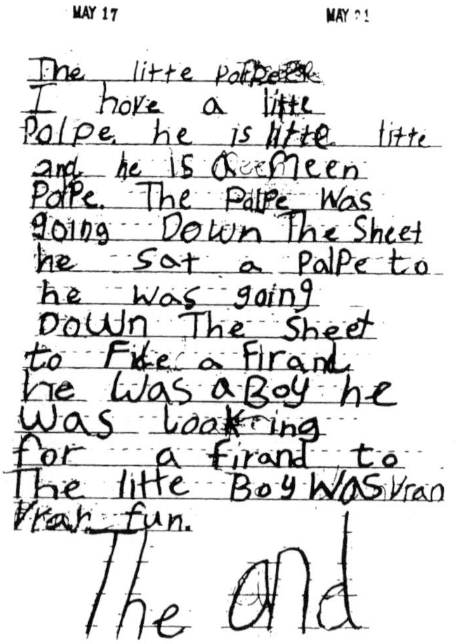

MAY 17 MAY ?1

The litte Polpe
I hove a litte
Polpe he is litte litte
and he is a meen
Polpe. The Polpe Was
going Down The Sheet
he sat a PolPe to
he Was going
Down The Sheet
to Fike a firand
he Was a Boy he
Was looking
for a firand to
The litte Boy Was Vran
Vran fun.
The and

FIG. 6–5 *Joseph's Puppy Story*

Joseph was tough. He needed to be tough to survive in his family and neighborhood. He told us, "My brothers beat me up for crying." He also was the frightened little boy who wailed in the hall the first day of school. In his writing he included the types of encounters he had in his everyday life. Joseph rarely wrote about these experiences in the first person. He often used animals as characters acting out things that may have happened to him. He still liked to use predictable structures in his writing, as he did in many stories that were similar in format to his first-grade stories like the one in the previous chapter: "'I can. Can you?' 'Yes,' said the pig." He worked on the following story, in addition to several other pieces, the entire month of May.

> The Dog is going to the park. The Dog is going to. play in the park. I like playing in a park The cat cam to play in The park Dog said wet are you ding [What are you doing] I went to play with you dog said cat in [and] cat in dog is going to play at the park the Dog what [want] to go home the cat do nat went to go home the Dog said if you went I do I'm going home then the big Dog and the cat is going to fighting the Nice cat ane dog What do you wonce We come to play or the playscate [on the playscape] What do you do fon we went to play with you can play bat do't figt we will nat fight dog went hom ane den't nat [didn't not] come back

"I'm not so worried about Joseph"

If this had been the first year of the study I may not have chosen to study Joseph. He didn't stand out as having overwhelming behavior or academic problems. There were other students in the class whom I was more worried about. I became aware of his problems and progress because of the study.

What a different year second grade was from first grade for Joseph. I hadn't been overwhelmed with joy about the prospect of spending the year with Joseph. I had heard about his "hoodlum" behavior the previous year when Dr. Oates talked about his problems in a faculty meeting. Betty felt he had made progress towards literacy in first grade, but I didn't know what that really meant. I feared that he would create many problems in the classroom. The Joseph I had imagined was not the Joseph who spent a year as a contributing member of our community.

Joseph moved three times during the year. Luckily for him all of these moves kept him within the same school district. He really developed friendships in our classroom, something he had just begun to do in first grade. He told us in an interview, "I love to be writing with my friends." I think it would have been hard for him to develop the social skills that allowed him to be a friend if he had not been in the same classroom throughout the year.

I watched as Joseph grew in leaps and bounds in second grade. He became a reader and a writer. At the beginning of the year he struggled to write very short stories. In the spring he was able to work on pieces over long periods. He set goals for himself and modeled his work on real authors. He included a table of contents in one book he wrote. He reread and revised his work on his own. He also "wrote more talking in his stories."

Joseph's progress in reading sneaked up on me. He worked diligently all year reading fairly easy texts. One day in early spring he delighted us both by competently reading *Curious George* (H.A. Rey) aloud to me. I think we were both surprised. I gave him the book to keep and taught him about using book markers, as it is quite a long story. Joseph was really reading. He was also able to read the first second-grade reader from the basal series by the end of the school year. He had not only made progress as a reader but as a risk taker also.

Being a member of a community of learners had given Joseph opportunities to use his strengths and develop his weaknesses. I hoped that third grade would offer him the same supportive learning community, and that in spite of the frequent moves his family made, he would remain with us at Walnut Street School. I think he was beginning to trust this school world and to see his rightful place in it, as a reader, a writer, a learner, and a friend.

SEVEN

"I Been Going Slowly, But I'm Going"

Joseph in Third Grade at Walnut, Oak, Birch, and Walnut Again

with Margie Weiderhold

Walnut Street School

Joseph's family had moved increasingly closer to the school, almost like a wary puppy sidling up to an outstretched hand. Joseph visited the school several times over the summer, mostly to talk with Betty. This year, unlike the previous one, he seemed to feel more comfortable in a new room; there was no fearful crying. He moved into Margie's room, where he encountered the familiar structures of reading and writing workshop. Joseph moved immediately into an atmosphere of friends: Caleb from both previous years, and Violet, Hunan, and his good friends Cory and Jonathan from first grade.

But all was not peaceful. Two days into school there were four police cars at Joseph's house because, as his older brother reported, "My mama almost got into a fight with my neighbor's friend." Then we heard that the family would be moving out of the Walnut district. "We might not move," Joseph countered. "Hush up," his little sister corrected. "You know we're already packed."

By the end of the next week they were gone.

Oak Street School

Joseph had a rough beginning at Oak Street School. His mother didn't come with the children the first day. The next morning he came in crying, saying he had a bad headache and wanted to go home. "The principal really tore into him, and told

---

Margie Weiderhold wanted to be a co-researcher, but Joseph moved shortly after the beginning of school. When he returned, Margie was very helpful in describing her observations. At Oak Street, Ms. Gibbons (the resource teacher's pseudonym) and Ms. Bradley (the homeroom teacher's pseudonym) were interviewed twice by JoBeth, who authored the chapter.

him that his behavior wouldn't be tolerated. He was scared," according to one of his teachers. "He stopped crying, then got real quiet. He never mentioned his head again." The following day he didn't go to school; his sister told his teacher, "He just didn't want to come, so he didn't get on the bus." He did attend the rest of the week, however, accompanied by his mother several times. The principal noted, "He's having a very hard time adjusting to our school. I've never seen a third grader cling to his mother like this—like a toddler."

His teacher, Ms. Bradley, said, "He didn't make much effort to do the work at first, but now he is trying harder." At the end of October Barbara talked with his teacher. Ms. Bradley, a young teacher new to the district, said, "Some days he's very cooperative; others he's totally defiant. He picks on other kids, but he's not my worst discipline problem. Most of my black kids pick on each other. He tries really hard in reading; he always wants to read aloud to the class. He's one of the best readers in the *Adventures* (2.1) group and helps the others in the group quite a bit. We don't do whole language. We do some writing with story starters, the 'pretend-you-are' type. Joseph *will not* do it—he refuses. I wasn't prepared to have kids that can't solve five minus two, but one day he did regroupings perfectly. I think he's holding out on me."

Coincidentally, Joseph's resource teacher, Ms. Gibbons, had transferred to Oak Street. Joseph went to her room two hours a week. Joseph told Ms. Gibbons that Ms. Bradley lied all the time—"she always tells stories about me." "Joseph is really floundering," Ms. Gibbons told JoBeth in mid-November. "He cried a lot at the beginning of the year. It's taking him so long to learn how to trust again. He had learned to trust Walnut Street, but he doesn't trust the education system in general. I'm seeing more neighborhood behavior, like threatening and shoving, at school. He doesn't just let things go; he escalates any provocation to the point of aggression, especially with one boy in my class. I'd like to move him to another time and take him five days a week."

In a discussion later that fall Ms. Gibbons, Ms. Bradley, and JoBeth talked about Joseph's progress and needs. Ms. Bradley agreed that he needed more time in the resource room. "He's always trying to tell kids what to do, inappropriately. Last week he told me, 'My brother hit his teacher, and I'll hit mine too.' He was upset because he had to miss recess for not behaving in class. Later he apologized. It seems like he's sleepy a lot. He usually has his head on the desk, and some days he actually sleeps.

"I'm real proud of his reading," Ms. Bradley continued. "Compared to the other kids in his group, he's one of the better readers. I bought him a book at the book fair about a monster. He read it to a visitor recently. I knew he couldn't buy one, and I figured it was something we could read together every day. He's sitting at a table with lots of bright kids, good readers and workers. He usually asks them for help, not me. I'm glad they can help. He hasn't done much writing. We usually do one piece a week, like with spelling words. He hasn't written anything yet. Today they made up a story about a crazy field trip, but not Joseph. His spelling and English grades were both Unsatisfactory, as was his behavior. He had Satisfactory in reading, penmanship, and the rest, except science—he had a Good. He doesn't usually finish assignments. In fact, he often doesn't do them at all, even when I cut back on assignments."

"Some of the kids are being forced to work in books they just can't be successful in. Maybe I can help with his class work," Ms. Gibbons volunteered.

"I never knew why he came to your class. I didn't get any information on any of the special ed kids," Ms. Bradley said gratefully.

"I'm trying to use mostly trade books," Ms. Gibbons explained. "Some textbooks are just too frustrating. The classroom here is really different [than last year's], so he's really doing pretty well, considering the differences."

Ms. Bradley agreed. "I was trained as a whole language teacher, but I've been told there's not much support for whole language here. I bet that [transition] would be hard for a kid."

"Joseph's a real heartbreaker," Ms. Gibbons sighed. "He's showing no remorse like he did last year. I asked him about the way he had been acting; I said 'This isn't the Joseph I knew last year.' He said, 'That was Joseph Green [using his last name] at Walnut Street. This is Joseph Cecil [using his middle name], and I don't care.'"

Birch Street School

Shortly after this conversation Joseph's family moved again. His new teacher at Birch Street School was too busy to talk with us.

Walnut Street School

In early April, the family moved back into the Walnut Street district. Joseph was "back home," back with his friends and with Margie, the teacher he had begun the year with. She commented, "He was somewhat defiant the first two days. Since then he's been very cooperative. He doesn't listen well to whole-class assignments —he needs individual instructions—but he's *not* a behavior problem. I just don't know about his BD placement. I really haven't seen any bad behavior. He seems genuinely happy. He gets along well with the other kids, especially Jonathan and Cory.

"He's in class for reading workshop, but he leaves during writing workshop to go to Ms. Erdrich (his new resource room teacher). The Chapter 1 teacher, Ms. Kingsolver, works with our class during reading workshop rather than pulling kids out. We have three twenty-minute segments, with three rotating groups. One group reads their self-selected books at their seats, I listen to another group read their own books, and Ms. Kingsolver teaches basal skills and does magazine testing. Some days are for skills and workbooks; some days our lessons tie in with units, like the one on endangered animals we're doing now. We choose books or basal stories on this topic and read and discuss them. I've got one group in *Journeys* (3.2), one in *Caravans* (3.1), and one in *Adventures* (2.1). I've been thinking about working with Joseph individually to get him through the testing while my student teacher is here. He is by far the best reader in the group. He loves telling the other kids what words are, giving them hints, but I'm trying to help all of them allow each other time to figure out their *own* words and strategies. He loves to read."

There was no information from his Birch Street teacher, but his transfer sheet indicated that he had gone to special education for reading, spelling, and English. He went twice a day for a total of ninety minutes daily, compared with ninety minutes a week in first and second grades. At Walnut, he now went to Ms. Erdrich for forty-five minutes of academics every morning and to Ms. Welty for forty-five minutes of social skills every afternoon. "It's odd," Ms. Erdrich mused, "because he's staffed for BD, and there was no IEP (individualized education plan) written at his other school. He can read—he's a good reader. He outshines the other readers in *Adventures*. Margie and I want to test him out of *Adventures* and into *Discoveries* (2.2). According to district guidelines he shouldn't pass third grade if he's not through *Caravans* (3.1), but by then his IEP will be different. It won't require that. And thank goodness the CRT will not be used for promotion this year!"[3]

At the end of the year Margie was pleased with Joseph's progress. "He's doing surprisingly well in reading, although officially we only got through *Adventures*. He hasn't been writing a lot because he leaves to go to Ms. Welty. He needs his reading and writing in the classroom, although he does need help with spelling. He has remained a cooperative kid. It amazes me that his behavior was ever a problem. He almost never knows what to do when I give an assignment, but once he gets started he's very task oriented. On an assignment last week on the book *The Little Island* (Brown, 1946), his partner was all at loose ends and Joseph got him to sit down and do it, got the books they needed (we have a class set), and they got it done.

"Right now he's going to both Ms. Erdrich and Ms. Welty because his papers still say two segments a day; the three of us will decide what's best for him next year. Joseph isn't BD. So what will he end up doing—little tiny segments or what—next year? I wish, in a school like Walnut Street with so many needs, we could just have fifteen kids per teacher, and have them all day. It would really make a difference."

Continuing Worries

What will become of Joseph? Will he be at Walnut Street again next year, or will he have another three-school year? Will he "need" special education, or will it simply happen because its on his record? Will he have an opportunity to reestablish himself as a writer? Will he be allowed to display his competence as a reader, or again be relegated to incompetence in a low reading group? Will his strength display itself in threatening other children, or in leading them in shared reading and writing experiences? Will he be a bully or a king?

3. See other sections for a full discussion of the special education/promotion/retention paradoxes. The statewide Criterion Referenced Test (CRT) had, up until this year, been used as a promotional exam in third grade.

JEREMIAH

EIGHT

Jeremiah in His Own Voice

First grade with Ms. Shockley, Walnut Street School

September

I'm learning to read, by the letters. Nobody is helping me; I just learn it. Oh, I mean my aunt is helping me, she helps me by the letters. Next I want to learn to read that book, *Monday, Monday* [Martin, 1983]. I'll learn it by the tape. See, you put your hands on the paper and he reads the words. When I'm a grown-up, I'll read that same book, *Monday, Monday*.

I'm learning to write books, like *Monday, Monday*. I'm learning it by the books. That's what I want to learn next in writing, and I'll learn it by myself. When I grow up, I'll write the same book. Will you bring me a book to keep? What kinds of books do you have? Can you bring me one, for my *very own*? And I'll give you one? You can make me one, can't you?

December

I'm learning to read "A Day to Forget" [a basal story], want me to show you? I wrote it. See, here *I* wrote it, and there, *they* wrote it [points first to self-initiated version he copied, then to the actual book]. Let me find it [in the index]—here it is—want me to read it to you? [He reads several pages of the play, struggling on a few words, self-correcting for meaning.] Shannon reads this part, I read this part of the play [he continues reading]. Oooh, this my favorite part! We did this when Shannon come over my house [he reads through to the end, gets his copied version, reads up to the point he has stopped copying, then tries to leave interview to continue copying].

I don't know how I learned to read this. Well, I learned it in kindergarten, like I learned "I," then my teacher learned me how to say "this," and I was on *Trumpets* and now I'm on *Parades*. Next I want to learn "Jed, Go to Bed," then "A Pet for Dan" [basal stories]; here they are in *Trumpets*. I already know how—listen . . . [He reads several pages of the story.] When I'm a grown up, I might read that book Ms. Shockley reading us, *The Twenty-four Days Before Christmas* [L'Engle, 1984].

I'm learning to write by reading the book, and then I think it, and then I write about it. Next, I'm going to write "The Christmas Day," like Shannon told me. She talking about she going to help me. She tell me, "Jeremiah, you can write 'A Christmas Day' after you write 'A Day to Forget.'" When I grow up, I'm gonna write like Shel Silverstein, poems.

April

I'm learning to write stories, and read a little story about this man and his daughter and he turns things into gold. I ain't learned how to read it. I can read *Parades* and almost *Carousels*—and the books I made. I'm learning by trying and sounding the letters out. Ms. Shockley helps me sound the words out, and Shannon help me, she knows some words. I'm going to try to read some more books, like *Jack and the Beanstalk* [Pearson, 1989], and the newspaper. I learned how to read the funnies; my grandma taught me. She get me the paper on a Sunday and teach me how to read some words. When I grow up, I'm going to read the newspaper, *Jack and the Beanstalk*, a Easter story, and Christmas and St. Patrick, and summer vacation story.

I'm learning how to write my words good like I did today and yesterday, write them in neat in my book. When I write, I'm thinking in my mind, like "The Little Rabbit" I wrote. Then close my eyes and think for one minute, and I be thinking and I write about the bunny and the little caterpillar and little frog. I write "The little Easter bunny was very shy." I write little books, and staple them, and put them in envelopes and send them to my pen pal, like my St. Patrick's Day story. And then I'm going to write about "the colors got to match," like green on St. Patrick and red on Christmas, and match the colors on the months. I'll make all kinds, like the one I made on the rainbow. I'll use a square paper. Shannon sometime help me; she think of things in the mind and help me think of stuff. When I grow up, I be a author, in New York.

June

I'm learning to do words like this: Jan-u-ar-y [one finger, two, three, four], March [one finger], A-pril [one finger, two], Ju-nuh [one finger, two]. I wrote a new story—want me to read it to you? [He reads.] Ms. Shockley taught me how to sound out Silly Syllables. Oc-to-ber—three! Next I want to learn how to make things, like a house, like them apple pigs in that book, now where is it? Here! You take a stick and you put a apple on the stick and then you . . . [He explains the process.] I'll learn it from the book that show me how. Colin made one. When I grow up I'm going to read all the Shel Silverstein books, and Bill Martin, and then I'm going to learn how to write, and it will be "By Jeremiah"!

I'm learning how to write a little story, like I wrote about Snoopy, and Scooby Do. I'm learning from the Bill Martin and Shel Silverstein books. I like that *Monday, Monday* book. Like Bill Martin, he love to play with words: "Monday, Monday . . . " Sometimes I play with words, like "chicken, chicken" in that story I wrote. I want to write more better—write like a author. I'll learn that if I look at their books, like look at Maurice Sendak books. I could learn how to make pop-up books. When I'm a grown-up, I'll write about months of the year and days of the week and parrots and parrots and parrots and parrots, like I been studying for my special animal. I'll have a school job—I'll be "Mr. Jeremiah." I'll write about schools, look at them.

Second grade with Ms. Michalove, Walnut Street School

November

Whenever I read, I make something. If there's something special in a book, I make it, like *The Three Little Pigs*, I make a pig. I just think up how to do it. Next, I want to build something, like a house. I'll get some friends to help, and Latonya and Bunny. When I'm grown up, I'll read in my fun time *and* in my job, like in a bakery. I'll read something you can make.

I'm learning how to do a play in writing. I looked it up in play books from the library. The same old persons going to help: Vickie and Latonya and Bunny—and Weston. Then I want to learn how to *perform* plays. Latonya said when she's grown up, she'll help me, and Vickie—all four of them. I'm going to write about Christmas when I'm grown up, for my grandmother. I told my daddy and stepmother I want skates for Christmas, and a tape recorder.

January

I learned to read a lot of funny stories, and some of my friends read with me. I'm learning by looking at the funny things. I'm always looking for books with funny things, like that new book—I forgot the name. When I get a funny book, I look at the pictures, and I tell my friends how to read it. When I grow up I'll read about how to make stuff, like cookies.

I'm also writing about funny things, like my story I wrote about "the terrible thing happened on TV"; this a funny story. I started up when Bunny said she looked at Jason [a horror show villain], and then Latonya, Bunny, and Vickie make me thought up good things. I'd like to learn how to make little people houses, like saying and writing and making books. My brother help me, he's going to make houses, gingerbread houses. He stays with my daddy. I go there on the weekends, but not my sister. That's what I'm going to do when I grow up, I'm going to write about something you can make houses out of.

February

I'm learning how to write long stories, and Valentine stories. Vickie is helping me, and Diana and Teena help me spell words. The ideas come from thinking and from books. I want to write poems—funny poems. And I want to build things with my writing, like puppets.

June

I'm learning to read plays. My fifth-grade reading buddy helps me, and Dr. Allen reads *my* plays sometimes, and Ms. Michalove and Bunny and Teena. They help me remember my part in a play. I want to learn how to read like I am *in* the story. You read for a long time, and soon you feel like you're in the story. My friends next year will help me.

I'm learning a lot in writing: write about TV things, write long stories, write funny stories, spell things by myself, and write plays. Diana helps me think of topics. Weston helps me get my talking onto the paper. Latonya helps me put periods, question marks. Ms. Michalove helps me spell things, put periods in the right places, and get questions right. Dr. Allen, too, by helping me read my story over to tell if it's right. Sometimes I write at home, like my poem about spring; that rhymed. My mother helped me. Next year I want to write some more off of TV shows, and funny stuff, and to make plays. My friends and teacher next year will help me.

Third grade with Ms. Gilcrest, Poplar Street School

March

I'm learning how to put compound words together, and put the apostrophes on the words and stop when the period come. I learn like in our reading group; we at the last magazine in our reading book and we been learning how the newspaper get written. I want to learn how to read hard words, like in this book [*The Burning Questions of Bingo Brown*, by Betsy Byers, which he had just checked out of the library]. I'll learn it step by step: easy, and a little bit hard, and hard. My friend Makeeta tell me how, like if I make a mistake she cover part of it and then I know it.

I'm learning how to illustrate my words and write my title neater, and don't forget my periods and question marks! When I think out what I'm going to write, I think it in my head and whenever a question come, I write it down a question on paper. I want to learn to write more faster, because you get finished more easier. I'll go slower, then fast. When I grow up, I'll write bigger words.

NINE

"Make Me Happy"

Jeremiah in First Grade at Walnut Street School

Today I (Betty) feel like Jeremiah must have felt. JoBeth says it's time to write and I just can't seem to commit to the task. So . . . I get some more coffee . . . convince myself that I didn't eat too many calories at breakfast so I can have one more piece of homemade bread and jelly. If anyone here would talk to me I'd have lots to say, but both JoBeth and Barbara are dutifully running their fingers over keyboards making wonderfully productive-sounding tapping noises. I turn my computer on and off four times so it would look like, and maybe sound like, I was doing something important too. We're writing together at the beach. I have the best seat in the house. The only thing between me and the ocean is this computer screen and a sliding glass door—both easily bypassed. I find myself thinking that each new wave might be the one that rolls in with just the right lead to help me share with others Jeremiah's story. Wait . . . here comes another one. It did have an effect on me—all that moving water—ahh—time for a bathroom break!

Constructing realities

All writers have those days and times when it seems more difficult than others to get started, but Jeremiah needed a jump start every day. As early as the third day of school I was aware that he might need some extra support—he was the only child who needed to be individually led through our checkout procedures for classroom books. A common example of his initial engagement difficulties can be seen in an excerpt from my journal, written during the January 4 morning writing period.

> The children had started to write, except for Jeremiah. First he went to Shannon's table, to see what she had written about him in her story. Then he went to Trisha's table and got some scratch paper. He wrote the word "Trisha" and took it to Shannon. The paper tore a little, so he got the stapler to make repairs. Shannon then told him they needed to write "Brenda," so he went over to spell for her. A little bit later, Jeremiah insisted that Shannon "write 'Trisha' and do it now!" Shannon refused. Jeremiah grabbed the book back that he had loaned Shannon; she continued writing her story, obviously relieved that the constant interruptions had ended, at least for the moment. Jeremiah sat, in contrast, with a blank page and an angry pout.

After a short time of being ignored, Jeremiah brought a draft of "Tina and Mary" over to the table; he and Shannon had worked on it together on a previous day. He began reading, then composing aloud, addressing his suggestions for the text to Shannon. Finally in frustration Shannon told Jeremiah, "I ain't going to do 'Tina and Mary' today." Jeremiah left the table again, putting his "Tina and Mary" draft dejectedly in his writing folder.

He got a book cover and more paper and stapled them together. He made a cloudlike figure on the front, a copy of the book cover Shannon had been working on. He wrote a title inside and credited himself with "by Jeremiah." And then he was up again—over to Brenda this time to read what she'd been writing. By the end of writing workshop he had written only two words, and then erased both of them. The next day he tried to "take ownership" by sharing the piece Shannon had written, but ended up asking her to read most of the story. He had actually written very little of it.

Sadly enough, even at the end of the school year I was still saying to Jeremiah: "You can do this. If you need to get a book, get one. If you need to ask a friend, ask, but don't wander all over the room not getting anything done."

Judith Fueyo, in her article "One Child Moves into Meaning—His Way" (1989), offers a supportive context for me to examine some of my concerns about Jeremiah. Was I devaluing alternative ways for Jeremiah to develop and present ideas (Fueyo, 1989)? I could accept the idea that Jeremiah was trying to construct meaning for himself in a unique way, like her example of Stephen, but I worried: Did he have the same ability to invest himself in an idea, an interest, or a learning event that Stephen had? Stephen set his own learning agenda and was able to make it explicit for himself and his teacher. He wanted to learn "about airplanes and airports" in first grade. Jeremiah had the same opportunity in our class—everyone did—to claim an interest and develop it through multiple investigative opportunities. Jeremiah chose parrots as his research topic, but the only outcome connected to that interest was an early paper model construction made during writing workshop (see Figure 9-1). In fact, this was the first piece Jeremiah chose to share with the class. Jeremiah read, "My bird is green and yellow." Andrea asked, "Is it a eagle, a hawk, or a plain old bird?" Violet asked, "Is it a parrot? Do it talk?" Jeremiah replied, "It's just a bird." "Why did you make it so big?" Cory questioned. "I seen a bird that was so big, out in the country," commented Andrew. Rather than answer these questions, Jeremiah explained how he used two pieces of paper and glued the bird after he made it and cut it out.

Unlike Stephen, Jeremiah produced no "how to" books or instructions on the care and feeding or life habits of parrots or even a crayon mural representing the varieties. I too wanted a classroom "where invented oral texts were as legitimate as invented spelling and invented reading " (p. 137). I was open and willing to support his learning in whatever form it might have taken, but Jeremiah just wouldn't, for some reason, commit to an endeavor and become engaged.

Writing workshop provided us with plenty of visual examples of this process of constructing meaning, for construct is definitely what Jeremiah did. It was as if creating something more real out of paper was a necessary, perhaps more concrete, step to written authorship. Like Fueyo's Stephen, Jeremiah flew things that he had "written" around the room, except in this case the construction was not an airplane but a guitar! Jeremiah used writing workshop to make things to which he might add a little writing, such as a doctor figure: "My Dertr si Pru (My doctor is

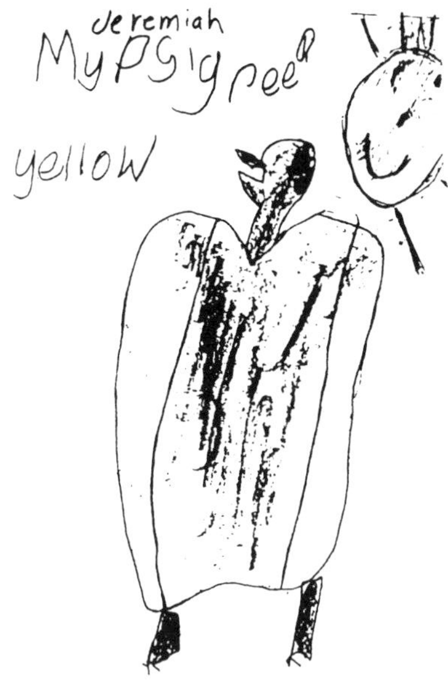

FIG. 9–1 *Jeremiah's Bird Model*

published; see Figure 9–2) a butterfly, a large smiling sun with three balloons, a hat with a large flower coming out of the top, and an intricate bird's nest.

When Jeremiah wasn't creating a three-dimensional object during writing time, he was usually complaining—"I don't know what to write"—and then he would sit and stare into space and do things like fumble with his crayons or just put his head down. He'd spend time worrying over the stapler or getting increasingly frustrated as the magic marker failed to yield to his intended designs. When I think of all the students I've taught I can recall other Stephen-like personalities—students on divergent paths but none the less headed somewhere. I never felt like Jeremiah had a direction in which he was headed. One of the reasons he is so difficult to portray is that there were no major turning points, no drama that I could identify in his year with me. I thought about something I'd read in *Ways Of Studying Children* (Almy & Genishi, 1979): "Because children in the early childhood period are developing rather rapidly and are learning a great deal, the teacher's picture of each child should change over time" (p. 55). This didn't happen. I continued to worry about Jeremiah all year and question whether he was making any progress. When would literacy become important to him, a meaningful reality in his life?

The victim or the antagonist?

As a repeating first grader, Jeremiah came to our classroom with well formed concepts about print. In fact, he was more advanced in this area than most of his

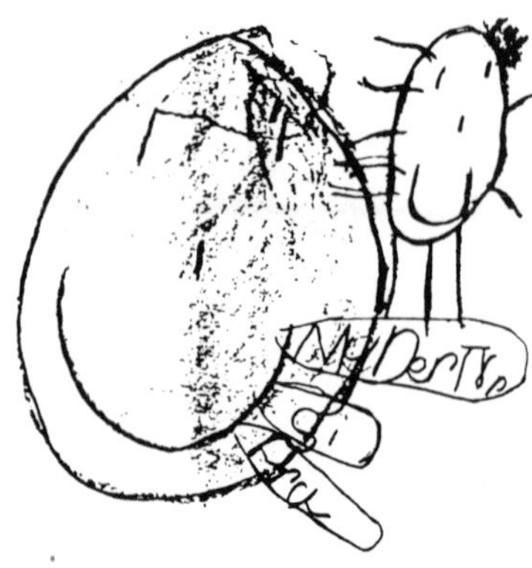

FIG. 9–2 *Jeremiah's Doctor Piece*

peers. There was an opportunity here for a good start. In the school's lingo, Jeremiah was a "one book behind" repeater. Promotion guidelines in our district were based on 80 percent mastery of four books—three preprimers and one primer. Jeremiah had successfully completed the three preprimers. He was not staffed for any special services. Perhaps for these reasons, Jeremiah did not stand out as one of the kids we were most worried about. His repeater status kept him in mind, but at first there seemed to be others with more striking needs. Before long, however, I found myself becoming more and more uncomfortable every time I was with Jeremiah. I confessed to JoBeth, "I am worried about Jeremiah's self-concept." Soon after, JoBeth wrote in her field notes: "I am really taken with how needy Jeremiah is. . . . Jeremiah just seems to need someone or something more." We were all beginning to notice. Here was a child who seemed to have adequate natural ability but for some reason was holding on idle.

Jeremiah seemed to be a confused personality searching for an identity. I wondered what could lead a child to write: "The Tree—The tree is singing—The tree stopped singing and cried—It got spoiled and dead." In another early piece he told us, "Some peoples happy. Some peoples sad. Some peoples mad. Happy, mad, sad." Of course this was true enough, but somehow you felt Jeremiah was trying to use his writing to understand his complex feelings. Not being promoted last year didn't help any in this regard. I know it was hard for him to understand why he had not passed first grade last year. For no apparent reason, Jeremiah asked me one day in November if he was going to "make my grades." And with another plea for some kind of understanding of the system he asked in February: "Why don't I go to no special classes?"

Jeremiah had difficulty being a friend. He struggled all year with his relationships with the three children he chose to be with most often—Shannon, Brenda, and Delia. He was always trying to organize them into writing groups or drama groups. I think he wanted to be a good friend but somehow he just didn't know how to be. He made a card one day where he put checks by everyone's name who was being mean to him—"Bad people who got checks by they name from being bad to me." Of course this power play didn't help things any. His relationship with

Shannon was a particularly rocky one, fueled by Jeremiah's decision to do such things as spell the word "monster" for her instead of the word she asked for, "monkey."

Big plans or storybook worlds?

More than anything else, Jeremiah seemed to be motivated by the idea of doing a play, but even this didn't turn out well for him. It was as though by creating a story world he could escape his real situation. He always had big plans but somehow even with support from me and others, he was not able to bring together a successful production. In April he took the initiative to assign his cast members the job of bringing in paper bags for costumes. The play was to be something about traps in the woods and a mean witch and a wedding between a prince and a girl. Hunan was cast as some Rambo rescuer. When it came time for the performance Jeremiah physically pulled and pushed people around the stage to get them to conform to his intentions, and as he did this he told them what they should be saying. Predictably, the characters did not appreciate this style of directing and the audience was confused.

One day soon after, JoBeth asked Jeremiah why he'd been in a bad mood. Jeremiah said he'd been feeling "bad because Shannon been aggravating me. When we had a show, I said I want to be in it, and she say directors don't be in plays." JoBeth asked, "Well, what can you do to feel better?" Jeremiah responded with, "I don't know." JoBeth suggested that he write Shannon a letter telling her how he felt. Jeremiah seemed pleased by the suggestion and set right to work. His letter to Shannon read: "Dear Shannon, I been so sad so lately. My leg is sore. Delia is making me sad. I'm not the director. Make me happy. Bye Bye." (See Figure 9-3.) "Please make me happy" was what he seemed to be asking of everyone he came in contact with. Being responsible for his own happiness was something he continually struggled with. Even in this letter he transferred blame and responsibility for his feelings from Shannon to Delia.

Jeremiah wanted to create happy endings. They were important to him. During a publishing conference with him I learned that this was his preferred conclusion for fiction, and I suspected for real-life dramas as well. When I asked why he wanted to add a new line to the story we were co-editing, he said matter-of-factly, "because that's the happy ending."

I believe Jeremiah had high expectations for himself as a writer. This may have been part of the reason he stayed so dissatisfied with himself in the process. He seemed to turn to published authors to provide that sense of direction he couldn't seem to create independently. By the end of this first year in a literature-rich classroom he had identified Bill Martin, Shel Silverstein, Maurice Sendak, and James Marshall as his models. The times he seemed most engaged as a writer were mostly associated with his choice to write variations of stories he knew and loved by these authors. He attempted variations on such books as Bill Martin's *Monday, Monday, I like Monday*, Maurice Sendak's *Chicken Soup with Rice*, and an Arnold Lobel story, *Ming Lo Moves the Mountain*. In Jeremiah's tale there was a huge strawberry that had to move because it was next to a mountain that was about to erupt. In January he said, "I'm going to make my books like James Marshall—you know with all those stories in it," referring to the George and Martha series. His version was

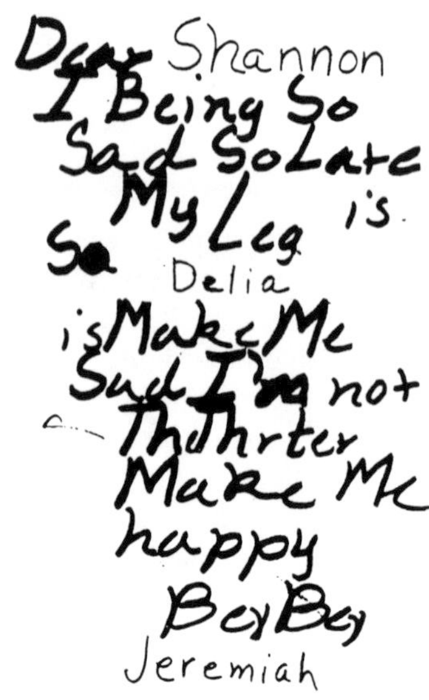
Dear Shannon
I Being So
Sad So Late
My Leg is
Sa
Delia
is Make Me
Sad I'm not
Thdhrter
Make Me
happy
BeyBey
Jeremiah

FIG. 9–3 *Jeremiah's Letter to Shannon*

"Tina and Mary feld trep [field trip]," shown in Figure 9–4. His use of storybook language and structures may have developed from this practice of imitating these favorite authors. He also said he was going to be a writer when he grew up. Frank Smith says published authors can show children the way. Jeremiah may be proof.

Jeremiah saw some personal benefits in writing too. He used it as a way to get things, like getting back at kids who were not being nice to him (as in his "bad people" checklist), or to get presents (e.g., books), or to get his mother to send a snack with him to school. He wrote his university pen pal and asked her to give him a book, stickers, and a surprise (see Figure 9–5). And when our class wrote letters to President George Bush, Jeremiah wrote:

> Dear President,
> You are a good President. You get to fix the homeless People. Please send me a Book.
> Love, Jeremiah

Jeremiah did get a book of his "very own" but not from the President—from JoBeth. He had asked her to bring him one. When she brought *Goodnight Moon* (Brown, 1947), Jeremiah hopefully asked, "For me to keep?" JoBeth nodded. Jeremiah got up slowly, as if to go for the book but instead put his arms around JoBeth's neck and hugged her for a long time. Later she shared the event with me: "As soon as my eyes cleared, I got my bag and let him take out the book. I told him it was my children's favorite book when they were about his age. I read the book to him and was immediately taken back to those days with my own children as I sat holding him next to me. Jeremiah said little and I couldn't tell how he was responding, but

FIG. 9–4 *Jeremiah's Tina and Mary Story*

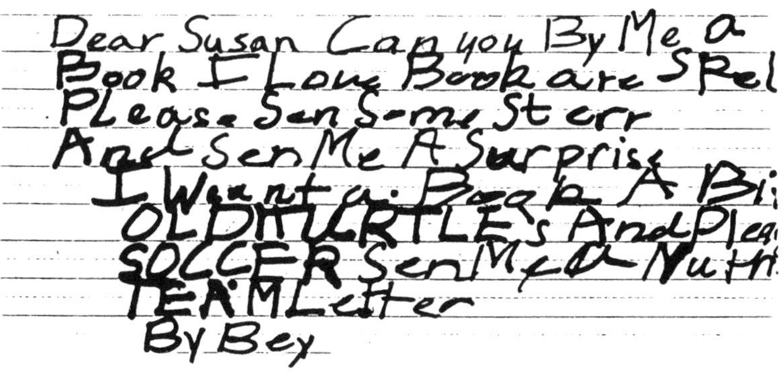
Dear Susan Can you By Me a
Book I Love Book are SPel
Please Sen Some Sterr
And Sen Me A Surprise
I Want a Book A Bi
OLD TURTLES And Plea
SOCCER Sen Me a Nutt
TEAM Letter
By Bey

FIG. 9–5 *Jeremiah's Pen-pal Letter*

when I asked him if we should read the book again he quickly answered yes, so I asked him if he'd help. He knew most of it already and joined in on over half the text." By lunch that day he was reading the book independently.

And he lived happily ever after?

The times I caught a glimpse of Jeremiah at his best were connected to verbal interactions. During the Christmas season the class cooperatively composed a story by adding a few sentences each day. Jeremiah was very good at this oral composing. One morning he came up with ideas to change our regular mouse character to a "wishing mouse" who "goes out to play and a magic snowflake comes. He runs and catches it. He sees some magic." When I asked what made it magic, Jeremiah confidently replied, "It twinkled!" This was a blessed moment. It wasn't that I needed Jeremiah to be the best writer in the class, or the best anything. I just wanted him to put some life into it, to participate positively and fully on occasion. He had so much to give and share. This was a rare display of self-confidence. Why did he seem to put himself so at risk with all the dependent behaviors and feigned incompetence? Jeremiah was hard to like. He was hard to work for because he didn't often work hard for himself.

JoBeth even dreamed one night that Jeremiah was dead and that she had killed him. We knew we had not bonded with him in the same way we had our other research children. We often engaged in positive dialogue as a research team regarding the other children but rarely included Jeremiah. Our notes were strained with references to him as whining and pouting and frustrating. We weren't even sure we had treated him fairly in our efforts to document his literacy development; but when we reviewed our data we were relieved to discover that we had indeed been just in our recording. He had simply not shown much change. As mentioned, there were no major turning points or pivotal events in this brief history, but a sameness that was dulling and trying. Yet this was the only child in our study who was not identified as needing support services through special education. He reached out. We reached out. We never really connected. He was our "regular" kid who still worried us and whose "irregularities" haunted even our dreams.

In April JoBeth and I visited Jeremiah's home. At that time he was living with his grandmother, a beautiful, young-looking woman who bore a strong resemblance to Jeremiah. They lived in a very comfortable and pretty trailer. The television stayed on throughout our visit; a well-worn family Bible had a prominent place on the coffee table in front of us. I had an immediate sense of relief when I got there—Jeremiah had a pleasant place and a pleasant person to come home to each day. His grandmother seemed genuinely interested in his school performance. I had seen his mom a few times when she had dropped Jeremiah off at school or picked him up and I knew she lived in a very rough housing area. I sensed that she was living with real poverty.

Jeremiah never talked about his father but we learned during our visit that he spent almost every weekend with him. The grandmother seemed hesitant to talk about either of Jeremiah's parents. She spoke of Jeremiah, however, as a "sweet boy" and expressed pride that he "reads great—even hard words—and is excited about his lessons."

As it turned out, I left a comfortable place with a not so comfortable question: Who does Jeremiah belong to? Jeremiah has another grandmother, who he stays with sometimes, and the grandmother we spoke with told us that he "might be going back to live with his mother." So between them all, where does Jeremiah belong? Did he feel he really "belonged" in our community? Did I?

At the beginning of this story, I was acting like Jeremiah by not getting down to business and using my time wisely. The examples I used were not actually the best for developing an understanding of Jeremiah's behaviors. Barbara reminded me that if I was acting like Jeremiah I would need scissors, cardboard, magic markers, and perhaps a stapler or some tape. So I suppose the best thing I could have done to share my year with Jeremiah would have been to make a big boxed gift for you—you know, the kind of present you get from your great-aunt. There's no question that it's special, but you're not quite sure what it is or exactly what to do with it.

Jeremiah liked to give gifts too. In October he decided to send his pen pal one of the books he'd authored as a special present. (He had even "laminated" it himself he said with layers of scotch tape.) His plan: "I'll put this in a piece of paper and she won't know it's a book and she'll open it and she'll be happy!" I hope Jeremiah's story will have a happy ending. But just like the James Marshall books he loved, there are still many more chapters to be written.

TEN

Dramatic Engagement

Jeremiah in Second Grade at Walnut Street School

Jeremiah impressed me (Barbara) the first day of school. He had only been in my second-grade classroom an hour when he was comfortably reading a familiar book with two friends from the previous year. After they read the book he said "Come on, y'all, we got to get ready! Rehearse it, we got to rehearse it!" During sharing he confidently led the class in a spontaneous group reading of *Peanut Butter and Jelly* (Westcott, 1987), laughing as he showed his favorite pictures, clearly enjoying himself.

Center stage

Jeremiah liked being center stage. He wanted to be the center of attention all the time. Often he was successful, but frequently for all the wrong reasons.

When he read *Where Does the Wind Go* (Vaughan, 1986), an accordion-type book, he wanted to open it to its full length and parade it around the room during reading workshop. After five minutes of arguing, Teena convinced him that it wasn't a good idea. He wanted to share first every day; when he didn't get a chance he pouted. He constantly whined and pleaded for help. "I don't know what to write about. How do you spell _______ ? I don't care how I write. Will you help me read this? I can't read it. I don't have time to finish." Lots of pouting, mock tears, tattling on friends, and physically leaning against any available adult accompanied his helpless behavior. He seemed to be saying, "I'm pitiful, give me a hug, do my work for me, make them like me."

Jeremiah's irritating behavior made it hard to like him. He constantly teased and tattled on other kids. He told Teena "That's a baby book" when she chose a book to read. When he had finished his spelling assignment he pranced around the room and sang, "I'm the first one!" He refused to take responsibility for his actions. He constantly bickered with the other kids at his table because he wouldn't clean up his messes. He clearly thought the world treated him unfairly. How could we possibly expect him to clean up his own mess, keep his nose out of everyone else's business, and not let him always have the first turn?

Jeremiah was artistic. He told us about his interest in creative responses to literature in the interviews. In November he said, "Whenever I read, I make something. If there's something special in a book, I make it, like 'The Three Little

Pigs,' I make a pig." Jeremiah's interest in creative responses to literature was influential in my decision to schedule time for these types of activities on Fridays. I provided materials and helped the kids when they asked for help. They provided the ideas and motivation. We used clay, paper, puppets, a box of costumes, and a variety of junk. Jeremiah loved this time. He was very creative making masks, acting out stories, and producing puppet shows.

Jeremiah rarely shared stories from home. In November I was shocked to learn that he had a younger sister in kindergarten in our school. Her teacher, Mr. Sams, called Jeremiah to the office to explain that their mother had to send a note to school concerning which bus they should ride home: Some days they went to their grandmother's house, some days to their mother's house. Mr. Sams had not been letting her get on an alternate bus without a note. Jeremiah had gone ahead to his grandmother's without his younger sister; she had ended up at their mother's house all alone.

Mr. Sams fussed at Jeremiah for not taking care of her. Jeremiah sobbed throughout the meeting. He had not assumed the role most older siblings assume with a younger sibling. Jeremiah acted as if the thought that he should be responsible for anyone else never crossed his mind.

I couldn't figure out why Jeremiah acted this way. I wondered if it was insecurity. He had the academic skills to accomplish any task he encountered. Was he so spoiled at home that he hadn't developed a sense of responsibility? Was he shuffled from house to house to such a degree that he felt he belonged nowhere and that no one really loved him? Did his moves from house to house allow him not to follow through on tasks, not to take real responsibility? Was he just manipulating all of us so we wouldn't be able to forget for a second that he was there? I didn't know why he acted this way, but could see that it hindered his academic and social standing in our classroom.

"It's mostly 'by Jeremiah'"

Jeremiah wanted to be part of the group, but couldn't seem to find his place in the social community. He played and worked mostly with girls. Teena, Diana, Bunny, and Latonya were his main group in both play and work. Sometimes Weston joined them. They argued, laughed, read together, tattled, complained, and attempted to collaborate with each other.

In October we overheard some boys talking to Jeremiah. Joseph said, "Everybody calls you a sissy." "Yeah, you play with girls. Girl," said Stanley. Jeremiah looked sad. "Just kidding," Stanley said. Later in the year Jeremiah wore a little girl's barrette on the short "tail" he was trying to grow. When the girls were dabbing perfume on their arms and neck, he joined them. The main characters in Jeremiah's writing were girls. Jeremiah was rejected by the boys because he chose to play with the girls, though most of his interactions with the girls involved fussing and fighting. The difficulty he had getting along with both groups often left him outside the community. He had very few friends. He assumed a male role in his writing only when he worked on a play with his friends.

Jeremiah wanted to be a leader. The day he attempted to join a group reading of a play was typical of the way things went when he tried to lead his group of friends. Jeremiah, Weston, and three girls were sitting in a circle looking in an anthology for a play to read. They decided on "The Gingerbread Man." Jeremiah was trying to direct things. He announced that he would be the gingerbread man. He tried to assign other parts, but the other kids wouldn't listen to him. He said, "Okay, Latonya is the gingerbread man." They argued over who would read which part. Weston finally said, "Let's do another story."

They all chose parts in "The Little Red Hen." They couldn't decide who would read the teacher's part. Jeremiah did "eeny, meeny" and ended on Bunny. He said, "I need to do it over." All the other kids said, "No, Bunny is it." "Then I'm quitting," Jeremiah pouted. He got no response. He didn't leave. He turned the page to a poem and said, "Let's do 'Five Little Pumpkins.'" He repeated it twice; everyone ignored him. When it was time to share they started arguing again about who would do each part. They were fed up with Jeremiah. He was still pouting. The previous day the rest of the group had spent their reading workshop time pleasantly reading a play together, without Jeremiah.

Jeremiah wanted to be in charge of things but he refused to be in charge of himself. He ended up being in charge of no one. He seemed to think that all his feelings and actions were caused by other people. His helpless behavior and irresponsibility in social and academic situations held him back from making the progress that he was capable of making.

Jeremiah's tattling and teasing continued throughout the year. He laughed at other kids when they got in trouble. The kids got tired of it, and of him. When I changed the seating arrangement in the room, I gave them the chance to list three kids with whom they would like to share a table. No one chose Jeremiah.

In January we started a class "Tattletale Book." If they wanted to tattle on somebody they had to write it in the book and sign their name. At the end of January Weston mentioned that it was mostly "by Jeremiah." Jeremiah came over and said "No, it's supposed to be your name." Keith joined in with, "Whose name's in it the most?" "Mine's just about two times," Jeremiah said. They asked for the book so they could check; it was mostly by Jeremiah.

When I looked over the field notes that JoBeth had taken on her weekly visits to our room, I realized that every one of them had an instance of Jeremiah tattling, teasing, or arguing with someone. She spent only a few hours a week with us, yet had observed numerous occasions of Jeremiah's difficulties getting along with others. It seemed as if he never stopped blaming others, tattling, and complaining. I understood why the other kids got so irritated with him. The last week of school we had planned a party. Jeremiah's friends told him he couldn't come if he didn't shape up. They were tired of his fussing. He had ten chances or he was out. He made a tremendous effort to be nicer so that he would be included.

The other kids tried to be his friend. They tried to include him. They invited him to write and read with them. They included him in their play at recess. They put up with his fussiness and self-centered behavior. They ignored his pouting. They gave him lots of chances to learn how to be a friend. He never took advantage of the many opportunities to learn.

I felt he used all these negative behaviors to manipulate people. He liked to direct the action, which came through in his writing. I had hoped that through writing he would be able to satisfy his need to control situations. His writing underwent a big change over the school year, but he continued to struggle with his controlling behaviors, as we will see in "The Play's theThing" section.

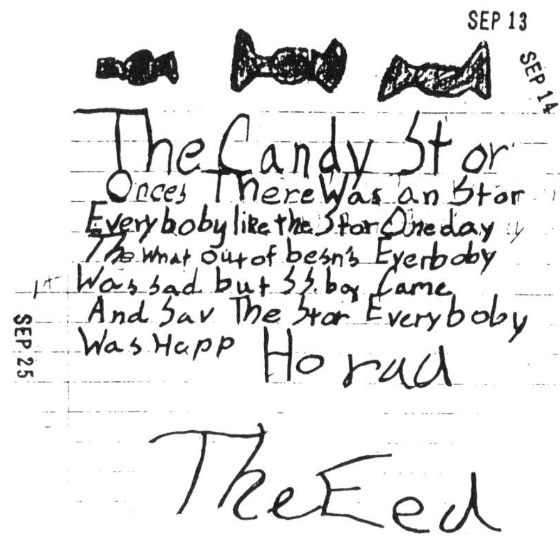

FIG. 10–1 *"The Candy Store"*

"Soon you feel like you're in the story"

Jeremiah stayed busy during writing workshop, but he had his own agenda. He spent his writing time making things. He stapled little books together, folded and cut paper, made rings for his pen pal and masks for a play. He appeared to be very productive. Then I realized he'd written very little the first month of school.

At the end of September I pulled him aside and told him, "You can't just cut and paste during writing workshop. This is our writing time. I expect you to be writing; don't tell me you can't." I put the stapler and tape in a drawer, declaring it off limits. When he kept fooling around I had him leave his writing group and sit alone. He wrote. He worked on a long story about Ramona, writing it for three consecutive days. He finished a story about a candy store, complete with super hero and a happy ending, that he had begun earlier in the month (see Figure 10–1).

After two weeks I let Jeremiah return to sit with his friends, and continued to insist that he write during writing workshop. I checked with him frequently, giving him praise and encouragement. He needed a lot of redirecting as his irritating behavior had not disappeared. He took every opportunity to tease someone and constantly asked kids at his table how to spell words, even words he knew.

It was hard to know Jeremiah. He rarely shared stories or wrote about his life outside of school, which was unusual for a second grader. One day he shared a story about his brother with me. I suggested that he write about it; he chose not to. Later in the year he excitedly told me about working with his grandmother. I insisted that he write about it. He did, doing a great job illustrating and writing about his experience. It was the only time all year that he wrote about his own personal life.

While most of the other kids were writing personal narratives, Jeremiah's writing topics came from books. Many of his compositions contained characters, titles, patterns, or themes from books he read. He wrote a story about Ramona after

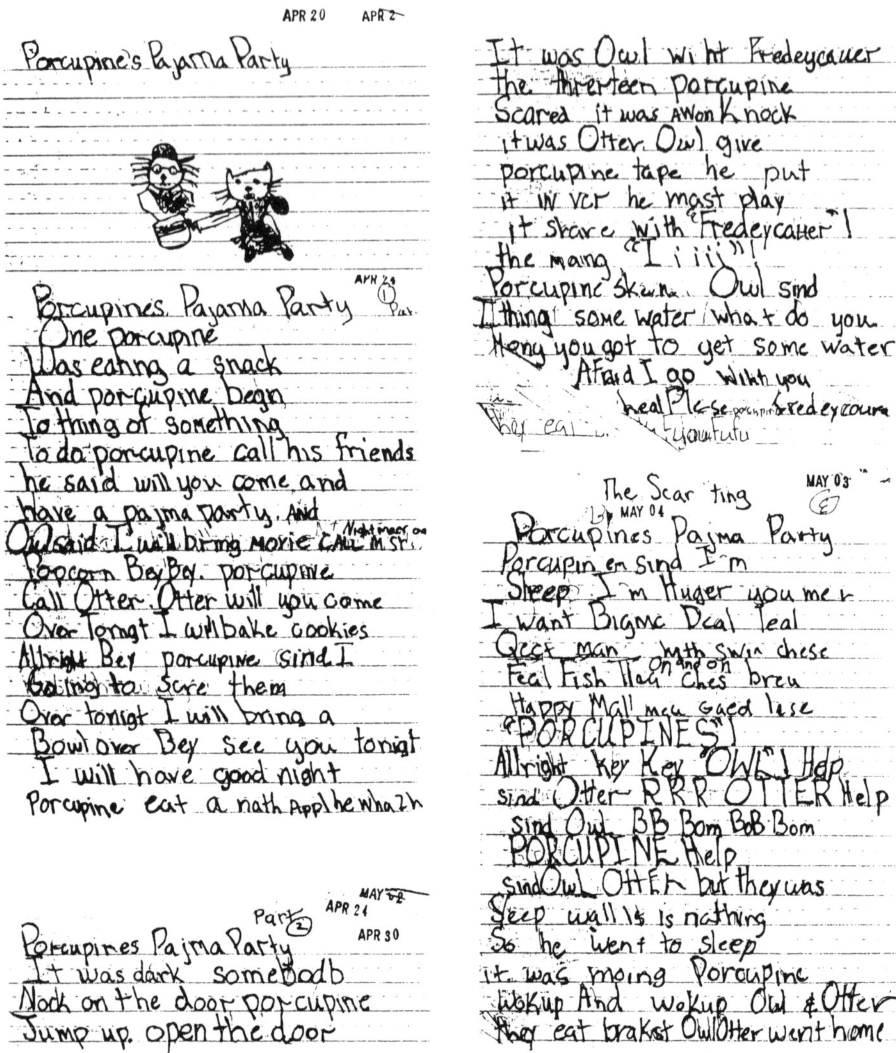

APR 20 APR 2

Porcupine's Pajama Party

Porcupines Pajama Party
One porcupine
Was eating a snack
And porcupine began
To thing of something
to do porcupine call his friends
he said will you come and
have a pajma party. And
Owl said I will bring movie call "Night mare on ..."
Popcorn Bey Bey. porcupine
Call Otter. Otter will you come
Over Tonigt I will bake cookies
Allright Bey porcupine sind I
going to Scare them
Over tonigt I will bring a
Bowl over Bey see you tonigt
I will have good night
Porcupine eat a nath Appl he whazh

Part 2 APR 24 APR 30
Porcupines Pajma Party
It was dark somebodb
Nock on the door porcupine
Jump up. open the door
It was Owl wiht Fredeycauer
the thirteen porcupine
Scared it was Awon Knock
it was Otter. Owl give
porcupine tape he put
it in vcr he mast play
it Stare with "Fredeycauer" !
the mang "I i ii" !
Porcupine Skean Owl sind
I thing some water what do you
Heny you got to get some water
Afraid I go with you
heal Plese porcupine Fredeycoure
They eat ... youtufu

The Scar ting MAY 03 MAY 04
Porcupines Pajma Party
Porcupin en sind I'm
Sleep I'm Huger you me r
I want Bigmc Deal Teal
Qecf man with swin chese on and on
Feal Fish Ha Ches breu
Happy Mall mcu Gaed lese
"PORCUPINES"
Allright Key Key "OWL" Help
sind Otter RRR OTTER Help
sind Owl BB Bom BoB Bom
PORCUPINE Help
sind Owl OTTER but they was
Seep wall is is nathing
So he went to sleep
it was moing Porcupine
wokup And wokup Owl & Otter
They eat brakfst Owl Otter went home

FIG. 10–2 *"Porcupine's Pajama Party"*

reading part of Beverly Cleary's *Ramona the Brave* (1975). He wrote a letter to the robbers in *The Brementown Musicians* (Plume, 1980). He read *The Terrible Thing that Happened at Our House* (Blaine, 1982), then adapted the title for his own story the following month. In April he copied the title from *Porcupine's Pajama Party* (Harshman, 1988), then said, "I'm not going to write that story, I'm going to write a different one." In first grade he had changed a few words in his own script to make it different from the published book. In second grade he borrowed the characters from the book but his story was different, as shown in Figure 10–2.

Jeremiah was aware of the influence of his reading on his writing. In January he told us, "I learned to read a lot of funny stories. I'm always looking for books with funny things. I'm also writing about funny things, like my story I wrote about the terrible thing happened on TV; this a funny story."

Jeremiah read well in the second-grade basal reader on those occasions I had the class read from it and when he chose to read it (usually for the plays it contained). He had little difficulty passing the periodic reading tests that we were required to use. When I gave him an assignment he was able to complete it on his own. What he did have trouble with was assuming responsibility for himself. He meandered around the room during reading workshop, picking up books, reading parts of them, then laying them down. He would join a friend reading, but often was unable to cooperate long enough to finish the book. Many times these shared book readings ended in an argument.

At the beginning of January I met with Jeremiah and four other students who had difficulty using their reading workshop time to read. I told them that I expected them to bring their books to a specific table during reading workshop and to read until sharing time. They could read together or even get another friend to join them, but they were restricted to that space. I spent a great deal of my workshop time there, listening to them read.

Jeremiah responded well to these clear expectations. He began to really read during all of reading workshop. He read longer books and seemed pleased with himself. After two weeks I allowed them to join the rest of the class in choosing where and with whom they would read.

I also had my instructional aide, who worked in our classroom for one hour a day, listen to these children read for fifteen minutes each day. Jeremiah knew that on Monday afternoons he read to Ms. Rossner. We continued these oral reading sessions for three months. All five of these children suffered from a lack of confidence in their reading abilities. The individual attention and help that Ms. Rossner was able to give them in these sessions helped them begin to see themselves as readers.

Jeremiah's irritating behavior and his continual need for encouragement and redirection made it hard for us to see how productive he really was in writing workshop. His behavioral difficulties overshadowed his academic performance. He appeared to be unengaged much of the time when he should have been reading and writing. He flitted around during reading workshop. He began many books but often laid a book down before he had finished reading it. He liked reading long books, but couldn't stay engaged long enough to finish many chapter books that he had started.

When we were able to look at Jeremiah's writing over the entire school year, we saw that we were wrong. He had stayed engaged over long periods of time, as much as a month, working on stories. He revised in response to his classmates' questions and suggestions. He struggled with editing so that he could publish his writing. He applied his artistic talent to the published pieces, as he did in his Christmas story (see Figure 10-3). The story is reminiscent of the group story that captured Jeremiah's attention in first grade; the difference was that this year he actually wrote it.

Writing workshop provided Jeremiah the opportunity to satisfy his desire to be the center of attention. One day in March he shared a funny story he wrote in which he had incorporated the teasing problem we were having in our classroom at the time. The kids loved it and thought it was hilarious. Weston told him, "That's the funniest story I ever heard in my whole life!"

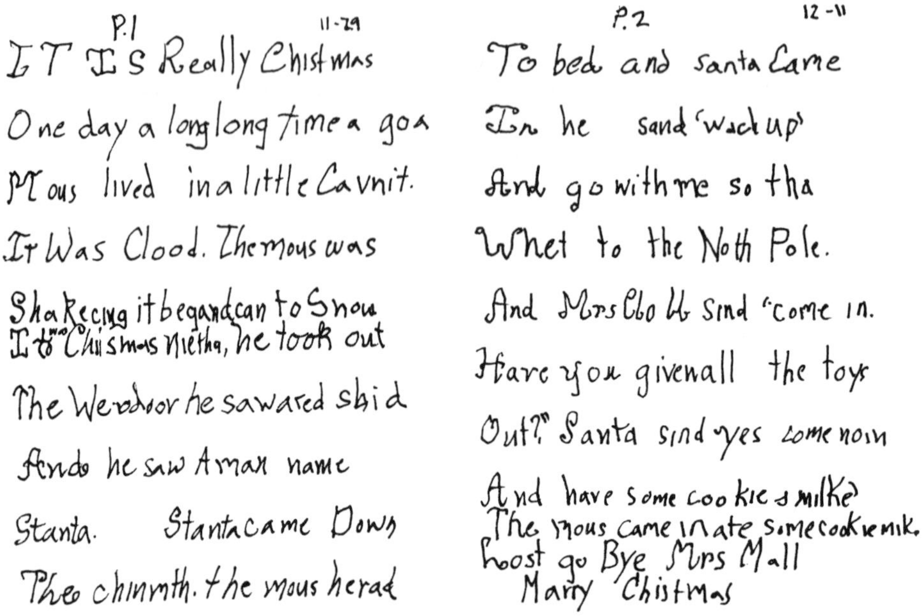

P.1 11-29

IT IS Really Chistmas

One day a longlong time a goa

Mous lived in a little Cavnit.

It Was Clood. The mous was

ShaKecing it begandcan to Snow

It's Chismas Nietha, he took out

The Werdoor he sawared shid

Ando he saw A man name

Stanta. Stanta came Down

Theo chimnth. the mous herad

P.2 12-11

To bed and santa Came

In he sand 'wack up'

And go with me so tha

Whet to the Noth Pole.

And Mrs Clo U sind "come in.

Have you givenall the toys

Out?" Santa sind yes come now

And have some cookies milke'

The mous came in ate some cookie mik.

hoost go Bye Mrs Mall

Marry Chistmas

FIG. 10–3 *"It Is Really Christmas"*

Jeremiah chose to read many different kinds of books throughout the year. His mother told me that he read to her and his younger sister at home. She also said that he liked to read hard books. Often she wasn't certain that he was really reading the text, so she'd sneak up behind him and check. "I was surprised that he was really reading them on his own."

The play's the thing

Although Jeremiah enjoyed a variety of literature, his passion was for plays. He loved reading and performing them. The second week of school he organized a group of children, made masks, and orally composed a script that they shared with the class. I knew Jeremiah had lots of plays in his head. We'd seen many examples of these. He would have been delighted if I had continued to allow him to produce plays after orally composing the script, but this was not the case: I insisted on a written script before performing in front of the class.

In November my student teacher, Ms. Gordimer, encouraged all of the children to sign up to produce a folk tale play. Jeremiah chose "The Three Little Pigs." He was joined by four other children. They dictated the script to Ms. Gordimer, who typed and returned copies to them. They tried to practice but Jeremiah made it impossible. He spent his time tattling and whining. He crawled under the table and made no effort to follow along when other characters were reading. He wanted to make the costumes before they practiced and refused to

MAY 23 a Play

The Witch and the cat

Staytell'er: Once upon a time there was a waketed witch that had a cat. the cat was nice.

witth: I will make a poscn

Cat: that's not a good Idia

Stoyteller 2: then the witch put a sipper on his moth

FIG. 10–4 *Individual Play*

cooperate when he didn't get his way. Jeremiah's difficulties cooperating with others even kept him from doing the things he seemed to love the most.

Jeremiah's interpersonal skills finally began to improve as we approached the end of the school year. I feel that his interest in being included in activities around plays gave him the desire to improve his behavior. For Jeremiah, the community was his cast, and he wanted not only to direct it but also to be a part of it.

We had many plays in our literature collection. Jeremiah sought them out and read them with friends. Toward the end of the school year students would invite Jeremiah to join them when they worked on a play. In April, during reading workshop, Latonya called, "Jeremiah, ain't you going to read the play with us?" Jeremiah quickly dropped what he was doing to join them.

As Jeremiah's ability to stay engaged increased he attempted to write scripts for his own plays and collaborated with friends writing plays. Jeremiah had become familiar with the parts of a script and play structures through his frequent readings of plays in our classroom collection, as can be seen in Figure 10–4—a play Jeremiah began on his own but abandoned to work with the group that produced "King Lawteafe" (see Figure 10–5). Writing a script for a play on one's own is difficult. Writing a play with seven other second graders seemed impossible to me until the kids in my classroom proved me wrong.

At the end of April a group of children started writing a play. The following day they immediately resumed working on it. As soon as Jeremiah realized what they were doing, he slapped his folder shut and joined them. Shortly after the group gathered together I saw that they were beginning to act it out. I told them, "Folks, before you ever do this play I want to see it written down on paper. Write the play today. Tomorrow you may get out the costume box and practice it."

After they had argued over chairs, Jeremiah attempted to get the group organized. He said, "Okay y'all, let's think about the princess. Storyteller, go. Diana

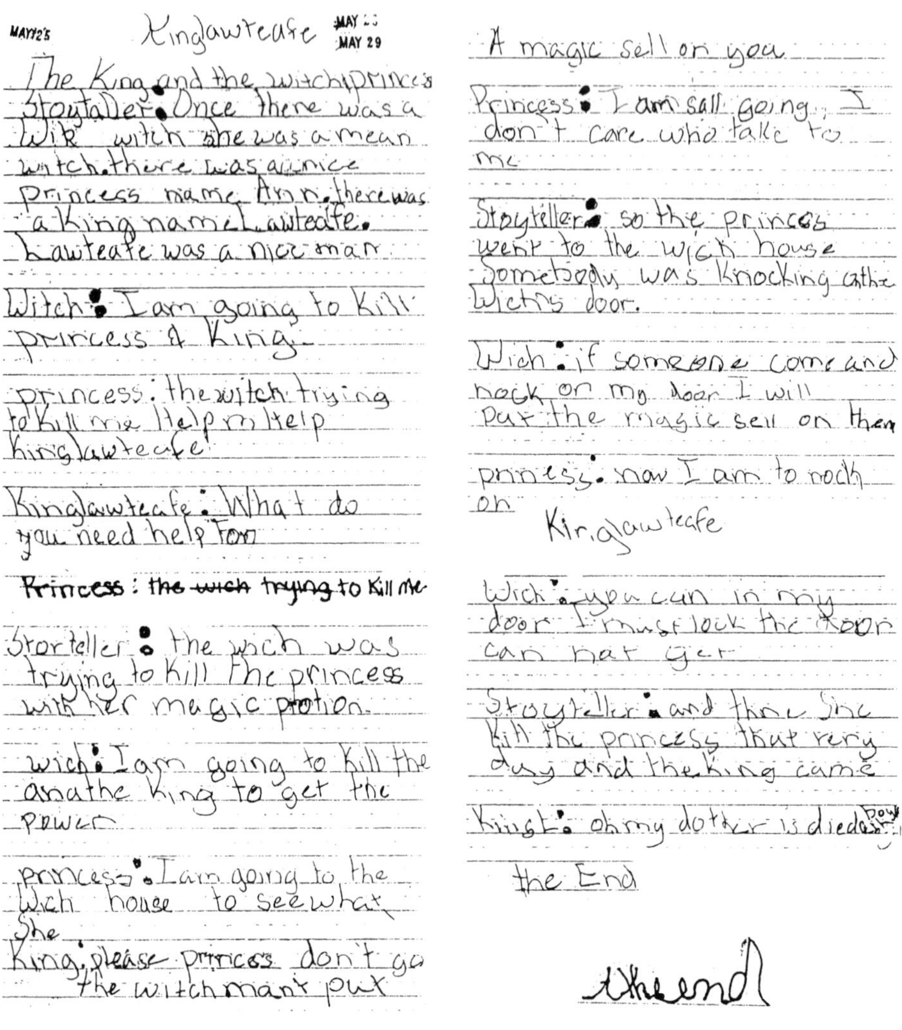

MAY 25 Kinglawteafe MAY 29

The King and the witch princess
Storyteller: Once there was a
Wik witch she was a mean
witch. there was a nice
princess name Ann. there was
a King name Lawteafe.
Lawteafe was a nice man.

Witch: I am going to Kill
princess & King.

princess: the witch trying
to Kill me Help m Help
King lawteafe!

Kinglawteafe: What do
you need help from

~~Princess: the wich trying to Kill me~~

Storteller: the wich was
trying to Kill the princess
with her magic potion.

wich: I am going to Kill the
anathe King to get the
power

princess: I am going to the
Wich house to see what
She

King: please princess don't go
the witch man't put
A magic sell on you

Princess: I am sall going. I
don't care who talke to
me

Storyteller: so the princess
went to the wich house
Somebody was Knocking at the
Wich's door.

Wich: if someone come and
nock on my door I will
put the magic sell on them

princess: now I am to nock
on

Kinglawteafe

Wich: you can in my
door I must lock the door
can nat get

Storyteller: and the Sine
Kill the princess that very
day and the King came

King: oh my dother is died Pow!

the End

the end

FIG. 10–5 *Group Play*

you got that part." Diana read several sentences as the storyteller. Other children in the group read their parts. The kids wrote their character's lines on separate pieces of paper as they orally composed the script.

After five minutes of concentrated work Jeremiah suggested acting it out. Diana replied, "We not going to act it out yet." "We can try. Let's try Diana, I know what I'm doing," Jeremiah pleaded. The other kids in the group continued writing their parts. Weston turned to JoBeth and said, "Dr. Allen, have you ever written a play before? It's hard!" Finally Diana said, "Okay, y'all ready?"

By this time they had become quite loud. I reminded them to use quiet voices. Weston whispered, "Okay, storyteller—one, two, three." The storyteller began reading, then the king. Cindy interrupted, "But Diana, we don't have a dragon."

They decided to ask Kenny to be the dragon. He agreed and the group returned to the chairs that they had arranged in a circle.

Jeremiah went and got a basal reader that had a play in it. He tried to get the group to copy a sentence from the book, with one change. Diana told him, "I don't want to be copy cats." Jeremiah left the group to pout. "Jeremiah, come on. . . . I guess Jeremiah don't want to," said Diana. "Y'all don't want to," Jeremiah shouted. "We don't want to copy!" Diana told him. He left and busied himself making a dragon. The rest of the group continued writing the script.

Jeremiah rejoined them and added a sentence to his script. They decided to read the play. "One, two, three, action!" Vickie shouted. The storyteller read three sentences, then stopped to revise. This had gone on for twenty-five minutes. I could see that they were getting bogged down in the mechanics of script writing. I decided to intervene.

I pulled up a chair and told them, "I'm going to help you because I think you're having a problem. It's hard work writing a play. Whenever we read a play it has a list of characters. You tell me the characters and I'll write it down for you." They named the characters as I recorded for them. "Now, who starts off?" I asked. The storyteller began reading; the rest of the characters read their lines as the story unfolded. I wrote their words down as they read. They really had a lot written and knew the order of their lines. Diana turned to me and said gratefully "You getting us all straightened out."

I retold what they had written so far. They began a discussion about what would happen next. Everyone was confused. I suggested that they continue talking about the plot during recess and I would help them write it down later in the day. They decided to take their writing folders outside so they could continue working.

They finished their script and practiced the play the next day. When our pen pals came to visit they presented the play. It was delightful. It had taken a lot of hard work, cooperation, and perseverance to produce their play. They were quite proud of themselves. For Jeremiah it showed real growth, not only as a writer and performer of plays but as a member of a cooperative group.

Producing a play gave Jeremiah a real reason to write and a real reason to get along with his peers. I continued to worry about his behavior and was glad to see that he could cooperate when he really wanted to. The challenge seemed to be presenting him with situations in which his desire to be included was strong enough to have an influence on his behavior.

At the end of May, Jeremiah, Teena, Diana, and Bunny wrote and produced a short play entirely on their own. They had all been part of the play group the previous month. They orally composed together as each child wrote a copy of the whole script, whereas the previous month they had just written their own character's part. They worked on it for two days. At the end of the second day they acted it out for the class. The only help they received from me was when I typed the completed script for them.

If we had not interviewed Jeremiah regularly, we would have painted a picture of an unhappy, often unproductive child: Jeremiah the pouter, the complainer, the one who couldn't get along in any group; Jeremiah the unengaged, flitting from cutting to pasting to stapling, but rarely reading or writing; Jeremiah the blamer, putting responsibility for his unhappiness on everyone but himself.

We saw a different picture studying his interviews over time. We saw a sustained interest in creative response to literature, creating "things" that for

Jeremiah were the story worlds he entered as both a reader and a writer. His interest in concrete response was also evident in his passion for plays—plays he wrote as well as plays he read. Jeremiah did indeed learn how to "feel like you are in the story."

Jeremiah had many literacy teachers. Even though we saw him as having difficulty working with others, he saw his peers as valuable resources for selecting topics, developing stories, spelling, and writing and performing his plays. In addition, in the interviews ("Jeremiah in His Own Words") he indicated the influence of his family on him as a literacy learner, like his mother helping him write a poem, and his grandmother helping him read the Sunday comics. He continued to have problems being a friend. His whiny, helpless behavior decreased somewhat, but continued to overshadow his accomplishments. He just didn't try very hard. He acted as if "someone else" should do it for him. I feared that with this attitude he would face failure in the school years ahead of him.

Several times earlier in the year I had wondered aloud if Jeremiah would be better off in a class with a different structure, one where the kids were all given the same thing to do, where the textbook work was sequential, where reading groups and seatwork allowed no moving about, or choices, or collaboration, which he had trouble with. But by the end of the year, with very clear expectations both from me and his peers, he was starting to learn how to take responsibility for himself as a member of a community of learners.

Now my concern was just the opposite. What would happen to Jeremiah in a textbook-oriented classroom, especially one with few opportunities for "creating"? I wished he were staying at Walnut Street, where I knew that by fourth grade he would be involved in the all-fourth-grade project of writing and producing a ballet. I even told JoBeth a prescription for Jeremiah's education. "I have studied this child's social, academic, and emotional needs, and this is my recommendation: He should go to a school for the performing arts, construct scenery, design costumes, and read, write, and perform plays. He would do well and really be valued at a school like that."

Jeremiah did go to a new school the next year, because of district transfers. But it was not a school for the performing arts.

ELEVEN

"His Behavior Is Getting in the Way of His Academics"

Jeremiah in Third Grade, Poplar Street School

October

"Jeremiah's having a really hard time with third grade, mostly because of his behavior. He tends to everyone else's business, then loses out on his own work. He's really disruptive in reading group. He just demands attention, like the other day in the middle of reviewing for the social studies test he raised his hand repeatedly. When I finally called on him, he tattled on Nicole, said she was writing cuss words. I got him to tell me. It was 'ass.' I told him it meant donkey and was not a cuss word. I told him he had been silly and had disrupted the whole class. He makes sure I always know what others are doing, but of course he never has any part in the disruption.

"He really has a negative attitude about school. He's always complaining loudly and slamming his books down. It's really hard to be positive with him because he's so negative. He creates a problem with whoever he sits by. The other day he came off the bus really upset about Dana, a new girl, who said she'd sit with him then didn't. He wanted me to deal with her. People aren't things you own—he doesn't seem to understand that.

"He doesn't follow directions. As a group, the class said our rules are 'Do the right thing at the right time.' He doesn't do this. Much of what he does wouldn't necessarily be wrong in other situations. His behavior is getting in the way of his academics. He's one of the poorer students in reading. I know he can do third-grade work when it strikes him, but often he just doesn't do it. He could be doing much better.

"He doesn't do much writing—none on his own. All the kids have writing folders and can write during quiet times, but he doesn't. He did one story. I had the kids write on a special person. We did a web first—here's his web (see Figure 11-1).

As told to JoBeth in interviews with Ms. Gilcrest (his homeroom teacher's pseudonym) in October, March, and June. JoBeth spliced and edited the interviews for what we felt was pertinent and for narrative flow. The teacher read JoBeth's field notes but not this narrative version.

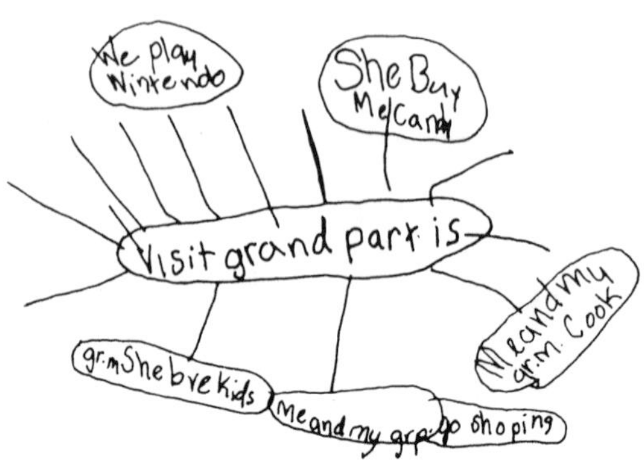

FIG. 11–1 *Jeremiah's Web*

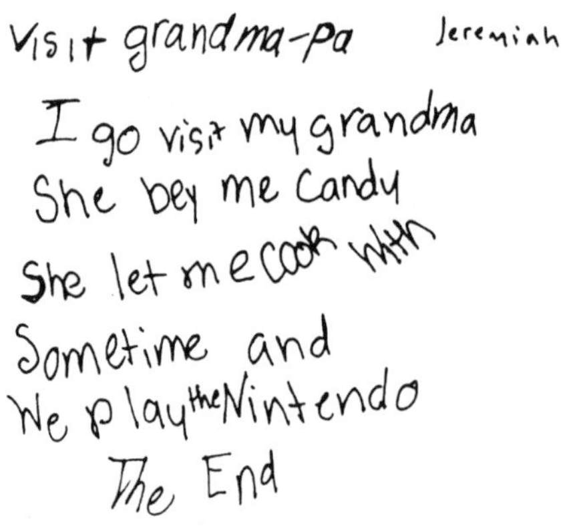

Visit grandma-pa Jeremiah

I go visit my grandma
She bey me Candy
She let me cook with
Sometime and
We play the Nintendo
The End

FIG. 11–2 *Jeremiah's Story*

"Then here's his story (see Figure 11–2). The only other writing in his folder is this homework assignment in spelling, 'If I was a fish.' They were supposed to use their spelling words, like 'pond, luck, lot.' We introduce a theme and the vocabulary words that go with it and they do different activities with it.

"We did proofreading paragraphs from the English book. He copied the wrong paragraph. I mostly use the English book for seatwork, like having them identify telling and asking sentences. Sometimes we do the enrichment sections: 'Pretend you work in a cereal factory . . . invent a new cereal.' It's kind of like you don't have to have training to teach any more, just open the book and teach.

"I haven't been in contact with other teachers at Walnut Street, but I would like to know more about Jeremiah. I send home weekly notes for the parents. At first Jeremiah's were signed by his grandmother, but none of the rest have come back. Since his behavior is out of bounds, I'm worried that the notes are not coming back. In one I even asked his mom to call me. I didn't realize they had no phone. He spends his weekends with his dad, but most of the time I think he's with his grandmother. His dad and mother or grandmother, I don't know which, both came to open house. I think I'll try to get in touch with his dad."

The class returned from music. Jeremiah went over to JoBeth and hugged her, then continued to lean on her—a familiar posture. JoBeth was invited to go to lunch with the class. She sat across from Jeremiah and the student teacher, who asked Jeremiah about reading and writing workshop last year. He didn't remember a particular book he'd read, but told her about a play he wrote and *The Princess and Prime Minister* (Olson, 1986, in *Discoveries*), a play that the class had performed. His eyes brightened as he recalled the story he liked best from his own writing, *The Terrible Thing that Happened on TV*. Then he clouded up again. "We don't get recess after lunch anymore. Now we do math after lunch. I wish I was in second. They got two recesses."

March

"Jeremiah is doing better, I see some improvement. His attitude seems better; there is still some pouting, but not like at the first of the year. His behavior is still really immature. I have real concerns about him passing the CRT. He's erratic, inconsistent. He's been sitting next to me in reading group and that seems to help him do better. But his independent work is still not so good. He's too 'cool,' and it's cool to be finished quickly. I've told him it's not cool to make a fool of yourself. I've seen some change since then.

"He has the ability to pass the CRT but there are real gaps, especially in math. Some days he does okay, others he does not. He rarely has his homework done. Last week his mother signed his homework, but it was all done incorrectly. They were two-step word problems, and he just hadn't taken the time. The answers made no sense. He could fail either the reading or the math on the CRT. The question is, will he focus in or play the 'cool' game?

"Jeremiah doesn't have many friends at all, particularly guys. I moved him by a gifted boy, but he copied his social studies paper. I told him that asking for help was fine but copying wasn't. He claimed innocence at first, was very defensive. One girl he hangs out with doesn't have any friends either. They fight like cats and dogs but keep seeking each other out."

JoBeth interviewed Jeremiah in March. He read to her from the library book he had just checked out, *The Burning Questions of Bingo Brown* (his choice), and from both *Journeys* (3.2) and *Flights* (fourth-grade basal). He read fairly fluently on all the texts, with 98 percent word recognition on the 3.2 passage, and 95 percent on the fourth-grade passage. He discussed and retold parts of the stories accurately.

June

"Jeremiah will repeat third grade—he just isn't making it. He thought batting his eyes would work. His ITBS [Iowa Test of Basic Skills] score was below grade level, his *Caravans* [3.1 basal] magazine scores were below, his CRT was below—all of them were kind of borderline. [A practicum student from the university] worked one-to-one with him in May, but he didn't seem to respond by working harder. I did some diagnosis, had him read from *Journeys* (3.2); he was really struggling with decoding and comprehension. Some of the decoding problems fit the pattern of his language—he slurred his words and left off endings. I think he had few role models at home who spoke clearly. Although he seemed to be doing well with his group, he seemed to miss the security of the group in the testing situation. I think he's brighter than he wants people to know.

"He had been having a lot of behavior problems. He's really immature and has this constant need for attention. The stories he's written are all about a mother and a baby who pee-pees" (from an assignment to write using spelling words about the beach):

> One day me my self and I was on the/ beach This Lady she was behind my/ back!!!!!! She sind [said]/ I what you talk one laok [want you to take one look]/ in my car I sind it is a baby with/ sun glasses on driving a car of cores she/ had tiws [twins] the othe was pul his parer [pants?]/ of and peepee in the sand He laef/she ran behind him He blow [writing illegible] . . . / The other baby in the car his parer/ had fod becoe [falled because of] number 2 They went home/ with they moth drag behind the car so I what home The End

"Maybe it's for shock effect; sometimes we share the writing, although he didn't share this with the class but with a few individuals. He's always stirring others up. They just got tired of him.

"I felt it would be an injustice to put him in fourth grade, that it would be unfair to him. I can't say I feel bad. He just wasn't convinced he needed to do work. And there was no response from home for a conference about the problems.

"He didn't say much about it, even after I talked with his mother. But one day he wrote in his journal, 'I've been thinking about what my mama told me, that I'm going to fail third grade. It made me cry and cry and cry.'"

Continuing Worries

Jeremiah failed. He failed to have a winning personality. He failed to make friends with his teacher, or with peers. He failed to "be a man," to be one of the "strong" boys; he was a "sissy" who played with girls. As Raphaela Best (1983) points out, this is the cardinal sin among young males: "No self-respecting boy would play with a sissy lest he himself be considered a sissy by his peers" (p. 78). He failed to use Standard English in a classroom where his dialect was not considered acceptable by his teacher.[4] He failed to have parents who responded to requests from school, thereby seeming disinterested and uncooperative. Most of all, Jeremiah failed to convince the school that he was trying. Perhaps he wasn't. There was no evidence in his scant writings of the kind of intensity he had shown the previous year; but neither was there choice of topic, responsibility to extend and revise his work over time, or the expectation that he write daily and show growth over time. A parallel situation existed in reading.

4. For many teachers the language patterns of African-American children is viewed as a social and cultural deficiency. The teacher's lack of understanding and intolerance may actually make the teacher hostile toward the child using the vernacular (Lightfoot, 1978).

Jeremiah did not make the transition from whole language classrooms to a textbook-driven system successfully. Would another year in a whole language classroom have made the difference? Two more years? He was just beginning to engage with genuine literacy, just learning to become a member of a community through writing plays when both of those support systems were changed. But who really failed? Is it not our responsibility to make elementary school a place for every child?

SHANNON

TWELVE
Shannon in Her Own Voice

First grade with Ms. Shockley, Walnut Street School

September

I'm learning how to read and draw good, and how to draw hearts, and get better doing work. Ms. Shockley, she get a book and sometimes she read them. And we learning to take care of Hunan [a new student in the class]. I like this class better than last year's class. I like writing really. That's my best. And doing work, but not that hard work.

I might want to learn about being a police and a singer and a body builder, but I might change my mind about being a body builder. Ms. Shockley, she help me, and other kids help. I help other kids spell. I help Summer with her words. I help her see it and spell it.

When I grow up, I'll need a tablet. I'll save some paper and pencils, and read about the caterpillar and the gingerbread man and Curious George. I'll have to read the Driver's License book—my mama did.

I'm learning how to spell hard words like "flower." I already know "help." Want me to spell it? *H—E*—right?—*L*—I learned it—oh,—*P*—that's the last one! Ms. Shockley teach me. She a good teacher. Sometimes I look on her paper, how she spell things. I know "to"—*T O*. Want me to spell all the words I know? *A N D*, *A*, *I S*, *H E L P*, *E M*—oh, me—*M E*. I'd like to spell the biggest word. I'd like to do a program, *The Fox Went Out on a Chilly Night*. I want to learn to spell surprise—*S E R I*—two *I*s? I'm learning better from Ms. Shockley. I know how to spell "bat" and "sat," and I put them in my backpack to take home. See. I'm learning a lot from Ms. Shockley. Wallace, he know a lot of words. I forgot some words and he say, "You can get that!" He know how to spell some big words, and my mom know how to spell "surprise party," and I put it in my backpack and look it up and read it over. I'll need to write in cursive when I be grown-up, but I don't know, and when I be happy . . . I wish we never get old so we can have a long, long time.

December

In reading, I'm learning how to spell "dinosaur" and "Christmas." It's fun and sometimes I don't know the words, but I try to spell. I'm doing good in reading, but I don't do no bad words. Ms. Shockley, Ms. Ansa [the instructional aide], and Jeremiah, and Brenda help me. Me and Ms. Ansa read almost a whole story in one day. Sometimes I be staggering over the words, and Ms. Ansa let me tell her and she say it for me and tell me to read. We read a story about a apple: "No I won't turn red if I eat the apple!" You know Ms. Shockley Teacher of the Year? I hope all the teachers in here get Teacher of the Year!

I want to learn how to spell "surprise." It's *S U R P R I U E S*, or something like that. Next I'm going to learn—you know that purple book [*Trumpets*, third basal preprimer]? I learned "Go To Bed Jed" in that book. You learn if you just read what you know and ask Ms. Shockley the new words, and sometimes I figure them out, like in *Parades* [primer]. I want to read *Parades* when I grow up—like that page and that . . .

I'm trying to learn to spell "Ms. Shockley." I looked how she spelled it. Delia and Ms. Shockley and Gavin and Jeremiah and Missy and Colin helps me. At my table Missy and Karen helps. Next I'll learn "surprise," that's a long word. When I grow up I write: "I be a police." And I'll write everything I'm doing.

April

I'm learning to put question words and periods, and new words. And the words I don't know Ms. Shockley helps, and we might sound it out. I learn from Ms. Shockley and friends and books. Some of the words I already know. Sometimes we skip on or sometimes we sound them out or Ms. Shockley helps us. Ms. Ansa and Ms. Hood [the student teacher] and Jeremiah, Brenda, and Gavin and sometimes Trisha help.

I want to read big books like Ms. Shockley be reading, that you go and borrow, that she reading to herself—and *The Night of the Twisters* [the chapter book Betty read to the class]. I'll learn if I pay attention, listen to Ms. Shockley and Ms. Ansa or Brenda or Jeremiah. I ask words; Trisha sometimes don't know. When I grow up, like I read my own books and other folks' books, my friends' books, and some Ms. Shockley has.

In writing, I'm learning songs and how to write poems because Gavin write one and I keep on asking him to help. I found "rain," and he helped me write "rainbows." When I asked him how to write a poem he said, "It's just a little story." I still need to learn where to put question marks and how to write big words. I don't know how to spell "dinosaur." When I grow up I'll need all of my books I wrote, poems and stories and songs, because I want them to come out with good illustrators, and I'm going to publish them in New York!

June

I'm learning to read new words and read *The Doorbell Rang* [Hutchins, 1986]. I learned it last night because Ms. Shockley gave me the book to keep, and I read to my sister with no help while she was in bed. But when I first didn't know, my sister and my mother helped. I want to read long words and how to spell them. I'll learn if I listen to the teacher when she be spelling some words on the board and on paper. When I grow up, I read monkey books [her chosen research topic]. I can be president of the whole wide world! I'll read monkey books and a president book!

I'm learning to write gooder. You should look in my writing journal. I been practicing. I write almost all the time at home. I want to write in cursive. I can learn by a teacher if she help me. I'm going to write monkey stories or stories like a president.

Third grade with Ms. Willis (August–February 6), Walnut Street School (promoted directly from first to third)

October

I read big words. Ms. Willis and Ms. Shockley reading books, and I read and they tell it when I don't know a word. I like to learn to read more gooder, read more words. I'll learn if I read—read. Ms. Shockley and Ms. Willis and my sister, my eleven-year-old or my older sister, will help.

When I grow up I want to read my own stories, ones I write when I was a kid, and some new ones. My job will be to read stories and write your own. If you want to be a writer, you got to read stories and poems.

I want to write in cursive—a cursive *S* and *D* and *H* and *T*. Ms. Willis give us a tracing sheet. I want to write little and not leave out words and capital letters, and I like to write in cursive more gooder. You got to listen, and if you get more work, you learn more. I want to learn how to be rich when I grow up. I'll be rich and get shoes every day. I'll work, make a song, maybe a lot of songs.

January

I'm learning to read good because I read. Ms. Shockley teach me. At home I read a bear story, and a girl and a fox, and *The Doorbell Rang*; that was my favorite story, but I lost the book. I want to learn to read in cursive next. I'll learn if I try to read in cursive—I can read that! [She reads interview sentence JoBeth has written.] When I grow up I'll read everything.

I can't say it, but in writing I'm learning to put periods at the end of the sentence or question marks and punctu . . . exclamation marks. If you're asking a question, you put a question mark; if you're asking a punctuation—I don't know what you put. I'm learning it by my teacher. I don't know how. My mama, she told me, I was just trying to get it right and I said, "When you asking a question you put a question mark, and when you ain't asking a questions you put a period?" And she said, "Right."

I want to learn to write in cursive. I don't know how I'll learn it— yea—my teacher. She give us a cursive handsheet—but that won't do it because you'll forget. Practice is a better way.

Third grade with Ms. Smith (February 6–June), Walnut Street School

June

I'm learning to read more books like this one [she picks up the book she just read]. I don't know how I'm learning it. Ms. Shockley helped me. Words I don't know she'll tell me, like at the end she'll tell me to go back to a page—like *The Doorbell Rang*—and I got used to it. I want to learn to read in cursive. I don't know how I'll learn it. When I grow up, I'll read my books and be a police, and a teacher, and a singer, and the President of the United States. I'll help the poor, and the Africans, and I'll bring them to America and buy anything they want.

I don't know about writing. I hardly write any. I'd like to write in cursive but I don't know how to learn it. I like to write now at home some.

THIRTEEN

The Girl with the Black and White Face

Shannon in First Grade at Walnut Street School

The girl with the black and white face she lived in New york City. And She lived in a scairdr (scary) house. She you (use) to go to a skary (scary) school and at the skary (scary) schocl (school) she mat (met) one scairdr (scary) frind (friend). Then she mat (met) one More and his Name was bad luck Jason. The girl with the black and white face skinned up her black face Then her frinds laughed at her so she stopped playing with Them. Then A nether (another) girl with The black and white face she jeast (just) told the orther (other) girl with the black and white face told I am sad me to said the orther (other) girl with the black and white face and said do you want to go away with me why yes I do want to go away with you so They want (went) to hawall (Hawaii) and when They was Flying up In The Air They saw A Volcano and The First girl with the black Face Fell in The Volcana. Then the Orther girl with the black and white face fell in the volcano too.

Out of place

Shannon wrote this story in the spring. It was indicative of the personal struggle she had been engaged in throughout the year. Shannon was eight years old, and this was her fourth year in school and she was in first grade! She had been at another school for the past three years, where she had spent two years at the kindergarten level and was now assigned to repeat first grade. How could she possibly overcome such beginnings? She was out of place in school, a place that was supposed to be for everyone, and her struggle to claim acceptance as a capable student was constant (see Figure 13-1). Many times I (Betty) echoed her friend Delia's comment, "Lord, I do hope this child make it to second grade."

Shannon had learned to view reading as a black-and-white issue of print analysis rather than a process of discovery, and school success as a pass/fail proposition. She seemed insecure about herself as a learner and a person. School had failed to support this child successfully in her emergent literacy development. Almost daily she experienced real highs and lows that naturally affected her academic performance and personal relationships. In between these crises she mumbled and grumbled about herself and others. Her conflict of confidence fostered a compensating strategy of learned dependency.

FIG. 13-1 *Walnut Street have too many kids. Look at that girl's faces.*

Beverly Cleary (1988) provided me with a base of understanding when she wrote about her childhood: "Even though adults had troubles, I was secure. Yamhill had taught me that the world was a safe and beautiful place, where children were treated with kindness, patience, and tolerance. Everyone loved little girls. I was sure of that" (p. 65). Shannon was a child who did not seem sure about anything. I would have been extremely happy for her if she had just believed something as simple and positive as "Everyone loves little girls." She was so needy. She sought assistance and reassurance constantly. I worked with her all year to encourage risk taking and self-evaluation. Helping Shannon believe in herself and her special abilities was a daily struggle for me too. I counted on her friends to show her that there was a place in this new, crowded school, even for a girl who was so unsure of herself. But Shannon found it very difficult to trust us, or to trust herself.

The frightening release of pressure that this situation generated occurred on April 13. I wrote in my teaching journal: "The most terrible thing happened today. Shannon and Jeremiah kept announcing ways they were going to kill themselves! At morning recess there was a conflict between Shannon and Jeremiah, and I asked them to sit on the sidewalk. Immediately, Shannon responded with comments like breaking her leg so she wouldn't have to come to school anymore. Right before afternoon recess, they both stayed back in the room after I had announced the final call to line up for recess. I told them they'd need to sit out for five minutes for not following instructions. When they came outside, they started complaining louder about all the terrible things they were going to do to themselves. I had to separate them. I moved Shannon to the bench and Jeremiah to the railroad tie seats. Shannon began to yell louder so Jeremiah could hear her and pick up on her lead. She said, 'I am going to run into a nail pointing out from a wall. I am going to tie myself to a railroad track and let a train run over me. I hope Freddy Krueger really comes to my house and kills me. I am going to fall and break my neck and die!'"

Significantly, in my opinion, this explosion of emotion came on the heels of our weeks of standardized testing. I had tried all year to offer her learning alternatives that were more open-ended and meaningful. It only took one series of tests for her to look at me as if I had been deceiving her all along. The last day of testing for the Iowa Test of Basic Skills had been the previous Monday, April 10. Once again, she had been forced into a school situation of black or white, right or wrong, and she had had to face it alone.

Later in April, Shannon came over and sat down with me on the bench at recess. She said, "I'm kind of shy about this but yesterday [at home] I had a talk with myself and I sang about believing in myself. I believe in myself now!" Up and down, black and white, I can't/I can—that was Shannon.

Shannon seemed to feel out of place in her family too. She lived in a very small frame house with her mother, stepfather, sixteen-year-old sister, a brother twelve and in the fifth grade, and another sister eleven in the third grade. Shannon had a different father than her siblings, and she was lighter skinned than they were. She shared a small, porch-like room with her brother and eleven-year-old sister. Her brother slept on the top bunk and she and her sister shared the lower bunk. She had one torn, zippered bag for her personal things and a basket where she kept old completed workbooks from previous years. She sadly complained to me throughout the year that her brother and sister teased her about being so old in the first grade and not being able to read yet. In the afternoons after school she would go home and sleep, so her brother "wouldn't mess with me." Her mother worked in a laundry and left the house each morning before Shannon went to school. When we talked at parent conferences, she seemed overwhelmed by the demands and stresses on her as she tried to work and support her family.

Getting to know Shannon as a person and a learner developed into a study of conflicts and contrasts in which the significance of others and her on-again, off-again relationships with them was a continuous issue. Shannon wrote about her family saying:

> My family By
> Shannon
> Hi I'm talking about my family.
> First with my mother
> When my Mother
> Cook She do NOt
> burn up my hot
> dog To
> day my mother
> going to Take my
> Sister to The
> blullu prler (beauty parlor)
> and my sister
> get her hair
> fix and I don't

and she do

look on
The next
pade (page)

second my
Father he did
Not want me
to got (get) my
her (hair) Fix and
my Father like
to play with
me
Third my sister
She lke (like) to
play with me to
and she call
me Wan Way
and my sister

fourth my Other
sister She
had a baby
and She want to
be sand (stingy) with
It

fifth my brther
my brther
are 12 and
This monring (morning)
my brther haved
a scarache (stomachache)
and That is all

The
end

In January, Shannon's sixteen-year-old sister had a baby and Shannon was displaced as the resident baby of the family. This was new cause for concern for Shannon. What would her place in the family be now? Her concerns were expressed in her longest piece up to that point:

The Long, Long, Long, Book (By Shannon, 2–21)

Me and my friends we are so happy together. I had to move. Then they were so, so, sad because the look on their faces told me so and I met some more friends. we was so, so happy together. So I invited them to a party at my house. so we had the party and my friends went Home. My mom had a baby and I was happy that my mom had a baby girl but I had to move again. The baby was happy. Then my friend named Brenda had to move. Now I was to, to sad to talk to my friend today But I talking to Them anyway. Then I told Them The bad News they said what I am shocked that Brenda had to move So I had three friends . won I had four friends and one had to move and I was still sad Then one more of me friends had to move. Her Name was Delia. She had to move So I had one friend left So me and Jeremiah went to the movies and we had fun at The movies Then I whant (went) back home Then my mom said Shannon did you can (come) back from the movies said my mom Yes I did mom. "OK" said my mom go to dad now. ok mom. Now me and Jeremiah woke up and went over to Delia's House early. This morning Delia said why are you ouer (over) my House early in the morning because I got something to tell you said Shannon. OK Shannon tell me said Delia OK Delia we got to go ouer (over) Brenda's House SO we went ouer (over) to Brenda's house Then I told Brenda x and o (kisses and hugs) Are you finich (finished) with your Book? yes [] mother I am finich (finished) with my Book. SO will you say The End so The End

Shannon worried about herself as a learner, and so did I. At a time when many of the children were delighting in their emerging independence as readers, writers, and learners, Shannon was only laying down shallow literacy roots that often had to be replanted. In early October she lamented, "I forgot all the words [last year's teacher] taught me." At the beginning of the school year she often had trouble remembering my name, JoBeth's name, or her pen pal's name. She still had to recite the alphabet to recall certain letters and could not discriminate between some similar letter formations. She often struggled to reread her own writing, but was always eager to share her attempts with a teacher or with the class during sharing time.

One thing was certain: Nobody worked harder than Shannon. She wanted to learn. She was conditioned to fail, not to failure. She had not shut down on us yet. In *The Education of Little Tree*, Little Tree said, "Once you give up on something, then you are kind of an onlooker" (Carter, 1976). Establishing reading and writing workshops as the primary arenas for literacy learning and not using the basal in a programmed way were, in my opinion, the principle reasons Shannon did not become just an "onlooker" in our community of learners.

Shannon needed a great deal of support to learn, but the workshop framework provided her a consistent, daily time to write and read. Choice of writing topic and reading material offered her necessary rehearsal time at her own level that did not label her in any way. She was a writer who struggled with getting ideas down on paper, just like everyone who has ever practiced the craft. As Little Tree's grandma wisely informed him, "Always when something is born, even an idea, there's fret and fuss."

Despite much diligence, learning to read and write were stressful for Shannon and caused a lot of fretting and fussing. In February she hugged her spelling tablet saying, "If you tell me they ain't all right, I'll cry." However, through her writing she made a place for herself.

"I can write that!"

Shannon's growth as a writer was really quite remarkable. She moved from labeling pictures to extended text writing and story constructions. Her writing folder bulged, indicative of her progress. She worked incredibly hard, and her motivation was high. Writing gave her concrete evidence of growth. She used her time well in class, focusing on her writing, ignoring interruptions. She added on to pieces over time and wrote at home and school whenever she had the slightest opportunity. She was engaged with, to, and by writing. Her community respected her efforts, and she surrounded herself with a network of peers; some were her models and some looked to her for specific support. Delia and Garin were her co-editors on many pieces, and Brenda and Trisha requested her help or copied from her often. Jeremiah was an occasional collaborator, but most of the time he was an interruption. Shannon was both a respected teacher and learner in her community.

I often worried about Shannon as a writer because I couldn't understand how language worked for her when I looked at her encoding patterns. Even in December she was writing the rhyme "rain, rain, go away, come again another day" as "ralien ralien go a weaiu come beik a neol dau." Was this transitional spelling? If so, it seemed like a very long transition. Nonetheless, she worked it out for herself and steadily moved toward conventionality in many aspects of her writing.

Examples from early October provide additional glimpses of Shannon's early efforts and struggles with written communication.

Page 1: The Flower
pink in green (pink and green
every CL (every color)
is goe reain (is gone raining)
Page 2: now
The
teu (tree)
ni The (and the)
Fleidus is bog (flower is big)
Page 3: now
The
hieas (house)
is
big
Page 4: now
every
Thing
is
The
same

As she attempted to reread what she had written, she erased often. I counted sixteen erasures in this example. The first week of school we noticed that she could not reread something she had just completed a few minutes prior. Many times when she couldn't read what she had written she would write something else, a self-editing strategy she acquired out of necessity that aided her production of more conventional writing.

The following paragraphs describe Shannon's attempts in an early writing workshop, providing examples of her strengths as a writer, as well as her struggles. We saw constant monitoring for meaning leading to self-editing, both verbal and nonverbal; Shannon's interactions with her peers, both as a teacher and as a learner; her joyous interaction with the text itself as it came into being; and some of the struggle that was to haunt her as a speller the entire year.

Shannon and Brenda worked at a table where JoBeth was observing. Shannon began to write, saying, "'I like' . . . how you spell 'like' . . . 'l—i . . . i?'" JoBeth confirmed her attempt. Shannon continued, "L—L?" JoBeth suggested she say the word. "Li—ke—k?" JoBeth nodded. "I'm going to finish this and write the song on the bottom of the page. How do you spell 'but' . . . b? . . . but . . . " She reread the whole sentence. Delia asked her about her writing so Shannon reread again. Delia told her that she needed "n" then "t" to make the word "don't." Shannon erased her first attempt, "dot," and corrected it to "don't." Then she reread the whole piece again and wrote, liLLk for "like," the same spelling as her earlier attempt. She continued her oral planning with, "'don't like me' . . . m—e" and began to sing, "so I . . ." Brenda and Delia joined in by singing, "I like you." Shannon wrote, "I love you," and reread by singing all the text again. Delia jumped in with, "I love you dinosaur . . . ain't that funny?"

Shannon excitedly said, "I can write that," and they read all she had written aloud together. Brenda began copying Shannon's story; Delia also began to write, but she did not copy. Shannon explained, "I'm making it like the dinosaur singing and the boy singing." Again she reread from the beginning, got lost, reread again to find her place, and then tracked carefully until she got to what she needed next, "love me." She wrote.

Several minutes later she again read the entire piece. She talked about an ending where they got married. She had written "I det" and read it as, "Yes I do." Brenda requested help in spelling "said." Shannon offered, "s—ai? Do you have 'e'?—d."

Shannon turned to read her song to Violet, and as she did discovered an omission and added "you." She talked her way through yet another section with, "so can we get married." She wrote "con" for "can," "me" for "we," but said, "I know 'get,' g—e—t." She said the alphabet and checked the alphabet wall display to confirm her attempt at the letter "g." Next she looked in her writing folder to an earlier composition in which she used the word "married," and copied "mrerd." I called for clean-up time. Shannon prepared her papers for sharing time.

Shannon had worked nonstop for twenty-four minutes and had used many resources to support her learning. Such an exchange demonstrated the opportunities for rehearsal and peer support that a student like Shannon desperately needed. The number of times Shannon was observed rereading her own writing gave us more understanding of the importance and power of time, choice, response, and community, opportunities that were not usually connected with fill-in-the-blank worksheets or follow-ups to reading group instruction. From this example one can also see the contrast between insecurity and security as Shannon questioned so many of her invented spelling efforts while simultaneously building a base of key words to nurture her confidence. Shannon had invested in the process, as evidenced by her willingness to write, read, rewrite, and reread until she was satisfied with the results.

Shannon still had real problems with encoding and decoding, even after four years in school. She did not have dependable spellings for words she must have encountered over and over again, in basal presentations as well as in her own reading and writing, such as "like," "can," and "we." Shannon showed me what she needed as a learner; she sharpened my belief that all children need to be able to use the school setting to escort their learning to fluency.

In the initial stages of writing workshop, Shannon often supported her pieces and herself by using the names of friends as co-authors. These credits did not represent true collaborative enterprises, but by naming people who helped her she could be a part of something. Maybe she was creating a place for herself. The list included:

November

- The Indians and The pilgrims (By Shannon and Delia)
- On a dark dark Night (By Shannon and Karen)
- Did you see my monkey? (By Shannon and Friends)
- I do Not Love you I love you Colin (By Shannon and Colin)

December

- The rain Book (By Shannon and Trisha)
- The Christmas cat and Christmas dog and Santa (By Shannon and Karen)
- Untitled (By Shannon and Frances [her mother])
- Untitled (By Shannon and Frances)
- Untitled (By Shannon and Frances)
- I Love You Santa (By Shannon and Frances)

January

- The Christmas Book (By Shannon and Jeremiah)
- I Love Jeremiah For The 100000$ (By Shannon and Jeremiah and Brenda and Trisha)
- The day of The Weeks (By Shannon and Delia)

Shannon no longer seemed to need to designate partnership in her writing after January. She knew her community of writers and she identified herself as a valued member of that community.

Another interesting feature of Shannon's writing was the number of times successful topics were revisited. By doing this she rehearsed words and story structures that were comfortable. Perhaps Shannon's biggest success, at least in terms of impact on the rest of the class, was one of her first stories, titled "The Bils" (The Balls, shown in Figure 13–2). We had just completed our first author study, featuring Donald Crews. Her story was an extension of the ideas in his book *Ten Black Dots.* She wrote her interpretation over three days in early September. This

FIG. 13–2 *"The Balls"*

was the first story with a definitive beginning, middle, and end that was produced by any member of the class; her use of half a dot (ball) on 9/7 to indicate motion delighted all of us. Again in September she stretched to use new vocabulary in her dependable format:

The Dieas and The cmamas gone
(The dots and the comets gone)

The cMaMas. gone and Dieas.
(The comets gone and dots)

The Dieas gone.
(The dots gone)

The and
(The End)

In November . . .

The Flower Book

"The" Flower grew
and grew It grew
into a big "plant"

The Flower dinsaper now
(The flower disappear now)

The
End

In December she added a twist on the structure by adding dialogue:

did you see my Biel

did you see my Biel
no said Marcus

did you see
my biel
no said
Jeremiah

did you see my
Biel Nora
I see it
The end

Several of the other students imitated her useful style of story development. She was a successful writer in her community, although she still had trouble reading what she wrote.

Perhaps because she had an understanding of these elements of story, she was most receptive to a series of mini-lessons I used in the spring to illustrate story planning. One day we focused on possible titles, then on lead sentences, then on setting, next on playing with problems and solutions, and finally we learned how to freewrite on a chosen topic before deciding to invest totally. Shannon's plan ultimately generated her "girl with the black and white face" story. She wrote the following plans:

> Possible titles:
>
> The black bake Fox
> The girl with The black an white face
> black face girl
> The girl Thay will laf at
>
> Possible leads:
>
> The Fox had a cripel black
> The black girl had a black bake NO byt (body) could NOT help
> The girl Srapd (scraped) but It did NOt come oof (off)
>
> Possible settings:
>
> take plays a school
> One day The girl
> with The black
> facs she went to
> school and Thay
> cap (kept) on looking at
> har facs
>
> The town is in
>
> New york city
> and It Takes places
> in New york City. It
> going to be in
> a scairdy houe.
>
> The problem:
>
> The problem
> is everybody
> keep picking
> on her
>
> The solution:
>
> she is
> going to
> picking on
> Them back

And she began her draft:

> The gilr wiTh The
> blak face [is] eigh (eight)
> and she Thaink (thinks)
> she is to skinny
> and she Thaaink (thinks)
> her friends pick at
> her black and white
> face and she is

nice and She Thaink (thinks)
her face is to big
and Thaink (thinks) she
haves to meny friends

Shannon proved that writing was a real part of her life. By early December she had started rehearsing her writing topics at home. She returned from Christmas vacation with two stories she had actually written at home: "The Book" (copied from some other print source with glued on pictures from the comic section of the newspaper) and "Belibe" (Believe). It seemed to pull together all her many rehearsals of main ideas, patterns in stories, conflict, and resolving endings in a dialogue between Shannon and Kim.

BeliBe

I lik Christmas. why Shannon? be case Santnick. come But I do NOt like Christmas Why Kin? I do NOt BeliBe in Santnick be case my MOM is Santnick? OK Kin It is you do NOt BeliBe in Santnick I do OK Shannon

I do BeliBe in Santnick NOW Shannon yes you do I Love you Shannon yes I do I do Love you to

The end

I remember worrying during my Christmas vacation that my students would forget everything they had learned by the time they came back to school. How relieved I was to see verification that what children learned by doing and creating for themselves they truly internalized and could apply to more than one situation or setting.

Shannon had started to rely on words as primary meaning makers by January. Illustrations were not as important. She decided she needed her writing time for writing. Soon her story ideas developed a heavy focus on her relationships with her friends and her feelings about herself. One often had the feeling that she was standing on the edge, teetering back and forth, as she tried to find a firm foothold within her school and home community .

me and my day

mom I had a bad day. Come on let's go and have a good day. My mom took me to The mall and I was happy. Then I told Them I had bad luck because I am sad because I need to be happy. Nora tryed to Cheer me up. Then Delia tryed to Cheer me up. But my mom tryed me some jokes But I was NOt happy will you be happy yes[] are no[] SO I will be sad so finally chilld (cheered) me up The end one two three

I Like you Darnell
do you like me No
I do Not like you Shannon
so I do Not like you Darnell
so who like you Karen and
Jeremiah like me and Brenda to
But you do Not like me so
so I do Not care do you care No I

Dear Mom, and Dad
I am doing
good In school but
I have a problm
of being grumpy
and I still right
good and I wish
I had more snack
please Mom and Dad
I copy sanack but
I need a snack every
day and Mom
and Dad

p.2

and I am going to
do good on my
test do NOt worry
mom and Dad
Love

FIG. 13–3 *Shannon's Letter to Her Parents*

do Not care so Shannon I do
you But I do Not whant to saia (say)
It can we go Home Now
The end

Shannon understood that writing could be functional too. One day she decided to write the principal about her rocky relationship with Jeremiah: "Dear Dr. Oates Jeremiah have been bad to me and he haved been good to me." In a prompted letter to her parents about her school days, Shannon wrote very insightfully (see Figure 13–3).

Shannon developed an identity as a writer in our classroom, as is evident from her interviews throughout the year. She expressed concerns about what she didn't know, and increasingly confident plans about her adult life as a writer. She even talked about reading as a grown-up, reading her own books and other people's books. Donald Crews remained one of Shannon's favorite authors. I had a snapshot of him, taken at the Georgia Children's Literature Conference, on our Author's Map. She imitated his style on several occasions, and often talked of going to New York to meet him and be a writer too. The multicultural literature we shared in our classroom offered many students what Calkins calls a "lifeline to literacy," and Crews seemed to offer that line to Shannon. Still, she did not see herself as a reader in first grade.

As one of her final writings of the year explained so dramatically, Shannon never did acquire the confidence in herself as a reader. She only read because she was supposed to. For some reason, she never seemed to make the connection between her increasing writing ability and her development as a reader.

> **I Like Books**
>
> I like books said Brenda and Shannon said I don't like books and Delia said why do you not like books Then I said I just do NOt like Books The next day when they got out of school they went to the Libraruy. But Shannon did not read a book and Delia and Brenda said READ A BOOK Then Shannon said No no I do not whant to read a book Then Brenda and Delia said Read a book now so I read a book but I skiped (skipped) some paiges (pages) I SAID I LIKE BOOKS

In this piece you can sense her frustration, as she really wants to cry out: "I know I'm supposed to like to read but I don't—it's still too hard!" But underneath these feelings of inadequacy, the desire to become a competent reader was still a powerful force. When I made a home visit in late March, I gave her a copy of *The Doorbell Rang*, a book by Pat Hutchins that we had read in class. She seemed pleased, but little did I know the time and effort she would put into learning to read that book fluently and independently. JoBeth had asked her to read the same book earlier in the year and she had stumbled on almost every word. By having her own copy of the book to practice and rehearse as often as she liked, she was able to share the story confidently with no errors by the end of the school year. We had a large classroom library that also provided continuity for emerging readers. The students were encouraged to check them out for nightly reading, but somehow literal ownership seemed especially important for Shannon.

"Do you like me?"

For Shannon, a student we really worried about, success rested on several key factors. The fact that she had a desire to learn was critical. I worked to match that desire with a daily learning environment and experiences that could provide exportable learning strategies, ones that would help Shannon be a successful learner in a variety of settings, and ones that would help her believe in herself as a capable person.

Shannon displayed a hungry need for approval throughout the year. When I took her to the library during the summer, she still approached me with the same sense of neediness. Looking up at me expectantly, she used her soft, high-pitched, younger-than-nine kind of voice as she breathlessly and pleadingly queried, "Do I look good, Ms. Shockley? Tell me I look good. I don't look good. I do look good?"

Obviously, Shannon did not have a perfect childhood or an exemplary educational experience; neither did Beverly Cleary. In first grade, Cleary recalls, "The class had been divided into three groups: Bluebirds, who found happiness in seats by the window; Redbirds, who sat in the middle seats; and Blackbirds, who sat by the blackboard, far from sunlight. I was not surprised to be a blackbird. The worst part of the day was the reading circle, where the Blackbirds in turn had to read words from the despised word lists. With luck, 'party' or 'mamma,' words I could read, were flashed at me. Oh the relief!" Cleary continues, "The best day of all in second grade was the day Miss Marius let me wash her little teapot after lunch. Then I knew for sure she loved me." To me, these kinds of events show the power and the promise of schools and teachers to help shape the lives of students. Sometimes instructional strategies such as ability grouping are taken for granted; we fail to question them, and thus fail to see their inhibiting impact on learners.

And sometimes it is the simplest gesture or comment that provides support for a lifetime choice. In the seventh grade, Beverly Cleary's teacher, Miss Smith, said, "When Beverly grows up, she should write children's books." Beverly heard her, and believed her. I hoped Shannon heard me, and was beginning to believe in herself, as she assured me that day in April (page 111).

Forrest Carter, portraying his childhood as Little Tree, also had a unique educational experience. He was taught at home in the mountains by his Cherokee grandmother and grandfather. Grandpa's core educational advice was about gift giving: "Grandpa said if you showed a fellar how to do, it was a lot better than giving him something. He said if you learnt a man to make for hisself, then he would be all right; but if you just give him something, and didn't learn him anything, then you would be continually giving to the man the rest of your life. Grandpa said you would be doing the man a disservice, for if he became dependent on you, then you taken away his character and had stole it from him."

As much progress as she had made, and as accepted as she had become in our community, Shannon was still out of place. She was a tall preadolescent in a child's world. I talked with our principal, Shannon's mother, and Shannon herself. We made a radical (*radical*— "at the root of, fundamental") decision: Shannon would skip second grade and move directly into third grade. She would go into a whole language classroom where she could continue developing at her own pace, an accelerated one as a writer, a more laborious one as a reader.

Shannon was evaluated and found to have a learning disability in reading, a real gap between her IQ of 87 and her reading development. She needed a stronger chance to beat the dropout odds, as well as the exemption special education would give her from state promotional requirements. We hoped a promotion, along with the extra help of a special education teacher, would be the support she needed for her changing self-image. When we asked Shannon what she wanted to be when she grew up, she quickly responded, "A writer and live in New York." I feel sure Beverly Cleary and Forrest Carter would join me in wishing her the best.

Shannon called me at home over the summer to tell me, "I thought of something I need to learn before the third grade—how you tell time." Shannon was accepting some of the responsibility for her own learning. Perhaps she was beginning to see her learning as something she could influence, rather than as a black/white, pass/fail process beyond her control. I hoped that she might someday see herself as a beautiful, capable, whole person, instead of the laughed-at Girl with the Black and White Face, falling into a volcano of fears.

FOURTEEN

"I Love You and I Will Try To Be Good"

Shannon in Third Grade at Walnut Street School

with Teachers Susan Willis and Judy Smith

> to Mrs. goodmen/ By Shannon./ Mrs goodmen is a/ goodmen said Kim/ Then she turned/ Lynn in to a Queen/ then Lynn said Mrs Willis/ I am diying hear/ yes you are diying/ said Mrs. Willis/ Then Mrs. goodmen/ turned Mrs. Willis/ In to a witch/ Then Mrs. goodmen/ said you are going/ to be on my side?/ said Mrs goodmen/ to Mrs willis/ Then Mrs willis/ said yes I/ do want [to]/be a witch/ Know doim little gilr [now dumb little girl]/ I am Not doim then Mrs 'Willis said/ you are doim then/ Then the witch stat [started]/ to chaiesed . . . (piece unfinished; written 9/13)

Shannon portrayed her new teacher, Susan Willis, as a witch in this and several other writings at the beginning of her third-grade year. In this story Mrs. Goodman (a woman who had made bread with the class that week) engaged Ms. Willis in the classic pull of good and evil ("Are you going to be on my side?"), with Shannon as the victim. Fear—fear of being chased by a scary person—and degradation—"you dumb little girl"—were very real parts of Shannon's life. Is she dumb, as her siblings and a school system that retained her in both kindergarten and first grade say or imply? Is a new teacher going to be like Ms. Shockley and make her feel safe and worthwhile, or is she going to be a witch that chases dumb little girls? Shannon was still the girl with the black and white face, unsure of who she was, distrustful of those around her.

Susan, like Betty, worried about Shannon's self-concept. "She had such a negative self-image, such a lack of confidence. We worked on it the whole time I was there." Mid-September, Shannon shoved her writing aside and said, "I don't like this story. It's getting boring—do you want to see it?" Later in the same writing workshop she said, "Nobody wants to hear it—nobody asks me any questions when I share it." With Susan's encouragement she did share, and two people asked questions; but this insecurity surfaced several times during the year when

---

Susan Willis is the actual name of the first teacher; Susan was an active researcher in the project until midyear, participating in both data collection and data analysis. Judy Smith is a psuedonym, requested by the teacher; she also was a participant in the research. Neither teacher was able to write the chapters for the four children they taught that year: Shannon, Reggie, Ricky, and Lee, although both contributed through observational notes, writing samples, weekly data analysis sessions, and feedback on drafts of the chapters. JoBeth is the author.

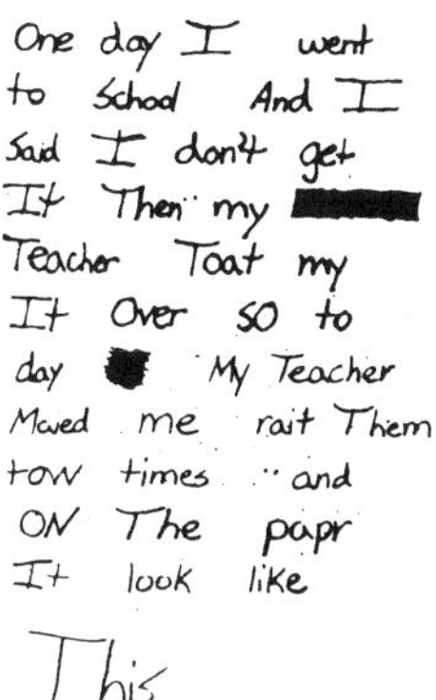

"**Sometime I get Mad**" by Shannon
Sometime I get mad.
"I don't get IT"

One day I went to school. And I said, "I don't get IT." Then my teacher told me IT over. So today, My Teacher made me write them two times, and on the paper it looked like this.

I can
I Can
I Can.

FIG. 14–1 *"Sometimes I Get Mad"*

she wadded up her paper in frustration because she couldn't read it, or it wasn't as good as what her friends were writing. At other times she was hesitant to share, like one day in November when she told Susan, "I don't want to read my story. I miss a word, that be bad." This self-effacement was also a plea for affirmation, reminiscent of her pattern from last year: "Do I look good, Ms. Shockley? Tell me I look good. I don't look good. I do look good?" Shannon seemed to hold this dual vision of herself as a permanent image; when Susan gave the class a sentence-completion questionnaire (Something About Me) in November, Shannon wrote after the lead-in "To be grown up," "I will be happy and sad."

Susan began working with Shannon on her self-image early in September, encouraging her use of positive self-talk. Several weeks later Shannon wrote about Susan's help (see Figure 14–1).

Where do I fit at home?

Susan worked hard, and Shannon worked hard; they had a great deal to overcome. Shannon's fourth-grade sister and middle school brother made it very difficult for her to believe anything positive about herself. Shannon told Susan that she hated her sister, that she was really mean to her. "Maybe that's why she's so hesitant to try things," Susan speculated. Concerned, she asked Shannon's mother and stepfather about the situation during the October parent-teacher conference. They said her brother and sisters told her she was dumb, that she couldn't do things. This certainly fit with Shannon's belief about how others saw her, as was obvious from her answers to two other questions on the questionnaire: "People think I *am stapt and dum* [stupid and dumb]," and "I'd rather read than *stay home*." Susan encouraged Shannon's parents to talk with their other children when Shannon was not around. "They need to know they can*not* talk to her that way," Susan urged.

However, things did not seem to improve at home. When each person had a chance later in the year to make a wish, Shannon's was "That I be pretty." Lighter skinned than her siblings, she had been told how ugly she was by them often. Like Pecola in Toni Morrison's *The Bluest Eye*, Shannon's beauty was not only ignored by the predominant culture, it was denigrated by her own family, her brother and sisters. Scary people were common topics in her writing. She wrote about teachers who were really witches, about monsters, a Thanksgiving turkey that "will skair me," and a boy in the class who "skarred my friends a way." In her October 17 story she wrote, "oneday I woke up and tow popcorn was in my bad. and I screamed and hallred. . . . Than I said I'm jast a littel gril with pigtells." She reminded us of nine-year-old Pharoah Rivers in *There Are No Children Here* (Kotlowitz, 1991), who told his mother when she tried to explain about his brother going to jail, "Mama, I'm just too young to understand how life really is." Shannon must have felt at times like telling the world, "Please be kind to me. I'm just a little girl with pigtails."

A highlight of the year for Shannon was when she won second place among all the third graders at Walnut Street School in the Invent America contest. As she proudly showed her ribbon around the room, letting her peers touch the satiny symbol of success, she said proudly, "My mama is going to hang this ribbon in the living room, and they're not going to call me dumb anymore!"

But they did. On March 7 Shannon called Betty (they still talked regularly) at 11:15 p.m., screaming. "Shannon, what is it! What's the matter, can you tell me?" Betty asked. "He's hitting me. He's jumping on my face! He's hitting—he's hitting my legs, my stomach, my . . . " she sobbed. "Who—who's doing this to you?" Betty asked repeatedly. Shannon was frantic, and would not or could not answer. Betty began guessing, and Shannon whispered "yes" when she asked, "Is it your brother?" Gradually she calmed down, cautiously answering Betty's questions. Her stepfather no longer lived there, and her mother had a new boyfriend. Shannon was really frightened when she was there without a parent, even though her sixteen-year-old sister could have taken that role. She hadn't had any dinner that night. Betty kept reassuring her that she could talk as long as she needed to and that she would talk to Shannon's mom about the situation. Betty said, "You keep your phone off the hook, and I'll keep mine off. It's lying right here on my pillow, and if you need me again, all you have to do is start talking and I will hear you, even if I'm asleep." Finally, after a long period of silence, Shannon whispered calmly, "Ms. Shockley, it's okay now. He's gone to sleep." Betty reported the incident.

The next day in school, Shannon got very frustrated and cried because she couldn't finish a class assignment. When Betty explained to Judy about the phone call, identifying the siblings, Shannon's teacher was shocked. "I didn't realize she was living with those two hoodlums. They both have ugly mouths, and they are really mean—nothing like Shannon. Shannon brought in cupcakes for Sonya's birthday last week; those two would never think of doing something nice for someone like that. I saw them at the Golden Pantry just yesterday, being run out for shoplifting. I talked to one of her brother's three Behavior Disorders teachers at the middle school, and she said, 'We just split his time up among the three of us; none of us can stand him.' Poor Shannon."[5]

Two weeks later, Shannon's sister told her teacher that her mother hadn't been home for four days. Shannon confirmed this to Betty, who had been checking on Shannon regularly since the harrowing night of the phone call. When questioned, Shannon also admitted that she hadn't been eating much; Betty noted that she looked very thin. The school went into action. Ms. Naylor, the assistant principal, called the Department of Family and Children Services. Police and a social worker went to the home and told the children to get packed to go to a foster home. Shannon was really upset. Ms. Dr. Oates (as the children called the principal) called to make sure Shannon had Betty's number, to see if the kids were alright. Betty called later, at about 8:00, and Shannon said her mother was home. She brought a man with her, her older sister's granddaddy. Her mother got on the phone and told Betty she was okay and was going to come up to school tomorrow (although she did not). Betty said that she was very concerned for Shannon's welfare. Shannon's mom didn't seem angry, and talked freely with Betty about the situation.

Shannon didn't talk much about her home situation unless asked, and she did not write about her family often. However, we wondered if her October 2 story (see Figure 14-2) was a thinly masked version of real life.

Where do I fit at school?

In the third-grade classroom

It is evident from the preceding section that Shannon's relationship with Betty was very important to her. On the questionnaire, Shannon responded to "My favorite place to be is *In Mrs Sckool room*" and "I look forward to *go to Mis Sockay room*," which Susan encouraged her to do on occasion to share her writing. Betty took her to the regional library several times during the year. Shannon never failed to return a book. After one trip, Shannon even got permission from her mother to spend the afternoon at Betty's house.

Now, however, she found herself in a trailer behind the school, far from Betty, with a new teacher. When Susan read to the class about the mean Mrs. Gorf, the teacher who turned children into various objects in *Sideways Stories from Wayside School* (Sacher, 1978) at the beginning of the year, Shannon wrote about "a skairy teahet" who turned Reggie into a dog. The next day she wrote:

5. We must note that it is really unfair to portray Shannon's siblings in such an unfavorable light, when we know nothing of their life stories. Why do they feel the need to belittle their little sister? What kind of self-concepts must they have? How does it affect a child to know (and surely he knows) that none of your three teachers can stand you? Still, this was the only information we had, and the effects on Shannon were dramatic.

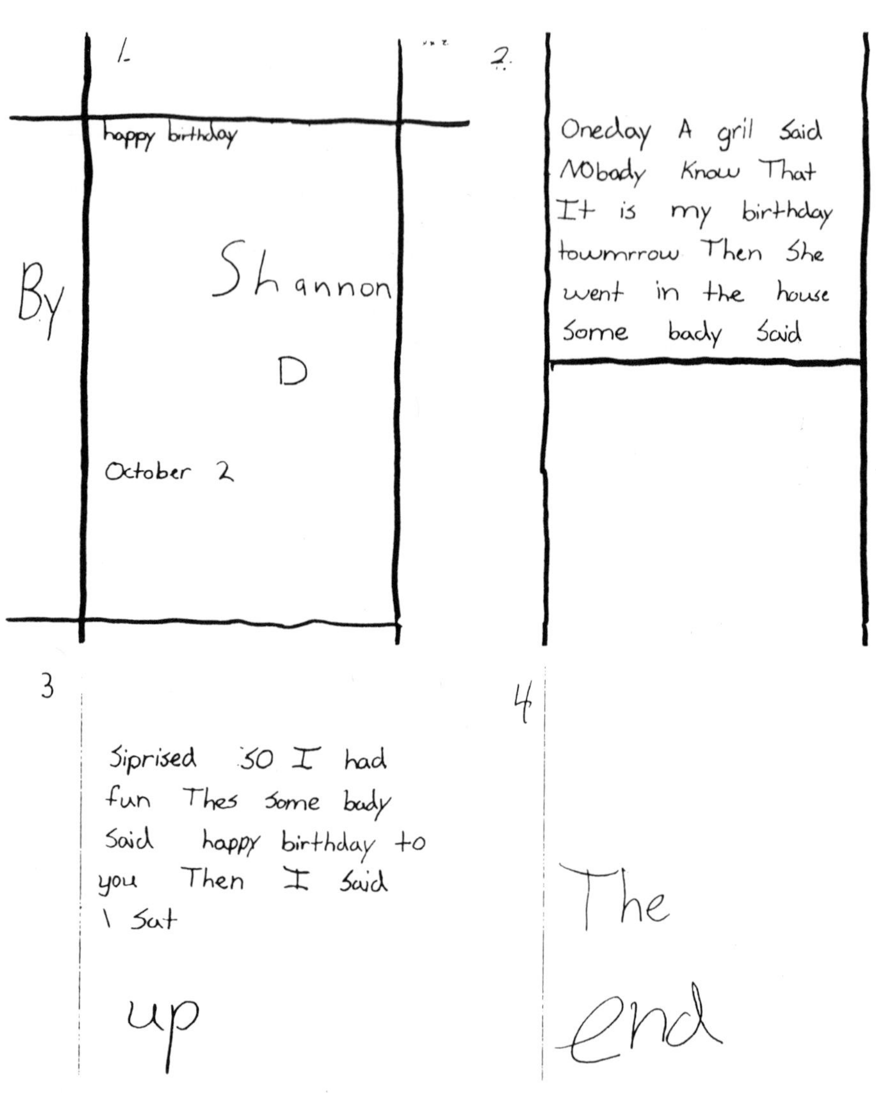

FIG. 14–2 *"Happy Birthday"*

> My mean teach/ Mrs Willis/ One day Shannon/ road [wrote] Mrs Willis a/ Nont and Mrs Willis/Came/ to/ my/ house/ and gave me/ a woeape [whipping]/ and I said/ aw/That haet [hurt]/ The end

Susan was sympathetic. "It took Shannon a while to warm up to me, to trust me. She wanted to go back to Betty. [When] she wrote about me as a witch in her story, maybe she was getting her anger out through writing about me that way, but she did share it with me." Susan worked to gain Shannon's trust, listening to her read self-selected books and her own writing daily, building up her image of herself as a capable learner and likable person. With Shannon's parents' permission and encouragement, Susan gave Shannon and a classmate several sweaters she no longer wore. Shannon was thrilled, and chose all the pink ones, her favorite color. She wore one the next day and even wrote about it. She began seeking Susan out, asking to read to her, confiding in her. On the same questionnaire where she had said Betty's room was her favorite place to be, she also wrote "My classmates are *Barbara Ann Mis Willis Lynn*," "Teachers I like best *Is Mis Sckoy and Mis Willis*," and "If I could do anything I wanted at school *I wold halp my tar* [teacher]."

Then, early in November, the warm, safe world in Susan Willis' classroom began to fall apart. Susan was diagnosed with Lyme's disease, struggled with the pain and weariness, and then got worse news: The doctor said she had lupus. Susan had no choice but to stay in bed and try to build her strength back up. She left the last week in November and did not return until after Christmas vacation. Shannon wrote her often. Her carefully handmade cards said, "We love you Ms. Willis and we hope you get well soon you are the #1 Teacher. We love Ms. Willis We love Ms. Willis." Another said, "I hope you get well soon and I love you and I will try to be good." Another promised, "We will be good." Did Shannon think she/they had made her sick, that this class, which was noted for its difficulty, had driven her away? Did she blame herself, as children sometimes do in divorces?

Susan returned in January rested and resolved. She would work only at school, rest when she needed to, relax rather than doing schoolwork at home— a tremendous shift for someone who had thrown all her energy into teaching for several years. But the plan did not work, and neither did her body's defense system. She grew more and more fatigued, and the pain became unbearable. On January 29, Susan was crying when the children returned early from a special class. The children were frightened and solicitous. Shannon made a card for her: "I hope you get well soon and I love you and I will try to be good. Love your secrt admie [admirer]."

Susan had no choice but to take a leave for the rest of the year. The children and a parade of substitutes had suffered mutually during her absence in December; this time Dr. Oates wanted someone the children knew, someone who would be there all year and could reestablish some stability for the children. Judy Smith had been a physical education teacher at Walnut Street for several years. She had recently become certified to teach in the elementary classroom and was eager to make a change. It seemed like a perfect solution. She team taught with Susan for two days, and on February 7 she took over.

At first Judy tried to maintain the routines Susan had established. "Due to the succession of substitutes," Judy explained, "the children were unsure of the length of my stay as well as the consistency of classroom rules and consequences." She struggled initially to get the children to respect her decisions, and soon decided that she had to establish her own routines, discipline plan, and instructional style. She explored several classroom structures; "It wasn't until May that I hit upon the routine I like best of those I tried," she explained. However, throughout her tenure much of her instruction was integrated around children's literature and author studies; she usually gave children related topics to write about.

Judy was very sensitive to how Susan's absence affected the children. Some mothers told her their children had been crying at home. One boy cried going to the bus on Susan's last day. Shannon was very negative anytime anyone talked to her about Judy. Shannon talked about Ms. Smith being a witch, just as she had written about Susan being a witch at the beginning of the year.

By mid-March we began to notice Shannon smiling, complaining less, and working more independently. One day after Judy herself had been out for several days (her own children were sick), Shannon said, "You know I always say I don't like you? Well, I like you better than the sub!" Another time she explained, "Even when I stamp my foot like that, I still like you." Judy worked with Shannon, and with all the children, on expressing their feelings verbally and in writing about Ms. Willis, and how they felt about her absence."Susan's loss was really hard on Shannon. She didn't really know me very well through PE. But I bragged on her a lot, her writing, her math, and her hard work. I reminded her, 'Remember, *I can—I can do this*. You're smart!' By the end of the year, she became really attached to me. She came to me for comfort when something went wrong. I can still see Shannon's face on the bus the last day, kind of dazed, like 'What am I going to do now.'"

In the special education classroom

Susan and Judy were not Shannon's only teachers. Shannon spent two forty-five-minute classes a day with Ms. Erdrich, who taught in an interrelated classroom (learning disabilities, behavior disorders, and mildly mentally handicapped: LD, BD, MiMH labels). At the beginning of the year, Shannon went from 10:15 to 11:00 in the morning, and again during social studies in the afternoon. She missed out on Susan reading aloud, reading mini-lesson, reading alone/with buddy, and most of sharing time. Susan was unhappy with the arrangement, and in October she and Ms. Erdrich reduced Shannon's time to one segment, at 11:00. Now she would be in class for all of Susan's reading aloud and reading workshop, the area where she needed the most help, but would miss part of writing workshop, the area in which she shone.

It was October 17, shortly after this change, at 10:57. "Ms. Willis, is it time? Is it time?" Shannon asked as she looked repeatedly from her writing to the clock. It must be difficult for children to get really engaged with literacy, engaged with learning, if they have to be watching the clock. In Ms. Erdrich's room, Shannon worked on a math assignment from Ms. Willis. She looked up with a smile and said, "I like you, you're a nice lady." "I like you too," Ms. Erdrich smiled back. "You're a nice girl. When you finish, maybe we'll read a little. Now you work on this by yourself—I've got to help other kids." Ms. Erdrich had worried that Shannon was getting too dependent on her. Her classmates were just finishing writing when she returned to the room at 11:52. Shannon wrote all through sharing.

Susan and Judy both noted that it was very hard on Shannon to leave class during writing workshop. "Her special class really interfered with her writing," Susan noted. "She missed a lot. She always tried to catch up when she got back into the room, but sometimes she couldn't." She began several pieces that she never finished, such as the one shown in Figure 14-3. She rarely got to share her writing, choosing instead to write, although sometimes Susan and Judy found extra sharing times during the day. Scheduling special classes was a nightmare for both classroom and special education teachers. Ms. Erdrich had children coming from various grade levels, with various needs, rotating in and out every fifteen minutes. Of the twenty-four children in Shannon's class, twenty-one left the classroom at some time for some type of special services.

As disruptive as this pullout program was all year, Ms. Erdrich herself was a good friend and supportive teacher for Shannon. She truly loved the children who

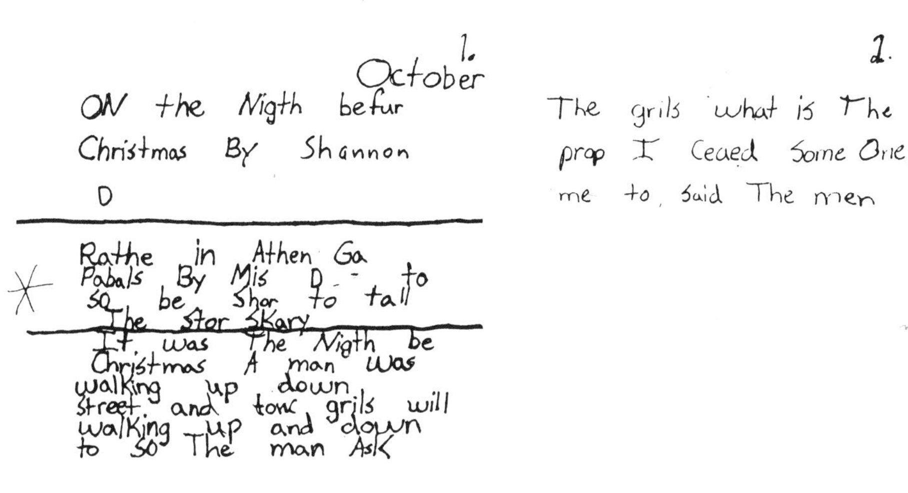

1.
October
ON the Nigth befur
Christmas By Shannon
D

Rathe in Athen Ga
Pabals By Mis D- to
So be Shor to tall
The Stor Skary
It was The Nigth be
Christmas A man Was
walking up down
street and town grils will
walking up and down
to so The man Ask

2.
The grils what is The
prop I Ceaed Some One
me to, Said The men

FIG. 14–3 *Unfinished Piece*

came to her, even those others found difficult to love. She often bemoaned the short amount of time she had with any one group, especially when she tried to get them involved in projects like her unit on animals in their environments. Shortly after Susan left, Ms. Erdrich noted that Shannon was anxious about the loss, and even asked to stay longer with Ms. Erdrich.

Soon Shannon lost that security too. Ms. Erdrich left for maternity leave early in April. Ms. Olson, who had student taught in the room in the fall, took over. On April 10, Shannon balked. "Do I have to go?" she pleaded, looking at the clock. "She said I don't have to." "Yes," Judy responded, as she prepared the rest of the class to go out to recess. "I hate it! I want to go outside." Shannon stomped down the hall.

She flounced angrily in her chair and announced, "I want to go outside." "Where is your spelling?" asked Ms. Olson. "I'm sorry, you *have* to work in here today. Go get your spelling book." Shannon got her book and returned, flipping the pages of the book with disdain. "Have you had a bad day?" Ms. Olson solicited. "I want to go out," Shannon scowled. Shannon grumbled throughout the period, but got her "behavior" folder when Ms. Olson requested it. After praising Shannon for following directions, she asked, "Did you speak politely? No, you have that attitude, like 'I hate school . . . '" "I do!" Shannon interrupted. " . . . so you don't get that check," Ms. Olson continued. "I hope you have a good day for the rest of the day." Shannon walked silently back to the trailer, where everyone else was reading, and dissolved into tears.

It seemed so important last year to have her tested, to see if those gaps we saw were really a learning disability of some kind. It seemed especially important to have her staffed to keep her from having to repeat third grade, after just being promoted into it. Everyone felt it would be difficult for her to catch up in time to pass the CRT. Everyone hoped some individual attention to Shannon's unique needs would be beneficial. No one was very happy with the way things turned out.

Shannon, in desperate need of some stability at school, had over a dozen substitute teachers that year, and did not have one full day of both reading and writing workshop.

"If you want to be a writer, you got to read"

The writer

One strong link for Shannon between first and third grade was writing. She retained her love of writing, as Susan observed at school and Shannon's mother reported at the October conference. At home, Shannon usually wrote when her siblings were playing. "She just writes about what the others are doing, and about monkeys—she loves monkeys [her research topic in first grade]—and the color pink," her mother told Susan. At school, Shannon often wrote fictional pieces to express her feelings, sometimes mixing third and first person, as she did in "My mean teach" (see page 128). Books and class discussions often prompted topics. The first week of school, Shannon read about "Ramona," a Beverly Cleary character who was also in third grade, and wrote the dialogue story in Figure 14-4.

At the first of the year, Shannon was often eager to share, which surprised Susan because she rarely acted like anything else she did was acceptable. She usually wrote alone, but often asked someone near her for spellings. She also used books frequently to find words, as she did one day in mid-September. She was writing the story at the beginning of this chapter, with Susan as a witch and classmate Lynn as a princess. She got *Sleeping Beauty* to spell princess, found "queen," and said, "That's better than a princess!" Lynn gushed her approval, having taken a great interest in the development of the story line. Later, Shannon looked for "dying." "Hm," she mused, "this has 'dead,' but not 'dying.' I need 'dying.'" Lynn helped her spell "diying," and many other words for the next several weeks. Susan worried that she was becoming too dependent and moved Lee between the two girls. They both began to help him.

Shannon was somewhat on the periphery of a group of girls who often read and wrote together. The group was friendly towards Shannon and tried with slow but increasing success to include her in their projects. They were delighted to learn that she could "talk country," and wrote a play in which she was the country grandma. "The kids loved her when they performed that play," Susan said. "She was really good!" By the end of the year she seemed an accepted member of the group. When she couldn't find a vocabulary word in a census article the group was doing together, a friend pointed it out. "It's right there, honey child." Minutes later, Shannon responded to a conversation about family members in the hospital by patting Barbra Ann's arm and cooing, "That's just too bad." This camaraderie extended to sharing books and occasionally writing together, when Shannon was there to participate. Shannon seemed quite confident of herself as a writer, and when the group rejected her suggestion she said, "I'm going to write it anyway—Sonya, you're on your own."

Shannon, experienced with writing conferences in first grade, also sought help from Susan. After sharing a first draft of a clever story about two popcorn kernels named "The" and "End," some of which was written and some of which she

FIG. 14–4 *"What's It Like To Be in Third Grade?"*

composed orally, she sat down and began to add the parts she had composed orally. "Ms. Willis, can I have a conference with you?" Susan moved to her side. "Do you know a special part I could add to it?" Shannon asked. After reading it aloud, discussing content, and adding a sentence, Susan had her read aloud for punctuation. "I wish I could read this to Ms. Shockley so bad," Shannon said proudly. Susan agreed.

As much as she loved to write, Shannon often became frustrated with her limitations. Spelling was still a tremendous struggle. Toward the end of October,

Susan noted that she was getting much better at hearing sounds in words; in recent stories she had used "sekre" for "scary," "cold" for "could," and "mad" for "made." The November questionnaire (Something About Me) provided an opportunity for interesting analysis of her spelling development. We noticed some of the spelling difficulties from last year. Shannon still tended to put in clusters of vowels when she was uncertain: "baid" for "bad," and "paias" for "plays." Even in this single-period writing sample, there were no stable spelling for some words: *Sckool*, *Sacik*, *Sckoy*, *Sockay* for "Shockley"—a very important person to her; *raied*, *raiid* for "read"; *raig*, *raiding* for "reading"; and *lit*, *lat* for "let." However, as Susan had noted, she was making progress in phonemic spelling (*stapt* for "stupid," *larn* for "learn," *halp* for "help") and included several transitional (Temple, Nathan, Burris, and Temple, 1988) spellings, including *somethan* for "something." She also seemed to have control of many more conventional spellings than last year, words like "room," "have," and "stay."

Shannon made steady progress, hampered though she was by a lack of uninterrupted writing periods at school. When Judy became the teacher, she was impressed by Shannon's writing. "She amazes me. Her writing is better than some of the kids on grade level. She writes a lot, and things make sense. She really works at sounding words out." Shannon also became increasingly secure as a writer, perhaps because teachers, peers, and her mother were interested in what she wrote. One day in April, Shannon read JoBeth's notes as she copied one of Shannon's pieces in progress. She grinned at her group of friends and announced, "Want me to tell you something? Shannon D. is going to be a famous writer!"

The reader

This view of herself as an author was consistent with what we saw from studying Shannon's first-grade literacy through her talk and writing. Her reading attitude began to change in third grade.

On the first day of school Shannon chose a long Ramona book by Beverly Cleary. She appeared to be reading, keeping her head down and eyes on the print, turning the pages at about the right intervals. JoBeth sat beside her and asked if she could listen. She struggled. JoBeth helped her with some of the words, especially the unfamiliar names. She read some whole phrases, such as "asking to share the meal," but struggled through most of the rest of the page. As she turned to the next page, she looked up at JoBeth with her quintessential worried eyes and asked, "Do you think I can remember all this?" She obviously knew that reading was more than just saying the words. JoBeth asked her if it was too hard. "No—Okay, it's about her ski clothes, and about being in third grade?" JoBeth nodded, amazed at her need and ability to check her own comprehension, hoping that she had proved to herself that she could read this hard, third-grade book and might now find one that she could enjoy more. She resumed her reading, again asking several words. When JoBeth didn't respond she seemed to tire, saying on several words, "I'll skip that one." Obviously, reading thick books fit Shannon's profile of the third-grade reader.

When it came time to share their books with the class, Shannon leaned over to JoBeth with a panic-stricken look. "I forgot about the book—I forgot it!" she whispered. She did not raise her hand to share.

Three days later Susan observed a similar despair. "Shannon was crying, and when I asked her why she said, 'Because I don't know my words.' Shannon really wanted to learn to read a page out of a Berenstain Bear book so she could share it with the class. We discussed several ways to help her remember the words. She said that when she gets home she forgets the words and can't practice them. I decided to draw a picture over the words to help her learn the words by sight. I told her that after she practiced the words she could erase the pictures and see if she knew the words. By afternoon she was able to read it with the help of the pictures. She took it home to practice."

Susan used several techniques to help Shannon develop word recognition, fluency, and confidence, the chief one being having Shannon read passages aloud to her several times before sharing them with the class. When Shannon realized she was losing the meaning, she often got an easier book—not just because she couldn't say the words, she explained, but because she couldn't remember the story. Late in September she read to JoBeth from an easy reader she had selected. After several miscues (some of them self-corrected) early on, she was not missing a word by the time she got to page 26. This contextual momentum (Bussis, Chittendon, Amarel, & Klausner, 1985) pleased her, as did the fact that she could retell the simple story line easily.

She continued to choose books where she experienced more success. One of her favorite stories was "The New Girl at School" from the 2.1 basal *Adventures*, a story about feeling misplaced and left out. Shannon read it several times throughout the year, perhaps in part because she also was the "new girl" at school, an anomaly who had come from first grade rather than second. Once, early in the year, Benton walked by and said disdainfully, "You still in that book? I used to be in that book *last* year." Susan, hearing him, said, "I enjoy the stories in there myself. Maybe I can get enough books that we can all read some of the stories." Later, during reading workshop, Benton got an *Adventures* off the shelf and read a story from it. Several days later the entire class enthusiastically performed a choral reading of a story from the *Adventures* Susan had gathered. Susan wanted the basals to be just books with stories in them, there for anyone to enjoy. But the children knew very well that success in their educational system was still measured by what book they were "in," and every child knew the sequence.

Shannon's insecurity about her reading was evident in her responses to several questionnaire sentences: "I don't know how *to raiid [read] good*"; "I wish someone would help me *raied and rat in kasas [read and write in cursive]"; and "I worry about my raiding*." She also had a strong sense of how she would become a better reader, as she told us in her October interview: "I'll learn to read if I read—read." She recalled several times during the year the first book she had learned to read, and noted on the questionnaire "Of all the books I've read, my favorite is *The door Bal raing*." She was also voicing a connection between her writing and reading. She wrote, "Better than anything, I like *I like rating and raig [writing and reading]*," and told us in the October interview, "If you want to be a writer, you got to read stories and poems."

By February there was a noticeable improvement in Shannon's reading. One day she was reading *The Mystery of the Lost Pearl* (Blake, 1979) silently. She asked confidently if she could read it to JoBeth, and proceeded to read such words as "dentist" and "special" haltingly but accurately. Ricky, a more ardent and proficient reader, sat down next to her and began reading along. Shannon held her hand up in a motion to stop him, and continued reading with obvious determination. Several pages later Ricky again joined in, laying his hand gently on her arm. She did not protest; neither did she allow him to set the pace. Shannon was developing a sense of herself as a reader . . . except on Basal Days.

Both Susan and Judy "did" the basal on Wednesdays. Susan did a few workbook pages but primarily worked with small groups, using the mandatory magazine (end-of-unit) tests in small sections to assess skills recently emphasized; this weekly testing seemed less overwhelming than the pages and pages of tests administered all at once. Judy maintained this plan, and also had the children read some of the basal stories. "Shannon got really frustrated in Wednesday's basal reading situations, especially magazine testing," Susan noted. Judy agreed: "Shannon worked hard as a reader if she selected the book herself and was very interested, but she became easily frustrated if she felt pressured. The basal really seemed to pressure her." The old school issues of black and white, right and wrong responses, were in direct conflict on basal days with how Shannon was learning to read.

Where will I fit in a new school?

Shannon was transferred to a new school at the end of the year. Third grade had been a rough year for her, even with Betty, Susan, Judy, Ms. Erdrich, and others who made special efforts on her behalf. What would it be like in a new school? Would she be far behind other fourth graders? Would someone look at her records and balk at the unconventional skip from first to third? Would she be encouraged to write and be supported in her reading development? Would every day be Basal Day?

And how would Shannon respond? There had been more instances of outright anger this year, such as the period after Susan left, and fewer instances of self-doubt and hatred than she had expressed in first grade. One substitute told us, "When I am subbing in Judy's room, Shannon is so defiant. She will not follow directions. If I give an assignment, she'll say 'so' or 'I don't have to do this.' She'll argue about having to copy out of the dictionary if the whole class has to do that for punishment; she'll say it's not fair for her to have to write [definitions] because two or three people got in trouble. She slams or throws her books on the desk and scowls a lot."

Maybe some of Shannon's anger and insecurity about herself was turning to anger toward the unfairness in the world around her. Two teachers she had gotten close to had left. She didn't get to stay in her classroom during times that were important to her; as she said sadly in the June interview, "I don't know about writing. I hardly write any." A dozen substitutes presided with a dozen different ways of doing things, and sometimes people asked things of her that were not right, like skipping recess and using writing as a punishment—and an undeserved one at that. We thought this change from anger at herself to anger at the world around her was a step in the right direction. What kind of step would Ash Street School be?

FIFTEEN

"She's Going to Make It"

Shannon in Fourth Grade, Ash Street School

November

"Shannon is a very hard worker. I'm really pleased. Her homework is *beautiful*. She's a very detailed person. The last two days she's been working on her solar system report—see this careful artwork? She is so meticulous. She struggles but she tries so hard—she *wants* to do well, and that's the most important thing.

"Sometimes she talks a little too much, but that's better than not participating. She's neat and well groomed every day. She makes wise use of her time; it might take her a little longer than others, but she really wants to do well. Shannon has a very positive attitude. She's always excited to share when she has learned something.

"Sometimes she seems afraid to ask questions, but I always encourage her to ask and she is getting better. I talk a lot with the class about not making fun of each other, questions are to learn from. I talk to them as adults. I have a rap tape about the times tables, and she likes to do that in front of the class. She always wants to do her recitations for class—poems like 'Dreams' by Langston Hughes, or our class rules [Be kind and loving, etc.]. She usually has them memorized. She especially likes the poem 'Persevere.' They get copies to keep. She says, 'I'm going to keep all of mine.'

"Her best friend is Theresa; they talk a lot but I don't want to move them yet. Theresa helps Shannon, not by Shannon copying, but Theresa tells her a word sometimes, things like that.

"The fourth graders are all working with the New York City ballet; they express themselves through storytelling and dance. Shannon's really excited about that. She's a member of the fourth-grade chorus. She really wanted a part in the school Christmas musical, but the music teacher didn't choose her. She mumbled under her breath a lot when she didn't get it. But she *will* get chances with this ballet, plus our class production of 'Peter Rabbit' and other plays in the basal.

"Academically, Shannon's below fourth-grade level. She struggles in the 3.2 reader, but she wants to do it so much that she's really working at it. She did part

As told to JoBeth and Betty in interviews with Shannon's teacher, Ms. Hurston (pseudonym), in November, April, and June. The interviews have been edited for what we felt was pertinent and for narrative flow.

of a magazine test today, and she did well—sixteen out of twenty. She has good listening skills. There are nine kids in that group; the other group is in the fourth-grade book, *Flights*.

"In spelling we have twenty regular words and five challenge words each week. She's doing ten a week and has been doing really well. I'll move her to fifteen this quarter. She studies on her own and shows me that she's written the words three times at home. She works so hard at everything. She asks to take things home if she hasn't finished. She is *always* on task—I sometimes even have to take work away from her.

"She has written some sentences, she is learning how now. We'll do paragraphs soon. We'll write about the 'Meaning of Thanksgiving'—jot down ideas, words, phrases. Next, we will turn that into sentences, then [into] paragraphs. She told me that she has a whole writing folder. At open house, her mom also mentioned that Shannon was a writer, that she wrote at home a lot."

"Her report card was mostly Cs, which is good for her. Her B in spelling was for only ten words. When she saw that, she said, 'A *B* is good.' This is the first year the kids have had A B C D F—even in art and music. There's no way she'll get Fs as hard as she tries. If all my students tried as hard—they don't; she does, but it's difficult for her for some reason.

"She was so happy after she went to Ms. Burns the first time [a special education teacher Shannon knew from Walnut Street]. She said she had learned so much. Shannon always reminds me when it's time to go, and goes cheerfully. I do worry about her asthma, though; she has missed several days.

"But Shannon's going to survive and do well because of her *attitude*. That's what I tell my students—and she has that positive attitude."

Near the end of the next quarter JoBeth shared copies of the children's quarterly interview responses with their current teachers. She told the teachers she thought they might be interested in the children's thoughts about reading and writing for the two years before this one, and said she'd like to interview the children again if their teachers thought it would be interesting to them and worthwhile for the children. Ms. Hurston was upset by the transcripts, but agreed to talk with JoBeth and Betty.

April

"I'm very concerned about what you wrote. Are you going to publish it? The language in here, the grammar, the articulation, this really bothers me. I know it's her words, but you could change it, write it in standard form. When people read language like this they stereotype. They think all black children talk this way. Case studies like this cause people to overgeneralize."

We had a long discussion of the pros and cons of recording or translating African-American children's dialects, an issue Ms. Hurston felt strongly about. We asked her to read our recently published *Reading Teacher* article. "Let us know, as an African-American teacher, how you think the children are portrayed here. What will other teachers think about the children? Will teachers who have African-American children in their classes have higher or lower impressions and expectations after reading this? We really value your opinion," we urged. Then the conversation shifted to Shannon.

"She has a lot going for her—she's going to make it. I purposely didn't read her records for the first few months. I saw her struggling, wanting so much to learn. She fits right in here. Her performance is below average, but so are some others. Her *effort* is above average. She'll eventually close the gap. I never thought she'd learn the multiplication process, but she really knows that now. It just takes her a little longer. She's still struggling in the 3.2 reader; I took her at a slow pace. She'll go into the fourth grade book next year in fifth. She'll definitely pass. I don't think she's too slow: sometimes we're just too fast.

"She loves to write. Her thoughts flow smoothly, although she has trouble with spelling. She did writing workshop in here for four weeks when we had a [practicum] student from the university. I teach writing with other subjects. For example, the children wrote in response to the ballet films they watched. Shannon was absent the day we went to the ballet in Atlanta, though.

"I took her to our faculty basketball game. My daughter was home from college and she also went. They did a lot of talking about college work, what they did in their spare time. Shannon was very interested. I just wanted to give her this extra opportunity."

June

"I didn't get a chance to read that article; things have just been so hectic. In fact, I really don't have much time to talk. Shannon is still very positive. I am going to work with her this summer on math and reading. I do that every summer for some who need the extra help, who can't afford summer school or a tutor. Her reading has improved, and I've seen some progress in spelling. She got a 73 percent on the last science test—she really studied for it.

"She seems really frail. She's been sick lately, been feeling bad, maybe it's asthma. I'm going to take her to my own doctor. I'm really worried about her health."

Continuing Worries

Shannon did, indeed, seem to be making it. There were signs that she was still a writer, albeit mostly at home now. Even though reading and writing were primarily textbook tasks in this room, Shannon seemed to be making the transition. She had found another teacher who took a special, individual interest in her. Betty, Susan, Judy, and now Ms. Hurston had all gone out of their way to help Shannon, both in school and out. Goldenberg (1989) found that just such singling out for special attention was sometimes the turning point for a child predicted to fail. In contrast to Jeremiah, who seemed to reduce his chances for success by his seeming unwillingness to try, Shannon tried, visibly and continuously. Teachers respond to that. Shannon was increasing her chances for success, and Ms. Hurston was helping her.

REGGIE

SIXTEEN
Reggie in His Own Voice

Second grade with Ms. Michalove, Walnut Street School

September

I'm learning how to read stories, like them little bitty books. I can read some big books, but I don't get all the words correct. My mama is helping me. She every day leave me some books. I got to read them before I go play. Next I want to learn to read a Santa Claus book. My mama got that book from the library, but she going to buy me that book. I like it but I can't read it. I get the first word, but I can't get the second. She read it to me every night. When I'm a grown-up I'll read some hard books, like the book come out the mail, like the *Zoobooks* the teacher got.

I'm learning to write my book about my story. My mama make me write some words and stuff. The teacher helps me learn it. I make a book and I write what I think, and when I finish I look in the second-grade dictionary and get my words correct. Next I'm going to learn to write in cursive; I can write a little bit in cursive. My mama going to help me. She tell me I can't do that. I try and I be writing fast and I took and showed her, and she said, "That be writing in cursive." When I'm a grown-up, I'll write letters to my uncles and my grandpa and my daddy. I'll write what they tell me at my job.

December

I'm learning how to spell words that I don't know and to read hard books, like *Carousels* and *Adventures* (basals). I can help other people with words, Nancy and Bonita and Lee and Van and Wendy. When they ask me a word, I sound it out and tell them. Every morning I come in and try to read the words in the dictionary with my friend Laneal. Sometimes Van and Norris and Kathryn and Vanessa help me. Next I'm going to learn to spell my words correctly. I'll look in the dictionary and find the word, and Vanessa and Kathryn will help me. I want to learn to read this thick book. It's a rhyming book, and I can't read those. Somebody will help me, or I'll try to read it every night. I got one at home; I got it at K-Mart. I don't remember the title, but it's a rhyme about a cat. When I'm a grown-up I'll read some hard books, like a book the teacher read in class when I was in first grade, *Perfect, the Pig* (Jeschke, 1988); it took three days. And I'll read in cursive writing, and I'd like to read Chinese writing—no, German. My daddy know how to read it and talk it.

I'm learning how to write some other people's songs, rock and roll and LL Cool Jay. And I'm learning to write neat. I got a lot of friends that help me: Lee, Laneal, Drew, Norris, Vanessa, and Fredrick. Some songs came on last night and I wanted to write it. It was Christmas carols, but I had to go to bed. I wanted to share it. I want to learn to write in cursive. I write with my friends. We look in our spelling books and copy the letters. My brother will teach me too; he taught me to do my times. When I'm grown I'll write about cars and motorcycles and a story about ABC to my favorite friend. And I'll write letters to my grandma, if she don't be dead. She down in Florida. My mama write her, and she let me write what I want to, like "I love you Grandma."

March

I'm learning to spell some long words, like "sentence." And I'm learning to read real hard, hard books. My mama make me study. She went to a store and got some books. I read them at home; my favorite is that karate book. Next I'm going to learn to look up hard, hard words in the dictionary. I'll tell my mama to buy me a dictionary, and she tell me a word, and I look it up. In class Vanessa and David help me. They be reading with me, and Laneal. I say a word and then go along and go along and then get to a hard word like "express," and they say "express." When I'm grown up, I'll read some hard books, studying about karate and about jobs and stuff. I'll look in the newspaper and see about jobs.

I'm learning to write cursive, and neat too. The teacher gives us a sheet of paper, and we got to do it ourselves. Wendy can't hardly do it, so Ms. Michalove write it and let Wendy trace it, but I write it myself. I don't have to trace it. I be making 100 all the time on my cursive. Next I'm going to learn to write Chinese. I got a Chinese friend that live by me, and he goes to the Boys Club. We be looking at some karate movies at my house. He say one day he take me to Japan, but that too far; I be missing my mama. When I'm grown up, I'm going to write some books about karate.

June

I'm learning to read hard books and how to learn hard words. I'm learning it in Ms. Michalove's class; Vanessa and David help me. Next I'll learn how to spell and read big books; my class will help me. When I'm grown up I want to be in the army. I'll read what they're going to do, and sign things, and I'll read big books.

I'm learning to write neatly in cursive. I'm learning to write letters you need, and those you don't remember go in the word, leave out. My class help me, and Chad. Next I want to learn to write a *J* in cursive. I'll study at home. I'm learning to write a play. My class help me. When I'm grown up, I'll write to people. I'll write phone numbers and write to sign up for the army.

Third grade with Ms. Willis, Walnut Street School

October

I'm learning to sound out words. I just do it by myself this year, ain't none of my friends sit by me. Well, Benton helps me sometime, and Sonya sometime, just sometime. Next I'm going to learn to do compound words, the hard ones. Somebody will help me on it. I'll ask them can they help me, like Tammy help me when

I ask her. When I'm grown up, I'll read big dictionaries, and big books that ain't got no pictures, and the newspaper. My mama be reading it all the time. Every time she go to the store she get a paper. She read who go to jail and who be bad.

I'm learning to write real good, like my friend Benton. He write straight up and it be neat. I look at Benton and he teach me sometime, and I just start writing. Next I want to learn how to spell "dictionary," and state capitals, because they big and hard. I'll ask somebody and then write them down and then study and then spell them. When I'm a grown-up I'll try to write a book about when I was little. When somebody call, or I'm going to be late, I'll write a message.

January

I can read some chapter books, like *Sideways Stories from Wayside School* [Sachar, 1978]. I kept on reading it, and every time I mess up I start over. My friend Kenneth help me sometimes. He tell me the words. Next I want to read grown-up books, big ones, like the one my teacher be reading. She said at home she got a big book she and her husband read. I'll go to the library with my mama and with Mr. Andrews, the other third-grade teacher. He's at my house plenty of time, like when my brother be bad, and to take us to the library. When I'm a grown-up, I might be able to read a Bible; I can read a little bit of the Bible.

I'm writing a good story about the Mike Tyson fight. I saw it on TV and I couldn't write about it at home because I didn't have no paper. Next I want to write to rappers in New York, with hard words; we going to make a record. My brother will tell me any hard words I don't know, because he's smart in reading and writing. When I'm grown up I'm going to write a chapter book.

Third grade with Ms. Smith, Walnut Street School

June

I'm learning to read chapter books, like *Honey I Shrunk the Kids* [Faucher, 1989]. My brothers read at home, a lot. I watch them and I practice. My mama make us study on Saturdays. I just take out the books my mama got, then I think it over, then I write about it. My favorite at home is a karate book; it tells you the karate skills. And a Mickey Mouse book, and *Honey I Shrunk the Kids*. We got it in our class too; I read it almost every workshop. Next I want to learn to read out of the dictionary and some of the newspaper. I can read some of it. I want to read ninth-grade books and twelfth and college. I don't know how I'll learn it, practice I guess.

When I'm grown up I'll read mail and the newspaper. My mama read the newspaper a lot. We call her nosey. She like to hear somebody go to jail, like my Uncle William and Uncle David and Uncle Lesley and Uncle Mike. On the other side my family they had a lot in jail. Calvin, they going to ship him off. One time I went to the jailhouse, my daddy in jail. My mama took me. They playing basketball. I hope I don't go to jail. I'm going to get out of this town. Police get you here, you don't do nothing. I'm going to another state. My friend go to Washington, D.C. and I might go with him, or New York, at my uncle's house.

In writing, Ms. Smith make us write a whole page every time we have writing workshop. We don't have it that much. I want to learn to write big words like my friend Jamail. He write in cursive, good. And like my brother too; he write in cursive neat. I'll ask my brother or my friend to help me, or just practice: I got *three* ways I can do it. I can ask my mama to help me too. When I'm grown up, I don't know what I'll write. I'm going to be a lawyer, like Mr. Willis [Ms. Willis' husband, who visited the class]. Or a lifeguard, like Mr. Smith [Ms. Smith's husband, who went with the class on a field trip to the swimming pool] and teach swimming. I'm a good swimmer. The lifeguard told me how to do a one-and-a-half, and I did it. He told me one time and I did it. He told me how to tuck and straighten out. I'll write letters, and if I be a judge, I'll write down stuff. I mean a lawyer.

Next year I'm going to Ash Street School. I'm going to have to walk. I be there in no time. It's a big school. I got to go through a graveyard to get there. Lots of my friends be going, everybody on my row. I got to walk with my sister; she in second grade, and she can't run fast. My best friends Jamail and Grover be going. We going to walk to school this year.

My teenage brother in the gang called Colours. He do whatever they do. I don't be around them. I play a slick game on them. They call me a sissy, but I just hit that path and go home. I don't want to get in trouble with the police. Every time we go downtown he be climbing on stuff, and riding bikes on the sidewalk.

I'm glad about going to a new school because there's a lot of people at this school, and they like to fight. I hope it be better.

SEVENTEEN

"My Class Help Me"

Reggie in Second Grade at Walnut Street School

Tough guy, tough time, and a mama who reads

I (Barbara) always know the children's names by the third day of school; I knew Reggie's by the third hour of day one. The first few weeks of school Reggie was extremely disruptive. It seemed as if the only time he stopped talking was when he fell asleep. He rarely sat down, didn't stay with the class when we went to various activities, and was very physical with the other students.

At times this physical contact was friendly; other times it became aggressive. In the classroom he kicked Norris, hard, for no apparent reason. On the same day he started a friendly shoving fight in line. This fluctuation between friendly contact and aggressive contact continued throughout the year. In March he karate-kicked Kent, breaking his finger. He didn't seem to experience any remorse over these aggressive incidents. He had a "don't mess with me, I'm tough" attitude, and felt as if he was always justified in responding in the way he had chosen; but he held no grudges and was soon ready to be the best of friends.

Early in the school year I sought out Reggie's teacher from the previous year. The picture she painted of Reggie in first grade was similar to what I was observing this year. Because of his constant disruptions, Reggie had spent the majority of time separated from the other students. He had also missed recess on many days because he would not attend to his assignments long enough to complete them. His kindergarten teacher reported similar problems.

Reggie had repeated first grade, making this his fourth year in school. He had experienced little success the previous three years. He appeared to have little or no confidence in himself as a reader. He had been tested for a learning disability but did not have one, according to the test results. In spite of this lack of progress Reggie seemed to have a lot of resilience. In nonacademic areas he showed much self-confidence. He was never shy or reluctant to try new things and was always willing to help in any way he could.

Reggie seemed to be a happy child. As I observed his interactions with the other students it became apparent that he was a very sociable and loving little boy. He was used to solving his own problems and setting his own priorities. His priorities did not always coincide with the school's.

Reggie lived with his mother and three siblings. Their mother worked at night and Reggie never spoke of another adult in the home. Reggie spoke of little extended family. Often he came to school in clothes and shoes that didn't fit or were inappropriate for the weather. Many days he was so tired that he fell asleep by 9:00 a.m.

When his mom came for a conference her responses to my questions about Reggie were very brief. She had difficulty providing information on Reggie's early development. She was quick to respond to the questions about discipline at home, emphatically telling me she used a belt, two times some days, saying, "He's a little boy, you know."

Reggie never mentioned getting a whipping at home. This was unusual; many of the children would mention getting a whipping for punishment. In November Reggie's brother came to school with welts all over his body resulting from a severe beating his mother had given him the previous night. The school reported the incident to the Department of Family and Children Services, and a caseworker was sent to the home. The brother told school officials his mom had said she would kill him if he told anyone about the beating. When I asked Reggie if he ever got a whipping he quickly denied ever getting spanked. I related to him the conversation I had with his mother in October concerning discipline at home. He then reluctantly said, "Well, sometimes if I'm real bad."

Although at times Reggie's mother appeared to be neglectful and violent, at other times her caring was obvious. A few times during the year Reggie came to school with new shoes or clothes bought by his mother. He knew his math facts thoroughly and said his mom helped him learn them. He also talked about stories she read to him and his younger sister at home. From the interviews we learned of Reggie's mother's strong influence on his literacy development. He told us of his mother helping him in reading and writing in each interview.

When we discussed drugs, Reggie told the class a story about watching a man shoot drugs into his arm and then die. The other students questioned him for details, which he readily provided, saying it had happened in his house at the kitchen table. He also told us a detailed story involving people snorting cocaine. From listening to Reggie's stories about his home, it seemed to be an environment where there was love and caring, but also violence and drugs.

"You and your friends can work together"

Reggie's tough, independent attitude disappeared when he entered the world of literacy. His reserve of resilience seemed to have been whittled away in his previous school years, where he had experienced so little success. He quickly displayed his lack of skills and confidence in both reading and writing workshop.

Reggie seemed incapable of choosing a book he could read. He wandered around the room during reading workshop, picking up various books, flipping through them, then putting them down. When I questioned him about this he replied, "I can't read anything, these books are too hard." I insisted he try, and found his reply to be fairly accurate. He truly could read very little, and the majority of the books on the shelf were too hard for him. Reggie did have some basic concepts about print, but making sense of it all was a source of great frustration to him.

When he came to a word he was unable to pronounce he just stopped reading and lost interest in the book. He appeared to have very few strategies for solving problems he encountered when reading. He used picture cues, and rhyming if the text allowed. He looked to me for constant help and reinforcement. He was easily frustrated, and often quit after one or two pages.

Reggie also struggled in writing workshop. He couldn't think of a topic and was reluctant to attempt to spell words he didn't know. He was very concerned about the neatness of his printing. His concept of writing revolved around correct spelling and neat handwriting. When we asked him at the start of the year what he was learning in writing, Reggie said, "Write neat."

My impressions of Reggie those first days of school were substantiated as time passed. His nonstop talking in the classroom continued. When I began to really listen to him I realized he orally planned his strategies for just about everything. The following took place during a spelling pretest on color words on October 17:

Reggie writes

red

blue

yello

(He is copying words from a wall display.)

Reggie: I can't see yellow from here. Pink, p, p. (He writes "p.") White, uh-oh. (White is not on the wall.)
Nancy: Just put a "w."
Reggie: Black, b, b. B-l-a-c-k.
Grey, g. (writes "g")
light (writes "look")
Light? Ms. Michalove, I got a good idea, our crayons!
Bright (writes "b")
Brown (copies from wall)
Colorful, K? K? I'm gonna leave that blank. "K"? Ms. Michalove?
Barbara: Just write what you hear.
Reggie: I don't want to get it wrong.
Orange (copies from wall)
Purple (copies). I can see that one good!
Rainbow r-rain-r
Nancy: Just put a "R" and a "B."
Reggie: OK. I put R—B—O and S. You got S? I hope I made me a 100!

Even though Reggie's ongoing dialogue could be annoying, I learned a lot about him by listening. In many classrooms this behavior would be considered totally unacceptable. It soon became clear that Reggie used his social skills to help him cope with his environment at home and at school. In the past years of his schooling this well-developed social ability had been a hindrance to him. In our community of learners it became his saving grace.

As Reggie began to see his classmates as teachers he began to seek their help when he confronted a problem. I encouraged this strategy. One day in early October he had not done his spelling homework assignment; at that time I had children write sentences using their spelling words. As we went to recess I reminded him that he had to complete his homework before he could play. I suggested he ask Drew (who was sitting out for another infraction) for help. They worked together on a bench outside.

Reggie: "sent"— I sent my dog to get the ball. (Drew spelled most of the words for him.) What's the next word?
Drew: "set"—I set my clock. Dr. Allen, how do you spell clock?
JoBeth: You can figure it out.
Reggie: C—O—L no AL—no.
Reggie: I can find it in the book.
Drew: Yeah, because it's a long word. (He leafs through the spelling book.) I swore I saw it in here.

I came by to check on their progress. I showed them the dictionary in the back of the book and asked them the first two letters of "clock."

Drew: I found it! Get ready, c-l-o-c-k.
Reggie: You got to stay out here a long time?
Drew: Yeah, now here let me look at this.
Reggie: I ain't finished.

Drew read some of the sentences.

Reggie: What's this?
Drew: "Well," like—well?
David: No, like you fall in a well.
Reggie: I drink out of well.
Drew: No, that don't make sense.
Reggie: I can get water out of the well. (He writes, then stops at water.)
Drew: "Water," that's one of my spelling words. w-a-t
Reggie: er -e-r, no, R.

They looked it up in the dictionary.

Drew: w-a-t-e-r. Reggie, you need to be out there running. "Yet"—the best is yet to come.
Reggie: I can't wait because—no, a short one.
Drew: The best is coming yet. Put it.
Reggie: That's stupid.
Drew: Yeah, but it gets you done with your homework, doesn't it?
Reggie: How you spell coming?
Drew: c-o-m-i-n-g. coming yet—that word—now let me read your sentences. "I have a dress!" Gallll, your sister may have a dress.

Reggie changed "have" to "halp." I came by and asked, "Almost done?"

Drew: Yeah, but one doesn't make sense—I halp a dress.
Reggie: No, have. (He changes it back to "have.")
Drew: Yeah, but you'd look silly in a dress!

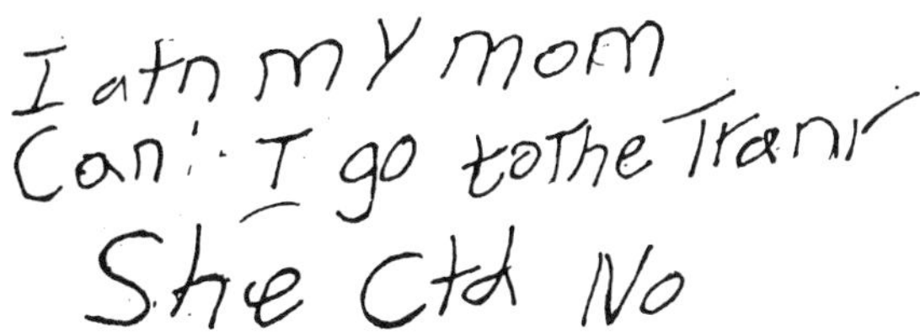

FIG. 17–1 *"I asked my Mom can I go to the store. She said no."*

Drew provided Reggie immediate response and encouragement. He helped him with his work, but he did not do it for him. Drew, a "gifted" student, accepted Reggie's contributions (well, most of them).

Reggie's initial reluctance to participate fully in reading and writing workshop left him on the edge of lots of the action in our room. He loved to interact with others. In reading and writing workshop the medium was print. He wasn't going to miss this opportunity to do what he did so well. He strived to learn the language so he could participate. This desire to socialize gave him a real reason to learn to read and write. Being part of the group was very important to him.

I provided numerous opportunities for Reggie to develop confidence in himself as a writer. Up until the beginning of October Reggie spent his writing time copying text and asking other students, "How do you spell ___________ ?" The first piece he wrote on his own became a starting point for a class story (see Figure 17–1): "I asked my mom can I go to the store. She said 'No.'" Each child in the class added a sentence like Reggie's: "I asked my mom can I ____________ ? She said, 'No.'" The book ended, "I asked my mom can I go to bed. She said, 'Yes, yes, yes!'" The book became a favorite in our classroom collection.

Reggie was flexible in assuming different roles within a group. At times he was the leader, like the day he organized a rap group to perform the rap he had written with a friend. Reggie stated: "I'll be the boss. Lee can make us all a ring." The group willingly complied with Reggie's plan. Soon he had the girls singing backup and the group performed for the class.

At other times he followed the leadership of other children. During reading workshop a small group of children were studying a piece about writing in code in the basal reader. Reggie got a copy of the book and joined them. They were writing a coded message. Reggie came to me announcing, "We have to go out before 10:00 to save the dog!" He went on to explain that it was a real dog, a stray on the playground. "She's real nice, she let us pat her." They had written their plans in code so no one would know how they were going to hide the dog when the animal control unit arrived.

As I worked with Reggie individually I found he needed frequent encouragement; without constant feedback he got frustrated and just stopped reading. It was impossible for me to give him the amount of individual attention he seemed to need, but by reading with students who were better readers he was able to have the constant feedback he sought. Fortunately, I wasn't the only reading teacher in the classroom. As early as the beginning of September we observed Reggie accepting help from a friend when reading a very easy book. When he came to a word he didn't know he asked for help from other children. He also accepted unsolicited corrections and continued reading the text.

Reggie also looked to peers for help and feedback when writing. The importance of getting his needs met immediately was vital for Reggie. He got frustrated and lost interest in a very short time.

One example of the way in which Reggie took advantage of working with other students to accomplish what he had in mind was a story written collaboratively with Kenton and Lee. The three had begun a football story the previous day. When our silent writing time was over Reggie quickly organized them so that they could continue.

Reggie: Come back here, Lee. (He had claimed the small table in the back of the room.) What you want to do, "Old Miss" ? What you gonna write? (He reread what he had written previously.) Put a "O" for old Miss.

Kenton: That be wrong—put a "E" right there where that "A" be.

Reggie: "And I went home."

Kenton: We got to put "we" there—"we went home." Come on man, read your story.

Reggie: (reading)"Going to the Georgia Game. I was selling cokes at the Georgia game. It was fun and Georgia win. The score was Old Miss 72 to Georgia 90. I went to home." [See Figure 17-2.]

As Reggie began to see his classmates as teachers he began to seek their help when he confronted a problem. In our classroom Reggie's need to interact with peers was encouraged. His ability to get along so well with other children helped him to grow as a reader and writer.

I am a writer—and maybe a reader

Reggie's "I can't, I don't know how" attitude and his reluctance to try to write initially excluded him from the excitement during writing workshop. It didn't take him long to find a way to become part of the group; by the end of September he began to collaborate joyfully in writing.

His first collaboration was with his friend Lee. They became very involved with a play on LL Cool J (LL Cool Lee, LL Cool Reggie) and were reluctant to stop for sharing time. I called them for sharing but they were so engrossed they didn't even hear me. After I went over and spoke with them individually, Reggie said, "Okay, we're just finished." They joined the class and shared their writing for the first time. Reggie's increasing confidence and engagement with writing were becoming apparent.

This collaboration seemed to be a turning point in Reggie's development as a writer. As Reggie began to collaborate with other students during writing workshop, he began to form more relationships based on his learning needs. His confidence in his abilities grew, and he began to be an active participant.

Reggie enjoyed collaborating with many different students on a variety of writing throughout the year. He wrote a story with Vanessa based on a book they had read together. He worked for weeks with David on a love song. He worked on

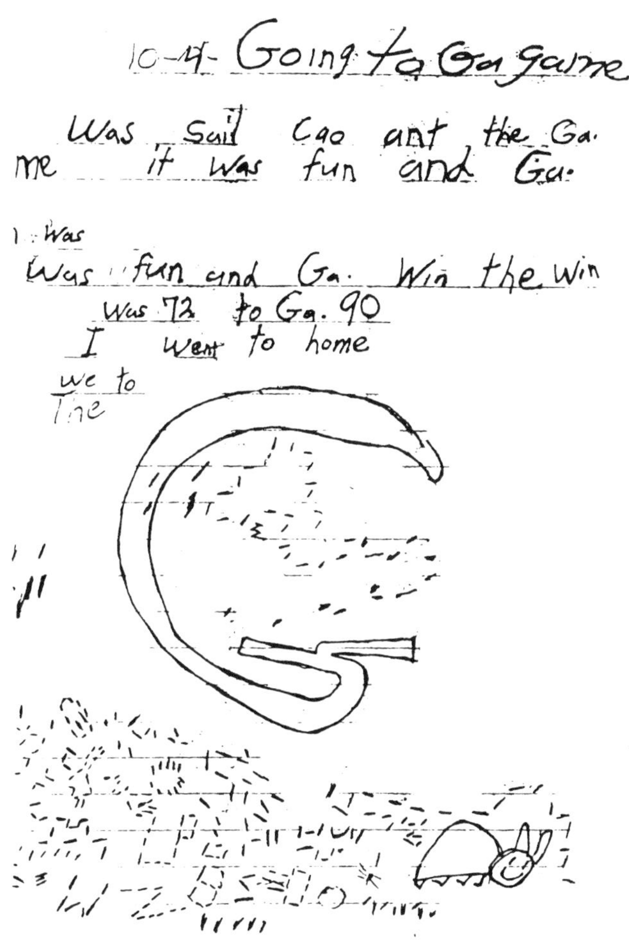

FIG. 17–2 *"Going to the Georgia Game"*

a play with Mary, Kenton, Laneal, and David. He collaborated with Thomas, Norris, Kenton, and David to write the plan to save the stray dog. It became clear that being able to work with others was of vital importance for him. His need to verbalize his thoughts—whether discussing ideas, letter sounds, or contents and sequence of the piece—became an appropriate and desirable activity within the writing community. As he experienced success in writing with others he began to take risks in pieces he wrote on his own.

By the middle of November Reggie's writing had improved considerably. On his own he wrote the letter in Figure 17–3 to his pen pal.

At the beginning of December, after a spelling test, Reggie said, "When we going to write. I want to *write*." His attitude had really changed! He chose to write during his free choice time. He had drawn a large picture of a car on Friday and said he was going to write about going to New York. On Monday he spent thirty minutes working on the story by himself. When we looked in his writing folder for the story

11-14-
Date

Dear Carol
I look at TV in I Look at Fat Bo'Y to my
Bothre he Don't Look Fat Boy
I went to tell my mom and
he had to get OFF a ponmosmit
he never caren about Fat Boy
a Gan boresi
Kelvin
I ge d
Love,
Reggie

Dear Carol,
I looked at TV, and I looked at Fatboy too. My brother he don't like Fatboy. I went to tell my mom and he had to get on a punishment. He never complain about Fatboy again.

Love,
Reggie

FIG. 17–3 *Reggie's Pen-pal Letter (November)*

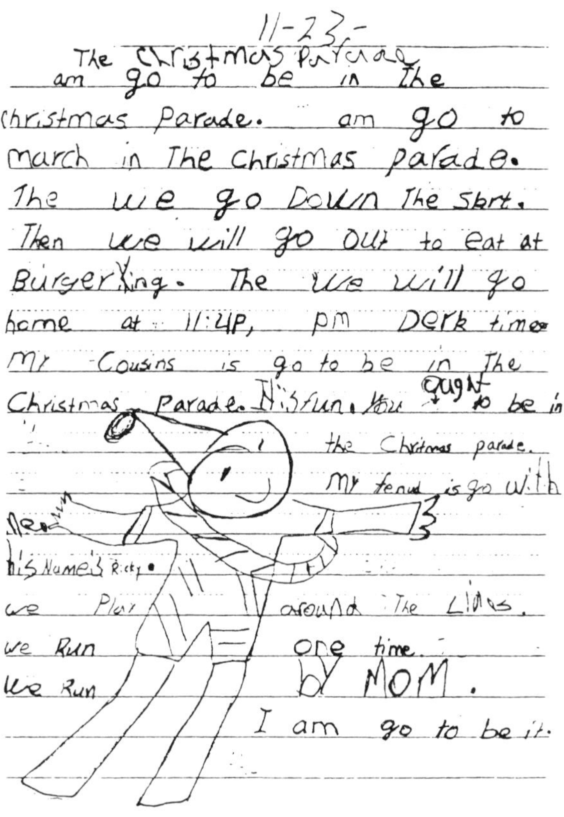

11-23-
The Christmas Parade
am go to be in The
christmas Parade. am go to
march in The Christmas parade.
The we go Down The Sbrt.
Then we will go out to eat at
BurgerKing. The we will go
home at 11:4P, pm Derk time
My Cousins is go to be in The
Christmas Parade. It's fun. You ought to be in
the Christmas parade.
my fenud is go with
me
his Name's Ricky.
we Play around The Lins.
we Run one time.
we Run by MOM.
I am go to be it.

The Christmas Parade
I am going to be in the Christmas parade. I am going to march in the Christmas parade. Then we go down the street. Then we will go out to eat at Burger King. Then we will go home at 11:49 p.m. dark time. My cousins is going to be in the Christmas parade. It is fun. You ought to be in the Christmas parade. My friend is going with me. His name is Ricky. We play around the lines. We run. One time we ran by mom. I am going to be in it.

FIG. 17-4 *"The Christmas Parade"*

we couldn't find it. I found it wadded up in his desk. When he read it he said, "I thought I had messed up. I thought I throwed it away, but it sounds pretty good!"

As Reggie's self-confidence increased he began to write longer pieces on his own. He wrote a story about being in a Christmas parade (see Figure 17-4) by himself, asking friends for help with spelling. Then he proudly shared it with the class when he had finished.

The response that Reggie received to his classroom writing was immediate and mostly verbal. The exchange of pen pal letters provided an opportunity for written response, which Reggie seemed to enjoy. On one occasion Reggie wrote to his pen pal:

> Dear Carol
> I want a rmkberncar
> I want to have to a
> kbeoE! but

Carol wrote to Reggie asking for clarification. He worked hard to make himself understood in his reply.

Dear Carol

I want a remotc untkcar (remote control car) in I will Try to save you a pess of cake in I will go to atlanta fou my Birthday in me in my frnd is going to atlanta in we or go out eat Love, Reggie

Reggie's increasing confidence in his ability to read and write was also clear in the interviews we held with him. Reggie responsed to our question, "What are you learning to do in reading?" in September by saying, "Learning to read them little bitty books." In June he said, "How to read hard books and how to learn long words." When we asked him "What would you like to learn next in writing?" he told us in September, "How to write in cursive." In June he said, "How to write a 'J' in cursive, and how to write a play."

He was changing his image of himself as a writer. At the beginning of the year he says, "I can't write, I don't know how." In the spring, for our class newspaper, he wrote the following about himself: "I am nine years old. I wrote two books. I am going to write a book about Karate." When Reggie's friend Laneal joined our class in October, Reggie confidently explained what we did in writing workshop. When Laneal asked what the paper in front was for, Reggie explained about the topic list. He told him, "Make up your own story, and you and your friend can work together." He took Laneal under his wing, helping him to sound out words and instructing him to "write more, or draw a picture" when Laneal had written one sentence.

By the end of the school year Reggie practically shouted, "I am a writer!" He told us in the interview about wanting to write at home. He had no problem generating his own topics and stayed engaged for long periods of time. He loved to share, and asked good questions of other writers. However, he wasn't quite so sure of himself as a reader.

After Reggie complained that he "couldn't read anything," I introduced him to a set of beginning storybox books (Wright Co.) that I had used in my kindergarten classroom. Reggie called them "the orange books" because of their bright orange covers, and was thrilled to have some books he could read on his own. There were twenty books in the set, and Reggie would choose a handful of them every reading workshop. His attention span grew now that he had some books that he was able to read successfully.

The books themselves provided him with the support he needed to practice his reading skills. Also, Reggie always chose to read with a friend. He and Lee spent weeks reading and rereading the orange books. By the middle of October Reggie began to be bored with the Storybox books. Again he began to complain to me, "I can't read anything." Together, we selected several books that I thought would interest him, although they were more difficult than what he had been reading. I sat with him and insisted he attempt to read. We began to read together. With my constant encouragement and immediate help with difficult words, he was able to read more varied reading material.

Reggie remained attached to the orange books. They were safe and he practiced reading them over and over. At the same time he began to choose harder books. He also began to vary his choice of reading partners. Up to this point he had read primarily with Lee, a less capable reader. Now he began to seek out children who read better than he did. He willingly accepted their help when they read together. This was a strategy that allowed him to choose a wider variety of reading material. He had also found a way to fulfill his need for immediate help and constant assurance that he was reading words correctly.

We observed Reggie reading with many students during reading workshop, but he developed a special relationship with Vanessa and David. He frequently read with one of these children, both of whom were very competent readers. Reggie continued his relationship with Vanessa and David throughout the year. As we studied the data at the end of the year it became clear that these students had taught Reggie to read. He also realized it. When JoBeth interviewed him in the fall asking, "Who helps you learn in reading?" he named his mom. In the spring he named Vanessa and David.

This was one of many instances where Reggie's social adeptness was influential in his learning. He was beginning to use his own strengths to help himself in school. He was developing relationships with children based primarily on literate activities.

Reggie's confidence in himself as a reader grew gradually. He had a clear pattern that we were able to see as we reviewed our notes. He started with "I can't read," then became very attached to books that he learned to read. He read the same books over and over, struggling at the start but persevering until he could read fluently. The only area in which he continued to come to me for help was choosing appropriate books. He still suffered from his image of himself as a poor reader. Every four weeks throughout the year I would spend some individual time with Reggie helping him develop the skills to choose books that he could read. I helped him by sorting and shelving books by difficulty and by repeatedly pointing out to him when he was successful. I encouraged him to try the first page of a book to discover the difficulty level. I also encouraged him to reread familiar books to build up his sight word vocabulary and fluency.

By using his social skills to help him tap the resources available in our classroom, Reggie began to develop a variety of strategies for getting meaning from print. Over the year we observed him reading to other students, accepting corrections from them, asking other students for help, reading in unison with friends, echo reading, choosing books that had been read to him, rereading familiar texts, rereading writing pieces in process aloud as he composed, rereading for fluency, advising Vanessa to "skip a word if you don't know it," telling Bonita "you cover up part of that word," using letter sounds and context to decode words, and self-correcting for both meaning and syntax.

As Reggie developed this repertoire of strategies his confidence in himself soared. At the start of the year he groaned, "I can't read anything." By spring he was scheduling appointments to read books to first-grade classrooms.

"Work quietly and stay in your seat" was an impossibility for Reggie, who thrived on interaction. During the times we worked in traditional basal reading groups, Reggie had a hard time controlling his behavior. He rolled on the floor and paid little attention to the lesson. This work, picking apart language, was a challenge for Reggie. Being successful in the basal was important to him; he was well aware that the county's promotion guidelines specified completing certain books for promotion to the next grade level. The structure of the basal program did not allow Reggie to use his strengths and he was lost. When asked to do the imposssible, he reacted by becoming a behavior problem during these times.

Reggie wanted attention from his peers. In the past his main way of getting attention was through classroom behavior that was considered disruptive. Sharing time in both reading and writing workshop gave him time to get attention from everyone in the class in an acceptable way. He took advantage of the opportunity. He wanted to share his work frequently and never hesitated to answer questions about his writing.

Time was a big issue for Reggie in developing literacy. Often he was not ready to stop writing when time was up. Although many times he continued working on his own, writing during sharing (a practice I generally discouraged), he asked thoughtful questions and contributed useful remarks to other students. It was just that he became totally engaged and had a hard time stopping when writing time ended. I have a mental image of Reggie during many sharing times with one hand waving in the air, signaling his eagerness to share next or ask a peer a question, and the other hand writing away. He also needed (and wanted) to read books multiple times to make them his own, books he could really read. Our schedule allowed him to have this extra time on a daily basis.

The reading and writing workshop setting was a haven for Reggie. Interaction with other students was encouraged. Discussion and collaboration were expected and nourished by the community of learners and our schedule. Reggie had a chance to use his well-developed social skills to help him acquire the academic skills he needed. His literate self-concept underwent a major overhaul in this environment. Whereas he had lacked confidence of his reading abilities at the start of the year, he now told his brother that he wanted "to read to the President."

My hope for Reggie was that his remaining years in school would provide him with the support and expectations that were an integral part of our classroom life. With that kind of support, I hoped he would develop the inner resources to overcome some of the obstacles that are part of his world.

EIGHTEEN

"I Want to *Write!*"

Reggie in Third Grade at Walnut Street School

with Teachers Susan Willis and Judy Smith

"My name is Reggie and I like to play *football!*" Football was how Reggie introduced himself to the new girl in October, what he wrote to his pen pals about, and what he did every chance he got. He was a good football player, an outstanding member of his YMCA team. Understanding Reggie's love of football, and identification of himself as a football player, gave us an insight into Reggie in school: When he felt competent, he engaged.

In discussing Reggie at the end of his third-grade year, Susan and Judy agreed: "If Reggie was doing something he knew he could do, he'd be very involved; he got in trouble when he felt he couldn't do a task." One area of competence was physical ability. Susan asked him to lead calisthenics the first day of class. He was a master of the back handspring and of flips. At the end of the year Judy took the class swimming; she noted, "Reggie was the star. He swims well, and can do cannon balls and 'fancy' dives off the board." But football was really his passion. He brought his uniform to share with the class one day and explained every part, from the markings on the helmet to the function of the pads. He organized the touch football games at recess nearly every day and directed the plays, even for the fourth- and fifth-grade boys in the group.

I am a writer

He also organized the writing of football stories in the classroom, just as he had done in second grade. He was excited about writing workshop the first day and every other day, Susan noted. "I would announce writing and he would say 'Yes!' with a high five to his neighbor, or a slamming shut of whatever book he was reading." One workshop in September was a prime example of Reggie's engagement with writing, an area where he had experienced success both last year and this. He was writing with Kenneth, his teammate from football and frequent reading and

---

Although neither teacher was able to write the chapters for that year, both contributed through observational notes, writing samples, weekly data analysis sessions, and feedback on drafts of the chapters. JoBeth is the author.

writing buddy. They talked about writing a Mike Tyson story. Each boy wrote his own story, with frequent discussion. When Reggie got to Round 3, Kenneth began to help him with the oral composition. They began at 11:22; when Susan called sharing at 11:57, Reggie had written three full rounds (and three full pages). Round 1 follows:

> **Boxing**
> I will lthee him/ out in the Round/ a I am going to give/ him a mike thentrnd/ hit and he go down/ Pere and I hait you/ go down in thens satlo/ otpek and I did/ othet him out hand/ hand was orpek/ and I oned a/ opapi gond Bant/ it is for me Boee

When Reggie got up to share, Kenneth went with him and helped him read in several places where he struggled to decode his own writing. He read, "I will knock him out in the first round, and I am going to give him a Mike Tyson . . . *punch* (I got *hit*) and he go down. Punch! and I hit—I hate you. Go down in the ring. Punch! and I did hit-knock him out. [He got lost here.] Okay, Punch! and I won a—oh, yeah, his gold belt. It is for me. I ripped it apart." Reggie continued with fakes, tricks, and a "punk" with a knife in his sock ("I made that up—it ain't in there") in Round 2; and he ended with, "This is your last time to see your mom. You better sit and rest for the fight, boy," and a flurry of kicks and punches. It was a great hit with the class. Reggie knew football, Reggie knew boxing, and Reggie knew how to write about them. As he would say of one of his stories in November, "It's a good one!"

Losing a predictable writing time was hard on Reggie.[6] When Susan returned after Christmas, Reggie and the others were excited about resuming writing workshop. She wrote in her journal, "Reggie is always the first one to start writing." Fifteen minutes into the first January workshop Reggie said to Susan, "I want to write more. Now I got something to write about." The next week he asked several times during the morning, "Can we have writing workshop? I want to write about the Tyson fight. It was a long time ago, but I never got to write about it."

One area of writing that was important to Reggie was good penmanship. In his interviews he consistently said he wanted to learn to write in cursive and to write neatly. He mentioned his friend Jamail and his brother as people who "write in cursive, neat." He often wrote with Benton, who had beautiful handwriting. His discussions of writing always focused on what he was writing about, even in the first interview in second grade; but at some point he emphasized that the appearance of the writing was also important. His penmanship improved markedly from the beginning of second to the end of third; and although he wrote well in cursive when asked, he continued to choose manuscript for his personal writing, with his own distinctive style (see Figure 18-1).

Some of Reggie's most extensive writing was to his pen pal. Denise, his pen pal from September through December, noted that Reggie really seemed to make a personal connection to her through his letters. He talked about football a lot, including a favorite book, *The Dallas Titans Get Ready for Bed* (Kuskin, 1986), and told her about what he planned to do, and about his brother. He used almost no punctuation, and she found his spelling difficult to decipher, as in this excerpt from

---

6. As explained earlier, Susan had substitutes for several weeks who did not conduct writing workshop.

2-6-

Feb 6

We have a game Wed.
against the georgiabull
dog.
We are going to bet the
georgabull dog.
We are going to have it at
the football feld.
My Coach Siade We is
going to Run the Wishboun
Formand.

FIG. 18–1 *Reggie's Distinctive Script*

his first letter to her: "then I get poheno am go the the Universer Gecome do you go to Gecome football Game I work ther and my benr is go to be srermer . . . I be at the adjective homue [he obviously thought he was copying something about the school carnival that night, because he later asked, "can you con come to the adjective homue"]. At first, he copied some phrases verbatim from her letter ("I am happy that you are my pen pal . . . attending the university"); later he did not rely on her letters for copied phrases, but was always interactive. He ended his first letter with "I love for a friend/ now by/ by Reggie." After several weeks, he switched to "Love." Note in the examples below the progress he made from fall to spring in increased content, more conventional spelling, and even a period, which in this case seems to indicate a new paragraph (topic change).

October

Dear Denise
We is go out to/ tenw [out of town] to play football/ and we get to play it good/ becamse it is a good tenme/but I am a runbake/ and I am read the DALLAS TITANS MY MOM/ sied she will tlak [take] me out to eat at/ MC br [McDonalds]
Love Reggie

April

Hi you been doing I have been/ fun [fine] and you no want [know what] I am go to the mall and we is/ go to timeout in the mall/ and we is go to Atlanta/ and I am go to see the /movies to see teenagemutantninjaturt [Teenage Mutant Ninja Turtles, probably copied from room]/house party. and we go/ over my cosin Marcus/ and cosim is in my cassroom/ we have fun I do not lot anybody/ mis with him I like and/ his brother Vernon he is/ dead Me and Marcus are/ first cosin We are Very/ soat [?] togetgat and I got/ a cosin in name Bernard/ and Ella We are Very/ soat to and Bernard is in/ my class to and I halp him to if he need some/ happy Eater

Love
Reggie

to Judy S.
happy Eater

(smiley face like
she put on his)
smile the End

Another area of writing where Reggie felt especially competent was illustration. He often sent elaborate pictures to his pen pals, illustrated his own stories, and helped others illustrate theirs. His spring pen pal noted when she met him that he seemed much more enthusiastic about showing his drawing than his writing, until she showed she could read (most) of it; after this success he even got another story for her to read.

But his favorites topic remained football. In one long story he described in detail various aspects of the game, including such terminology as "sidelines," "fumble," and "time out." This story, like many others on this topic, disappeared from his folder before we could xerox it. We wondered if there was a special spot at home for them.

"Can I read it to you?"

That was really a major question for Reggie. He often had trouble reading his own writing. He grew in his ability to spell phonetically, but often when he got carried away with the story his spelling deteriorated. Susan was surprised to find that one day when the kids were playing with magnetic letters, he was unable to put all of them in order. He tried twice.

When Susan had the children read basal word lists as a quick assessment early in the year, he started having trouble on preprimer 3 (13 words correct/20 possible) and primer (12/20) levels; they stopped after 1.2 (9/20), although Reggie had wanted to try them all. However, on September 19 when he was reading a self-selected book on karate, he read "self-defense" and "practice"; he self-corrected "could" to "told" and "bad" to "would"; and he had several semantic substitutions such as "started up" for "warmed up" and "bend" for "stretch" (although he still missed words like "talked," "with," and "warm."

"I don't want to read, I want to *write*," Reggie responded one day in October when Susan announced reading workshop. He did not experience the same consistent success with reading that he did with writing. "He came to me with a book to read only when he felt very successful, not every day like Ricky did," Susan explained. And he did *not* like "basal days," where he often experienced frustration rather than success. One day in January, Susan called his group to the table to do mandatory basal testing. "Oh, *man*," he groaned. Then he began to catch on. "Oh, I know this one," and "'take' makes sense," and "Oh! I got it!" as he built momentum (with Susan's help). He got all but one correct. "I'm ready to do some more—I'm ready to do forty pages! When we finish this, we going to be in another book?"

It wasn't that Reggie didn't like books, as some of his comments might have indicated. He listened intently when Susan read aloud every day, and often chose those books for his own reading. He was an enthusiastic listener, often predicting what would happen in a familiar text. One day when she was reading about dolphins he blurted out, "I *knew* it!" with a huge grin.

Reading books he had heard was a variation on another well-used strategy: rereading. On the first day of school Barbara sent *Little Bear* (Minarik, 1957), a favorite from last year, for Reggie to have in his new classroom. He picked the book up and hugged it to his face, like a father caressing a child after a separation. He showed it to Susan, who said he could read it right then in reading workshop. He read the table of contents aloud, then began reading the first page to himself in a soft voice, halting occasionally, but reading it all with storybook inflection. During sharing he explained to the others, "I read this book about four times; it's about his mom tricking him . . . " He went on to explain the plot in detail, his love of the book animating his whole body as he talked. When asked to share a favorite part, he immediately turned to a funny section and read it fluently for the whole class.

One day a girl from another class came to read to Susan's class. Reggie was impressed. He practiced a poem he especially liked, "Growing and Changing," for over two weeks. He told Susan he was practicing it so he could read it to another class. She listened to him several times over the next few days, until they both felt he was ready. He read his poem to great acclaim in his older brother's class and Barbara's second grade. On returning to his own room he proclaimed, "I read that story good!"

Whether it was because of his sense of competence in reading it or an aesthetic response, "Growing and Changing" remained an important poem to Reggie throughout the year. He memorized what page it was on, and turned to it several times throughout the year. "I like the thing about changing," he explained when asked about the poem ("I'd like to change places for maybe a week and look like you look like and speak as you speak and feel what you're feeling . . . ") Being allowed (in fact encouraged) to reread books in both his regular classroom and his Chapter 1 classroom continued to facilitate Reggie's reading development in third grade; Susan noted in November that he was really making progress as a reader. His reading of the 3.1 basal reader poem "My Dinosaur's Day in the Park" went from 66 percent word recognition in September, when he was able to read only three stanzas, to 78 percent in January and 86 percent in June on the full text.

Much of Reggie's reading took place in his Chapter 1 class, where Ms. Piercy held reading workshop every day. A typical day there demonstrates some of Reggie's reading strategies, as well as some of the constraints of a forty-five-minute pull-out program. It was October 10, and Reggie had selected a book he could read fluently. Although he began reading in a soft whisper, he was soon reading loudly. He read several sentences a second time to self-correct. He read with a vengeance, ignoring instructions and the commotion around him until Ms. Piercy called him by name and told him it was time to quit. He had two pages left. He was asked to choose another book to read; soon he seemed just as engaged in reading it. He asked the girl next to him for "heard," "hoof," and "giraffe," but read the rest aloud to himself. "I know this," he said excitedly at one point. "This like that rooster book!" He continued reading, building momentum in inflection and fluency, when once again it was time to stop. Reggie kept reading. The other children returned their books. Reggie kept reading. Finally he stopped, pointing out the word "build." "This one of our spelling words," he noted. Reggie asked if he could take the book home. Ms. Piercy suggested that he and Mary, who had read the same book, could talk about it. Reggie explained a long and complicated connection between this book and one he read about a chicken and a rooster. Then it was time for them to return to class.

In many ways Reggie's Chapter 1 situation was ideal. Ms. Piercy had recently taught in a regular classroom, where she had incorporated many of the whole language structures that Reggie was familiar with: reading workshop, writing workshop, teacher read alouds, buddy reading, etc. She incorporated all of these structures into her Chapter 1 classroom, with an emphasis on reading workshop, which made for congruence between Reggie's two classrooms. And yet everyone was frustrated. Reggie often asked not to go to Ms. Piercy's class, even though he went with several of his classmates. He usually missed all or part of writing workshop in his regular classroom, where the children had much longer periods to write and share. Several times on returning from Chapter 1 he'd ask, "Have you done sharing yet?" Not coincidentally, Reggie was often a problem to Ms. Piercy, demanding a great deal of her attention. Further, Ms. Piercy was frustrated at having the children for the short forty-five-minute period that made extended reading difficult, and writing almost impossible. Finally, everyone was frustrated with scheduling problems. Good instruction that interrupted other good instruction was still not the answer, both teachers agreed.

One aspect of both Susan's classroom and Ms. Piercy's Chapter 1 classroom that seemed important to Reggie was being able to choose his own books (a necessary condition for rereading books frequently). One day late in October he was reading a book about karate, when he explained, "My uncle know a lot of karate. Everybody in my family know karate—we *study* karate—except my grandma. My daddy learn when he was in the army." Talk about a real reason for reading! Another book he read often throughout the year was *The Dallas Titans Get Ready for Bed* (Kuskin), a book about football players and their gear.

A final vignette of Reggie as a reader of growing, but still shaky, competence reveals how central personal book selection was for him. He had gone out of the room to read to JoBeth on April 17. "I think I'll read one of those new books," he said, pointing to a nearby stack. "I've been reading *Wonders of the Forest* (Sabin, 1982) in reading workshop. It's stupid," he said as he leafed through it. "No, I can read this one good!" he decided. He read seven pages of it, with about five miscues per page, words such as "canopy" (can- cava- what?), "laurel" (later), and "skunk" (snake). He then picked up the 3.1 basal JoBeth used in the interviews and began looking through the table of contents. "Can I read 'You, Whose Day It Is'? No, this one on 143 [turned to page 143]. This a poem—I'm looking for a story. I don't want to read 'Green Thumb Thief'; let's read 'Winter Bear,' 170." He turned to the poem by Karla Kushkin and began reading.

The next week when JoBeth visited the class he asked her three times, "Can I read this book to you?" It was a book he had never read before. He never would have asked at the beginning of the year. "Can I read this to you?" was taking on a new meaning, more of a "May I" than a "Can I."

"Write what I write now"

One of the issues that changed for Reggie in third grade was his interaction with friends during reading and writing. Often, although not always, he wrote and read with his friends, usually Kenneth, Benton, Bernard, and sometimes Shannon and Sonya. However, on several occasions Reggie asked to go to the back table to write by himself, saying the first week of school, "I work better there." Was his love of writing superseding, at least for one period a day, his love of interacting with his friends? Or did he need less help? He usually knew what he was going to write about and didn't need others as much as he had in second grade to develop the story line, or to manage the physical aspects of writing.

What we believe may have been happening in third grade was that Reggie was developing a stronger sense of his own contributions, especially in a writing setting. He accepted help in areas where he knew he needed it (primarily spelling), but did not acquiesce in areas where he felt confident, as we can see from comparing an interaction with Kenneth on September 5 with one on February 6:

September 6, 10:42

Reggie: I'm going to write about cars, what you going to write about?

Kenneth: The game. [He wrote the name of one of the local high schools that had played its crosstown rival the previous Friday. Reggie copied it.] Do you know how to spell [the other high school]?

Reggie: No—write "game." [Kenneth wrote and Reggie copied. Reggie then began composing independently, orally planning and rereading frequently.]

Reggie: . . . wait, that don't make no sense.

Kenneth: That's a sentence. Put a period. How do you spell "afternoon"? A- f-t-e-r-n hmmm, we better look it up.

Reggie: I told you this game is too hard—we need to write about *cars*! [Kenneth agreed and they wadded their papers up and started new stories.]

Kenneth: Okay, you start first.

Reggie: Okay, write your name first.

Kenneth: We should write about motorcycles.

Reggie: I'm writing about cars. [Kenneth reached over and wrote "moctery" on Reggie's topic list.]

Reggie: Car and motorcycle—we-is-going-to-ride . . .

Kenneth: You are?! [Reggie has written "car and moctery."] You took my thing!

They had three more abandoned starts, then began writing in earnest at 10:58, hiding their work from Susan, and perhaps each other. Ten minutes later, during sharing, Reggie shared a story about riding motorcycles, and Kenneth shared one about his dad buying him a motorcycle. While both boys had abandoned their original topics, Reggie had ultimately chosen Kenneth's suggestion—perhaps because he wrote it on Reggie's list.

February 6, 11:56

Reggie, Benton, Kenneth, Bernard, and Marcus were writing together on the floor.

Reggie: I'm going to write about football. Trade me paper, I don't like these edges. [They discussed how to begin.] I'm going to say, "We went to play Madison County."

Bernard: How you spell "county"?

Reggie: C-c [Susan walked by, they asked her, and she helped them sound it out, reminding them about capitals, before moving on to help another child.]
Kenneth: How you spell "game"?
Reggie: G-e-m-e
Benton: G-*a*-m-e. "We-have-a-game-against-the-Georgia-Bulldogs." How you spell against? A-g-a-i-n-s-t. [Reggie copied the sentence Benton had written.]
Reggie: Write what I write now. I'm tired of writing what you write. [He and Benton composed orally together, both writing as they talked.]
Benton: Let's say we going to have a game at the football field.
Reggie: The *Georgia* football field.
Benton: Wait—you're going too fast.

The boys continued, with various writers asking for spellings from each other, and Marcus correcting Reggie's ever-present "they is" to "they are." Reggie lead the content, with sentences about the wishbone formation and the coach's instructions. When Susan returned and asked them to explain the wishbone to her, Reggie drew her a diagram and explained in detail. This time Reggie knew what he wanted to write about and what he wanted to say. "I'm tired of writing what you write" showed his growing ability to contribute to the collaboration. He also showed increasing pride in his independent accomplishments. In May, when he was writing about Teenage Mutant Ninja Turtles, he spelled "bulletproof vest" as "bliteproffvast" and was able to read it when he shared the story. He pointed the word out and asked, "Is that right? I spelled it all by myself!"

Sharing was a good forum for social interaction; the writer was always center stage, and there was always a lively question and comment period. Reggie seemed especially to enjoy sharing. He almost always wanted to share, and almost always had a question for the reader. Starting in November he and Bernard, Kenneth, and Benton often asked to perform raps that they had written, some original, some from popular groups. "It doesn't have any bad language in it," they would assure Susan. Reggie was always the leader. This additional area of competence gave him a way to be a leader among his friends, a leader at school. Such was not always the case.

"I'm in trouble . . . but not in deep trouble"

After the first week of school Susan said, "He's my worst behavior problem, but a sweet little boy." Soon, however, he was engaged most of the time with the classroom activities and community. "He never really talked back," Susan noted by the end of the year. "There was not instant compliance, but he eventually did what he was supposed to do." There were few entries for the rest of Susan's tenure related to Reggie's behavior. Those that she did note took place outside her classroom. Reggie skipped school one day to be with his brother, who had been suspended from school. He got in a fight with Marcus when Susan was out of the room. He got sent back from PE one day late in January. He was sent back early from Chapter 1 on several occasions. (Perhaps this was not accidental; he hated missing sharing and it often fell at this time, and he also liked writing much better than reading. Either way, Ms. Piercy often spoke of him as a problem.) But for the most part, he cheerfully participated in his classroom community.

This changed dramatically when Susan's illness caused her to resign and Judy to become the teacher midyear. After her first full week of teaching Judy was miserable. "I feel like the kids don't respect me. Reggie has an 'I-don't-care' attitude." When he was timed out in the office one day, Judy said with mixed emotions, "I hate for them to miss things, but it's really much smoother if Reggie, Benton, or Lee is out of the room. Reggie minds other people's business." JoBeth's notes began to record long periods of total disengagement with school events, especially the new structures Judy was struggling to make work.

His attitude was defiant, totally different from anything we had recorded previously. A substitute wrote, "Reggie would not follow any of my directions. He talked back to me several times, so I had him write 25 words from the dictionary. During Walk Across America he was supposed to walk right beside me, but he ran back to play with Benton. He wouldn't get near me. I put my hand on his back and walked alongside him, helping him along, and he accused me of pushing him. Then he had to sit on the steps during recess. He complained the sun was too hot. He told me if he went home and told his mother he got hot, and if he got a disease from the sun, she would 'get me' in the office. Later, he was picking on and calling another child names. I discussed school rules and home rules with him. He said his mother told him, 'If anyone hit you, you can hit the nigger back. Don't let anyone hit you and get away with it.'"

Reggie was not without remorse. On his "Something About Me" questionnaire he wrote, "I wish I hadn't *kick him*," a reference perhaps to breaking Kent's finger in second grade. He didn't seem to stay mad or hold grudges, although we saw more and more flares of temper. He seemed to be suffering from the instability of the school situation, but we suspected there was more to his disquieting behavior. Reggie also gave us several cues. On his questionnaire he wrote, "I'd like school better if *I go to sep [sleep] at niht*," and "Something that bothers me is *seep*." As he had in second, Reggie fell asleep in school frequently. Was it too noisy to sleep at home? With his mom working nights, was he unable or unwilling to go to bed at a reasonable hour? Whatever the problem, he knew it was one.

He lived in an atmosphere of violence. His brother, by midyear, was transferred to a center for severely disturbed children. "I know he's bad," his mom sighed of Reggie at the parent conference, "but he's not as bad as Derrick." One day in casual conversation Reggie noted matter-of-factly, "If they use weapons, you use weapons." He wrote one day about going with Marcus to take flowers to Marcus's brother's grave. "He died of a overdose," he told Susan. By the end of the year we had a new worry. In Reggie's June interview he talked at length about his family members who had been or were presently in jail. We were especially disturbed by his talk about the gang his brother was in and the pressure they were putting on Reggie to participate. What would he do with this daily option all summer? "Reggie could go either way," Judy sighed.

By the end of April Reggie began to participate in more positive ways. He began to scowl less, smile more. Judy noted the change, saying he talked with her more and got in trouble less; she attributed it to her Popsicle reward system, which Reggie loved. Another third-grade teacher, Mr. Andrews, was also helping Reggie. He was an important person in Reggie's life, the only African-American male teacher in the school. Reggie's brother Derrick had been in his room. He spent time with both boys outside of school; as Reggie said, "He's at my house plenty of time, like when my brother be bad, and to take us to the library." He worked out an arrangement with Judy and Reggie that when he had a really good day he could eat lunch with Mr. Andrews' class; if he had a good week he could spend a whole day with him. Reggie got to spend the day with Mr. Andrews twice.

Toward the end of May Judy passed Reggie sitting in the hall outside the art room. There was a substitute in art that day, and as usual, Reggie and the substitute did not see things the same way. When Judy asked why he was sitting out he smiled a bit sheepishly and said, "I'm in trouble—but not *deep* trouble." We hoped he was right. Most of our notes for the last four months of school referred to behavior rather than reading and writing engagement. Would this issue become the predominant one of his school life? His life in the wider community? Even with his behavior improving, we were worried about him.

We weren't the only ones who worried. Like Lafayette in *There Are No Children Here*, Reggie seemed to worry about his mother's well-being. Just as his interviews introduced Reggie's mother as a key literacy figure, several of his questionnaire responses revealed how important his mother was to him:

- My favorite place to be is *at home.*
- I feel proud when *I'm at home.*
- Better than anything, I like *you mom.*
- I worry about *I am [worried/] about my mom.*

Reggie seemed to love his mother very much and worry about her well-being; but he also hinted that he needed someone when she was gone: "I wish someone would help me *do my home work*," he wrote, and "I don't understand why *my mom [didn't?] come back*." At the parent-teacher conference Reggie's mom explained that she was working two jobs; she seemed almost asleep on her feet. She listened to problems Reggie had been having and said, "I know, that's Reggie." At the October conference she reported beating Reggie with a belt for skipping school when Derrick was suspended. She seemed resigned to her boys' behavior, but was still in there trying. When she left the conference in April she said, "Now I got to go find out about the really bad one."

Policy as risk maker

It was a difficult year for children and teachers alike, but even with all the unavoidable disruption, Reggie made progress as both a reader and a writer. He had another hurdle to leap. Every third-grade child in the state of Georgia had to pass both the reading and math sections of the Georgia Criterion Referenced Test, administered every spring.

Reggie worked hard on the CRT. He read most questions softly to himself; several times when he sensed that his voice was too loud he cleared his throat and began whispering again. He missed several key words that made responding almost impossible, but he kept trying. He missed most of the phonics questions, marking "cloudy" for the same *y* sound as "shy," and "kick" for the same beginning sound as "knot" ("Ooh good, that's easy"). Other questions dealt with main idea, explicit recall, series, pronoun referents, etc. He worked hard on words he didn't know, and there were many. Twice he reread the questions, and on those two he made the correct choice; but with limited time he rarely had time to reread. He continued to take the testing very seriously, even erasing a stray mark. Did he know what was at stake? Probably.

Susan had worried as early as November that Reggie would not pass the CRT. She referred him for learning disability testing because, "I am afraid he won't pass the CRT, and I don't want to see him retained again. Special education is the only sure way out." Many academic sections of the children's IEP stated that they were not to be held to state or district promotion guidelines. This Catch 22 situation affected all six of our children: If they no longer needed special education services, then they became vulnerable to promotional standards like the CRT for third graders and the 80 percent basal magazine test criterion at no less than half a year below grade level (e.g., the child must pass the 2.1 tests to pass second grade). Conversely, when teachers observed children who were making progress on their own schedules, but not on these mandated schedules, they often referred them for special services in hopes of preventing retention. In May Reggie was tested for potential learning and/or behavior problems, but it was too late.

Reggie failed the reading section of the CRT, although he passed the math. "I really think he could have passed it if he could have reread each passage several times," Judy lamented. Reggie was a reader whose strategy was to reread until he was competent, to listen to the teacher or a peer read, and then read it himself. During testing season he had to read totally unfamiliar material, written in disjointed sentences and paragraphs, with "tricky" questions. He was made to feel incompetent when he took the test, and his incompetence became public on the last day of school, when he learned that he had failed third grade and would have to repeat it the next year.

Reggie had already been retained once. This retention would put him two years older than most of his classmates (and make the statistical probability of his dropping out of school 90 percent). But he had been transferred to a new school, a bright new school right in his neighborhood—"I be there in no time." Maybe the stigma would not be so obvious; maybe not everyone would know he was repeating. "I hope it be better," he mused. So did we.

NINETEEN
Reggie in Third Grade—Again
Ash Street School

October

"I'm concerned about Reggie. I thought he'd be a behavior problem; I have had *none* of that. But he told me he went to Youth Detention Center two weekends ago. He stayed in the whole weekend. He was caught running from the police. He loves to talk with me about the little gang situation, and seems really wrapped up in it. The other kids say he's in the gang, but he says just his brother is in it. He wore a bandanna the other day and told his friend he had to get his 'blue rag and his black and white sneakers.' The name of the gang is the MPs; they steal, fight, beat each other up. The East side and West side gangs fight every weekend. Reggie told me, 'Ms. Walker, they try to kill each other.'

"He came in excited and upset today. There was an accident in front of his house. His mother's sister's boyfriend was running from the cop, and ran into a tree. His car turned over in the road, and they were afraid he was killed. The ambulance came; he was seriously injured.

"Reggie's mom came to eat lunch with him and his little sister today. He was really happy about it—talked about it all day. She said she enjoyed lunch, and wanted to know when parent conferences were scheduled.

"Reggie's working hard for me. He's weak in reading. He's in the brightest group—they're in *Journeys* (3.2). He's the slowest in the group, but I don't want to put him back in a slower group. I don't want to embarrass him, so I often call his group while he's gone to Chapter 1; then when he returns I say, 'Oh Reggie, I already called your group—come read with me.' We do the skill work, the story, whatever they're working on. He reads part of the story, then does the rest as homework or after he's done his seatwork.

"I've also been worried about papers going home on Friday with a sheet for the parents to sign. He only brought [them] back once. His mom said today she didn't know he was supposed to bring them back. He said he just gets so excited about the weekend he forgets to bring them back—he's real honest about it. He is more responsible now about homework; often before he didn't even take it home.

As told to JoBeth in interviews with his teacher, Ms. Walker (pseudonym), in October, November, and May. The interviews have been edited for what we felt was pertinent, and for narrative flow.

He's a very, very poor speller. He simply hasn't studied. His mom said he needs to take his spelling home every day; that's one of my requirements anyway.

"He writes in, tries to write in, his journal. We write stories. He's really trying —that makes me so happy. Sometimes we have writing as seatwork; it's not a routine thing. Sometimes they write connected with particular subjects, like language. Free writing is just when they have time, and that's private writing; they can write anything. The writing I grade or discuss with them is separate. I told them, 'That is your own personal journal. If you don't want me to read it, just write me a little note.'

"We had an English test last week. He asked me about it, said he tried so hard. I felt terrible handing it back with 48 percent on it; I told him I know he tried. It was on punctuation, subject and predicate, and they had to choose which groups of words were complete sentences.

"Reggie tells me he won't be in third again next year. I tell him that's right, he'll be in fourth grade next year for sure.

"He gets along with everyone in the class. He sits by Bonitra; she's a smart little girl and helps him a lot. He seemed excited when Vince joined our class; he said, 'Hey V . . . V . . . you in here now?!" Vince is a discipline problem; he also knows about the MPs. But they have not been a problem together. Reggie's attention span seems really short. Often he doesn't listen to instructions, he's so busy getting started on whatever he needs to do for seatwork. The class is calm; they know what they need to do. I think they've been a positive image for Reggie.

"We get along really well. There was a minor incident over an eraser last week, and Reggie had to go to the principal's office. He admitted to her that he broke the eraser. When I asked why he hadn't told me he said, 'Because I didn't want you to be mad at me.' I think he likes me and I do like him—I just worry about some of the things he is exposed to and gets into."

Ms. Walker got out Reggie's journal, which contained several pieces, all quite neatly written, some of them copied verbatim from a book about football. One original piece, written on September 27, showed us another glimpse of his world outside school, the things Ms. Walker worried about (see Figure 19-1).

November

"Reggie was observed in class today by the school psychologist, then he left with her for a while. This was a follow-up on a recommendation from Walnut Street last year that he be tested.

"He still had a good report card, but he's struggling academically and becoming frustrated. I'm seeing some outbursts, like 'Leave me alone man!' He was sort of like a zombie today; maybe he stayed out too long trick-or-treating last night.

"At lunch one of the boys said to me, 'Do you know that Reggie is on the corner selling that stuff?' Reggie shook his head no, but he had a little smirk on his face. Another boy said, 'Yes he is.' This time Reggie made no response. That would explain why he has all that money in his pockets.

"I'm really worried about Reggie. I'm planning to talk to his mom at conferences next week. I think she should know. Maybe she will have some other information."

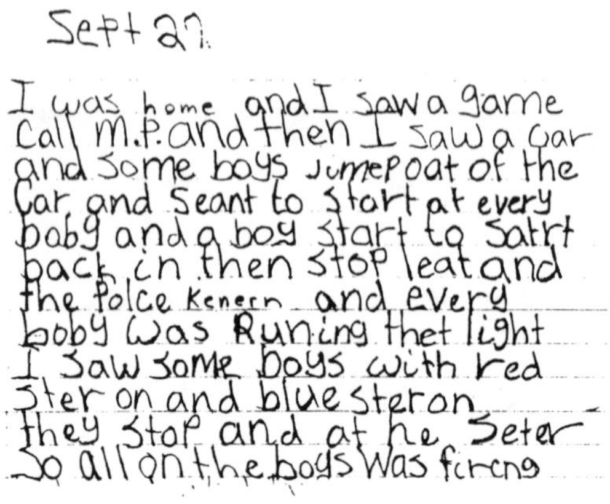

Sept 27.

I was home and I saw a game
Call M.P. and then I saw a car
and some boys jumpoat of the
car and seant to start at every
boby and a boy start to satrt
back in then stop leat and
the polce kenern and every
boby was runing thet light
I saw some boys with red
ster on and blue steron
they stop and at he seter
so all on the boys was fircng

FIG. 19-1 *A Neighborhood Event*

The class returned from PE just in time to get ready to leave. Reggie went immediately to JoBeth and said, "Can I read to you?" She had a book for Reggie to share with his friends, *Arthur's Pen Pal* (Hoban, 1982), and several for the whole class. Ms. Walker reminded them of their homework. Reggie seemed to pay no attention, but literally jumped for joy when she gave away local high school football tickets. Again he turned to JoBeth and said, "Can I read that book to you?" But his mom was there to pick him up. Another time, she promised.

May

"Reggie is doing fine. I'm so proud of him. He has worked very hard. He won 'Invent America' from our class. He didn't have to take the CRT; his ITBS scores were low, but I expected that. He's going to the fourth grade. He will struggle, but he tries so hard, and he asks for help when he needs it.

"He has said he's going to college because he really wants to be a PE coach. He said it over and over during the year, so I had him talk to Coach Conroy here at the school.

"He is a poor reader, his comprehension especially; his word attack skills are better. He got staffed LD and goes to Ms. Burns [who was at Walnut Street the previous year] every day—he thinks he's going to Gifted! She teaches him reading and spelling. His writing is coming together better for him. There's still no formal punctuation or capitalization, but the writing is starting to make more sense. My student teacher has been doing writing workshop. Reggie had a *long* section of an Arthur and Violet story (Marc Brown) that he copied word for word—he copied it very well, too. The student teacher wrote, 'Good! Maybe you could write your own story like this.' He also wrote about seeing a falling star the other night:

One day I saw a falling Sear

On night I was sened on my peirh [sitting on my porch] and SLeuLe [suddenly] something falling form the sky. And some one told me to whis [wish] upoupen it so id and she told me to skeep it a serek [keep it a secret]. and this help [happened] 2 or 3 day ago. and I liak [it looked like] it fall on Marks house. no one nice [notice] it but 4 pople

"Reggie hasn't said anything about the gang or drugs lately. He talks about helping his mama—moving her into a nice house, helping her pay her electric bills. I don't know. . . . "

Continuing Worries

Reggie worries us deeply. He had a good school year, with a teacher he obviously cared about and who cared about him. The home-school connection was strengthened, perhaps because this new school was in the neighborhood, and probably because Ms. Walker is African American (Hale-Benson, 1986). Reggie is struggling academically. He was able to write at times, but not the daily writing that he was responsible for improving. We know that neither frequent, unexamined writing nor skills exercises lead to real writing development (Hillocks, 1986). It does not appear that he is making as much progress as a writer as we hoped, and he also does poorly in more traditional language skills exercises. He is struggling as a reader in the basal system, although Ms. Walker made the effort to work one-on-one. He hasn't shut down. He is still excited about books, cares what his teacher thinks, and risks reading aloud to JoBeth, if only she had time.

But these academic issues pale beside the more urgent issues of Reggie's life outside the shelter of school. Our little university town has weekly reports of gang violence—gangs fighting each other and attacking people on the streets. Drug- related crimes are rising rapidly, and there are more and more reports of the use and sale of crack cocaine. Reggie appears to have been drawn into these dangerous worlds; it is, from all reports, the world his family and friends inhabit. He resisted for awhile, he told us last year. He has other goals, he told Ms. Walker and Coach Conroy. But he also has a tough guy image to protect, and he wants to take care of his mama, to move her into a nice house.

Judy Smith saw Reggie at a local convenience store recently. They talked about his new school, and he asked about his old one. Then Judy asked, "Are you being a good kid, Reggie?" He shifted his eyes, then turned his head away. "Well, I got some friends who aren't so good," he admitted. We are more worried now than ever.

RICKY

TWENTY
Ricky in His Own Voice

Second grade with Ms. Michalove, Walnut Street School

September

I'm learning to read a book, those little books. My favorites are library books. Nobody helps me. When I'm a grown up, I'll read some hard books, read all kinds of things.

I'm learning how to write in my book, about math. The teacher helps me. I want to write books. My mama might help me. She spell out the word and make me write it. When I'm grown up, I write in cursive. I write people name.

December

I'm writing about books. I want to learn how to study. Ms. Michalove help me. When I grow up I read books.

I'm writing about some people. I learn by looking in a book, like . . . [points to dictionary]. I want to write about Indians; I'll copy out of a book. Lee or Bonita will help me with the words. When I grow up I'm going to write about scientists. I'm going to be a scientist. I don't know what they do.

March

I just read. I read hard books, like *Goodbye Max* [Keller, 1987]. [He reads the book easily on request.] I learn alone. I want to learn how to study, and to read books at the library. They'll help me—and teachers. Kathryn and Sarah help some; they help me with words that I don't know. I'll read science books when I'm a grown-up, to learn about science.

I'm writing stories. I figure out some, and Kathryn and Sarah spell words. I want to write a lot of stories—like "The Big Race." I'll use my brain. When I grow up I'll write about people. On my job, like a police job, or a restaurant job, I'll write words, stories.

June

I haven't read no books since last week, but I'm starting *Sleeping Beauty* [Mayer, 1984], and *The Little Mermaid* [Bell, 1986], and *Lee the Running Bear* [peer authored], and *Jeffrey* [peer authored]. My teacher help me, Ms. Michalove, and Ms. Mason [the student teacher]; they tell me what the words is. My friends help some—Bonita, Harris, Terrance, and Stephen. They tell me the words when I ask them. I don't know what I want to learn next. I can read anything I want. I read *Cinderella*, "Gregor the Terrible Eater"—it's in *Adventures*—I already know how to read that. I figure out the words; I spell them out. At home, when I'm a grown-up I'll read science books, and at my job, if I work at the restaurant, I'll read the menu.

I'm learning how to write in cursive. Ms. Michalove give some sheets and I practice in cursive. I don't know, hmmm, I want to write a poem in the library—"Bear in the Refrigerator" and "Stop Thief" and [he names several Shel Silverstein poems that are posted in the library.] I'll copy them out of the book *Light in the Attic* [Silverstein, 1981]. I might make up my own; I might figure out some. When I'm a grown-up I'll write stories and poems.

Third grade with Ms. Willis (August–February 6), Walnut Street School

October

I'm learning how to say words, like a story about dinosaurs have hard words. I was thinking I couldn't read it. But I did. The teacher told me some of the words. I want to learn how to read that book that you gave me [brought in for the class that day], *Arthur for the* [*Very*] *First Time* [MacLachlan, 1980]. I'll learn by spelling out the words. When I grow up I read a book that be hard, like the encyclopedia.

I wrote a lot of stories. I share when the teacher call us, and then I raised my hand. It was hard if we be shy. I want to write a Halloween story, write it to my pen pal. I need to learn how to spell words. The teacher tells us sometimes. When I grow up, I'm going to write to other people. I'm going to write to a man from Africa—the whole class is—that's Ms. Willis' friend.

January

I'm learning to read a big old book. I spell out the word, and then I look at it, and when I don't know it, I sound it out. I want to learn how to read a scientist book. If I still be going to school, my teacher read it, some of it, and that's how I learn it. I probably be a reader when I grow up.

I been writing about policemen: I want to be a policeman. My teacher told me how to spell "policeman" and some other words. Sometimes Kenneth and Matthew tell me; I spell the first word and they spell the other. I want to learn how to be a helper in writing—help them how to spell it. I'll look in the dictionary—Ms. Willis got a lot of dictionaries.

Third grade with Ms. Smith (February 6–June), Walnut Street School

June

I'm learning to pronounce the words. I look at the last word and I spell it out, and then I say it. I want to learn how to read science books. I'll look in the encyclopedia to find the words. When I grow up I'll read dinosaur books, and president books. My favorite this year was *Stringbean's Trip [to the Shining Sea]* [Williams, 1988]. I read it to myself [after Ms. Smith read it to the class].

I'm learning to spell correct words. That's all. My teacher, she tell me the first word, then I figure it out. I don't know what I want to learn—a hard word? I'll use, like the encyclopedia. I don't know what I want to be yet. If I be a policeman, I'll write a ticket, write to other police. Next year I go to Poplar Grove School. I believe that's a good school. Frances, Matthew, Tanya, and some other people from Green Valley and the apartments next to mine will go there.

Third grade repeated, with Ms. Gilcrest at Poplar Street School

March

I'm learning about how to play football; the book tells you, *How to Play [Better] Football* [Jackson, 1972]. This the story I'm on in *Journeys* [3.2 basal]. We take turns reading, these four boys in our group, and sometimes our teacher reads some of it. Next I'll probably read this [he turns to next story in basal], "Winnie the Pooh." There are some hard words; my teacher tells us what the hard words is. Sometimes, somebody who sit by me help me, like Steven.

I'm writing a story about three boys. We write about water, we be going on a boat and we got a cup and see how much dirt in the water, and we keep it for a day and it evaporate—we did that in Ms. Smith class last year. I'm writing about it. Sometime we write in cursive, sometime she tell us write in D'Nealian. I'm probably going to write a president book. That's what I be reading, about the little Madison, George Washington, and Abraham Lincoln. I probably just read them, and then write them down, copying some words out of the book. The teacher help me; she be telling me some words like the hard ones I never heard of.

Is my class going to have pen pals? You remember when Ms. Michalove class visited the university and went around with our pen pals? We might be moving from the Valley [Green Valley Apartments]. They bad people there. You see Lee? What grade is he in?

TWENTY-ONE

"We Drew a Circle"

Ricky in Second Grade at Walnut Street School

A wall of distrust

I (Barbara) remembered Ricky from the previous year. I had noticed him among numerous first graders because his teacher always held him by the hand, he sat next to her in the lunchroom, and he frequently was required to sit out at recess. He was so violent and explosive, causing harm to the other students, that he couldn't be trusted to walk down the hall unescorted, his teacher said. She described him as a loner. He had remained uninvolved with the people and the environment in the classroom throughout the year. He completed his work only with frequent reminders and encouragement. His limited interactions with other children tended to be very aggressive.

Ricky lived with his mother, younger sister, and older brother in a subsidized apartment project on the outskirts of town. His brother had a school history of violent behavior and had been in the behavior disorders program for the majority of the time he had been enrolled at Walnut Street. At conferences Ricky's mom was extremely quiet. She seemed to be distrustful and rarely spoke, just nodded in response to statements I made.

A classmate's grandmother, who had taken Ricky to church with their family, asked me what was going on with Ricky's mother. She said his mother had barely spoken with her and would not open the door when they came to pick Ricky up for church one Sunday. The apartment complex in which Ricky lived was known for its active drug trading. There had been numerous incidents of violence and drug-related crimes at the complex.

Ricky's mother clearly cared about him. He was dressed neatly and brought books to school that his mother had bought for him. She always came to school for conferences for Ricky and his older brother. She seemed to be proud of his progress over the course of the year, although she spoke very little at our conferences.

When Ricky entered our second-grade classroom I was worried about him. It was Ricky's fourth year in school. I recalled his behavior difficulties from the previous year. He was scheduled to be staffed into the behavior disorders program, after meeting the criteria in the spring of his first-grade year. But it wasn't acting out behavior that had me worried, it was just the opposite: Ricky's lack of engagement with everything and everyone around him was apparent soon after school began. He wasn't just shy, he was extremely withdrawn and distrustful of everyone. He didn't want to be touched and withdrew physically from any attempt to make contact. He didn't participate in group discussions or volunteer to answer questions.

Ricky seemed to have no difficulty with second-grade work. But his reluctance to participate in activities made it difficult to know what he really could do. As I watched him the first weeks of school my concerns grew. I did not see any of the violent behavior that had been so frequent the previous year, but his lack of engagement continued. This reluctance to become involved with either people or learning experiences increased my concern.

Membership in the community

Ricky seemed to have surrounded himself with a wall of distrust. He kept to himself, not daring to take any risks in writing or with relationships. By the fourth week of school the other children were collaborating and sharing their work. Not Ricky. He avoided interactions with other people.

During reading workshop he often flitted. One day he sat down on the sofa and leafed through two new books. He got up and went to the listening center. He put on the headphones, then took them off. He left to show JoBeth his radishes. He went back to the listening center. He picked up a book and read it aloud, fluently. He went to a table, looked through a stack of books and chose three. He listened to JoBeth read one of his books. He went to the bookshelf and chose another book. Finally he "lit" when I called the class for sharing time. All of this flitting took place in fifteen minutes. He flitted on the playground also. He stayed on the periphery of the action. He'd run in and tease someone, then run back to the edge of the playground. He didn't join in; he acted like he wanted to be part of the group, but he didn't seem to know how.

When he did read during reading workshop he liked to crawl into the small space under my desk, physically isolating himself from everyone. As a real sense of community grew in our classroom it became harder for Ricky to isolate himself from everyone. When David and Reggie wrote a list of club members, they included Ricky. When Kenton wrote about dinosaurs, he asked Ricky to work with him. As the kids became aware of each others strengths, they discovered that Ricky could read "real good."

In the middle of January, when Laneal and Reggie cornered Ricky and demanded that he read a difficult book to them, he relented. He had little choice. They made it quite clear that they weren't taking "no" for an answer. He competently read *The Magic Fish* (Littledale, 1986) to them. It was a breakthrough for Ricky. He had engaged with friends and a book for a long period.

It was an instance where the community no longer accepted his lack of engagement, and demanded that he become involved. After that episode the word was out and Ricky didn't have a chance of resuming his isolated position in the community. He became a much desired reading partner. The cracks that had begun to appear in his wall became crevices; kids entered freely and Ricky began making tentative excursions into the realm of friendship and caring.

He began to develop relationships with children that extended beyond the reading workshop time. At the end of February I wrote in my journal that I was amazed at how much the kids taught each other. I had noticed Ricky still kept to himself during writing workshop and hoped he would begin to work with a friend.

I wondered how I could make this happen. On Monday I was delighted when Ricky wrote a long piece about playing and going to church with Ken, a classmate, over the weekend. It was the longest piece he had written. More important than the length of the piece was that he asked Ken to work with him during conferencing time. This was the first time I had observed Ricky invite someone to collaborate during writing workshop.

He started to become engaged not only with books but with classroom life in general. He wrote a letter to Kenton when he was in the hospital. He asked JoBeth to sit by him at writing workshop. When we watched a video one afternoon, he sat close to me and talked softly for forty-five minutes. By March he was playing for extended periods of time with friends on the playground. He continued to read under my desk, but now he was rarely alone. He always had at least one friend reading with him.

One spring day I brought a small snake I had captured to school. Ricky and Kathryn assumed ownership of the snake as soon as they walked in the classroom. They carried it around all morning and took it out at recess to put it back in the woods. As they released the snake, Nathan kicked at it. Ricky punched him in the stomach. This was not the out of control aggression his teachers had reported previously; it was a righteous anger at an injustice toward something he cared about. I was so thrilled to see his involvement, both with the snake and with Kathryn, that I had little sympathy for Nathan. Later Ricky wrote about the snake in writing workshop.

Ricky's concept of who helped him learn changed. When we asked him in September he said, "Nobody helps me." In June his response was quite different. He said, "My teacher and my friends," and went on to name several. The length of the interview responses shows Ricky opening up and showing more of himself toward the end of the year.

As with other aspects of our classroom life, Ricky appeared initially to be unengaged with books. Engagement with reading came gradually and primarily through relationships with people.

One day in September he asked JoBeth if he could read a new book she had brought to the classroom. When he brought the book back to her, she read the first page to him. He began reading along with her, then read the rest of the book fairly easily. When he finished, he asked if he could keep it. JoBeth told him she'd leave it for the class, suggesting that he read it to others. He left, then returned with a canvas bag. Inside the bag were five Dr. Seuss books that his mother had bought. He wanted to read them to her, but there wasn't time. Ricky brought the books back to school the following week when he knew JoBeth would be with us. He read *Green Eggs and Ham* fluently.

Ricky was always attentive when I shared new books with the class. He frequently requested to use them after I had shown them to everyone. He had no trouble choosing books for reading workshop and often asked me to read a book aloud to the class. His trouble seemed to be staying engaged long enough to read the whole book. In November he told JoBeth, "I don't always read the books I pick; sometimes I study the pictures or just read part of them." Working with friends helped Ricky stick with a book. He liked to read his favorite parts of books to me or JoBeth. By spring he approached one of us almost every workshop requesting to do this. Many times when he read aloud to us peers would join to listen. They began to join him when he read alone. When he began to develop friendships and work with other kids, he began to read whole books.

As Ricky felt more comfortable in the classroom he became more verbal about his interest in books I read to the class. At the end of April I read *Daisy Rothschild* (Leslie-Melville, 1987), a nonfiction story about a giraffe, to the class. Ricky was very interested in the book. He asked to read it, and then volunteered to share with the class what was going to happen next. He participated in class discussions and read it on his own and with friends.

Many of Ricky's pieces in writing workshop were influenced by his reading. He wrote short book reports and borrowed story structures from books he had read, replacing key words with his own. From January until the end of the school year he wrote about books to his pen pals. Often he told them a little about the books.

As his engagement with books grew his self-confidence increased. In the September interview he told JoBeth, "I'm learning to read a book, those little books. My favorites are library books." At the end of the year he said, "I read hard books. I can read anything I want."

Becoming a risk taker

As Ricky developed relationships with other students his distrust of adults, teachers in particular, became more apparent. He didn't seem ready to take the risks that he took with his peers. He made a few overtures, but retreated if we tried to push him. He continued to withdraw physically anytime an adult placed a hand on his arm or an arm around his shoulder. His reluctance to take risks was clear in his reading and writing also.

For months Ricky was his usual withdrawn self during writing workshop. While most of the children collaborated on pieces or read their stories to each other, he sat quietly at his desk, neatly copying text from books or lists in the room. He printed in very neat, small, tense letters, using only the left half of the paper. He would throw away a paper and start over if he thought he had messed up. By the end of September he had written only one piece on his own. It was a book review of *Cornelius* (Lionni, 1983). He never volunteered to share, never responded with comments or questions to other children's writing.

Ricky seemed to have a need for security and order. His desk and personal belongings were neatly organized. This need was also reflected in his writing. Many of his papers had numbered sentences (see Figure 21-1). Ricky's concept of writing appeared to be writing sentences, something he was familiar with from his previous years in school. As Ricky began to view our classroom as a secure place, he began to take risks in his writing.

The first time we saw him really write on his own was in a letter to his pen pal. From the start the pen pal correspondence gave Ricky a real reason to write. Ricky's first letter, at the beginning of October, was different from anything he had written previously. The words filled the page and his print was larger than usual. As this correspondence continued throughout the fall, Ricky shared information about his family and his interests with his pen pal (see Figure 21-2).

Ricky frequently copied texts, until the end of October when he wrote a four-page piece about Halloween. He had worked on it over a two-week period. He shared it with three other children. This was the first time that Ricky had shared his writing. Over the next two months Ricky began to write on his own instead of copying. He began writing in first person. He wrote about his feelings towards school (Figure 21-3) and about his father (Figure 21-4). Both of the pieces were

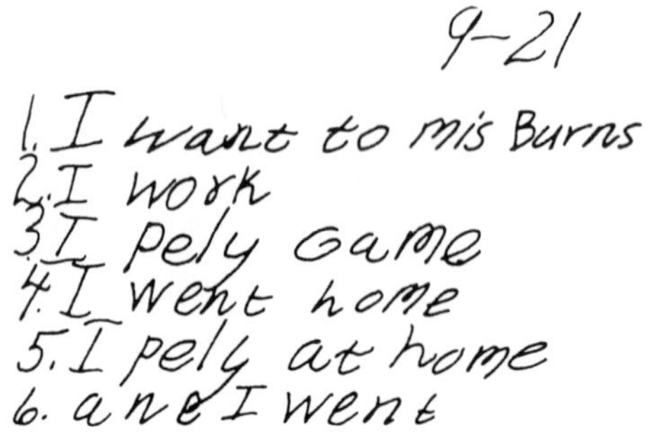

9-21

1. I want to mis Burns
2. I work
3. I pely Game
4. I went home
5. I pely at home
6. ane I went

FIG. 21-1 *September Writing, Numbered Sentences*

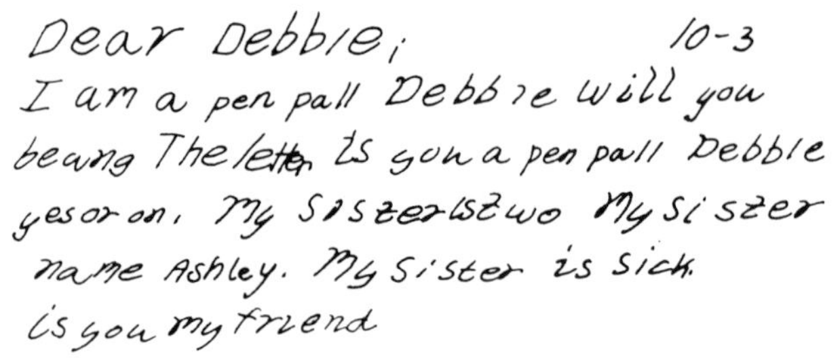

Dear Debbie; 10-3

I am a pen pall Debbie will you
beang The letter. is you a pen pall Debble
yes or on. My sisterstwo My sister
name Ashley. My Sister is sick.
is you my frend

FIG. 21-2 *Ricky's Pen-pal Letter*

11-7

I m Not go to this SCHOOL
Nex yer I her this SCHOOL
I go in gio Pepler Street
I do t lik this SChooL

FIG. 21-3 *I Do Not Like This School.*

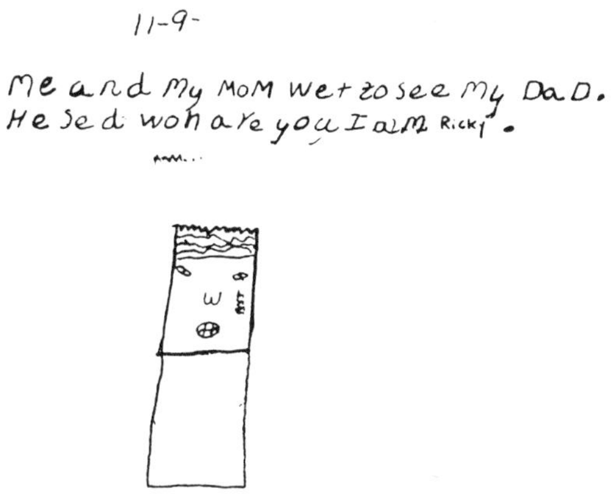

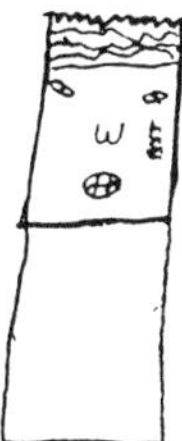

FIG. 21-4 *My Dad Said "Who Are You?"*

somewhat disturbing to me, but I was encouraged to see that writing gave him an opportunity to express his feelings.

Although Ricky rarely vocalized his feelings in school, in his writing he expressed his desire to be liked and to share love. He wrote, "I like Miss Green. She like me." In a letter to Santa he said, "Santa will you tell Mrs. Claus I love her" (see Figure 21-5). With all of his pen pals he eventually signed his letters "Love Ricky." He also began to take risks as a reader. In October he asked JoBeth, "Can I read this to you tomorrow? It's a hard one!" He told a friend about a book he had read. He showed interest in books that were challenging for him.

When we returned from Christmas vacation, Ricky went back to copying. I spoke with him about this, encouraging him to write his own ideas. He wrote two pieces in January. One was about his brother, whom he described as a monster. The other was a story he wrote on his own, then copied over neatly to share with the class. He read very softly and had to repeat it a few times for everyone to hear. This was a big risk for Ricky. He didn't share his writing with friends and rarely participated in commenting on other children's writing. He had made a lot of progress, but I still felt his lack of confidence in himself and his reluctance to trust people held him back from using his abilities to the fullest.

As Ricky became more competent his confidence grew; he began to realize that he knew a lot about reading and writing. He arranged to read a story to a small group of first graders. His writing also began to reflect this new improved self-concept. His pieces were longer and he wrote about his life outside of school. A breakthrough in Ricky's ability to trust adults occurred during this same period. Ricky developed a special relationship, through his letters, with his Winter quarter pen pal, Kay. She was a mother with young children. She always responded to what Ricky wrote to her and expected and encouraged him to respond to her questions. She would remind him when he didn't, gently insisting that he really communicate. They shared favorite books, information about their families, and wrote about what they were doing in school.

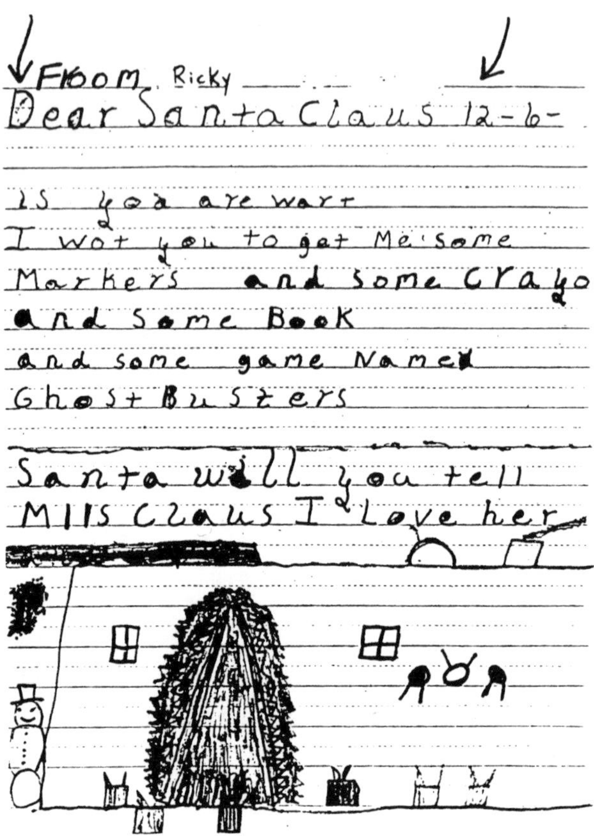

From. Ricky
Dear Santa Claus 12-6-

is you are wart
I wot you to get Me some
Markers and some Crayo
and Some Book
and some game Named
GhostBusters

Santa will you tell
MIIS Claus I Love her

FIG.21-5 *Letter to Santa*

Kay's letters were warm and caring. They meant a lot to Ricky. In the last letter of the quarter she wrote, "Ricky you are my special friend and I love you very much. I will miss you, but you will have another pen pal soon. I will think of you always." She included a small tablet and pencil for him. He spent an hour writing in it. I watched him with pleasure, excusing him from our regular activities.

Through this correspondence Ricky was able to build a loving relationship with an adult in a nonthreatening way. Her openness and caring came through to him, and he seemed to respond by becoming more trusting toward all of us. It was around this time that he started hugging me and JoBeth. In the past he had shied away from physical contact, moving quickly away from even a caring hand on his shoulder.

Ricky's relationship with Kay and his developing friendships with children in the class provided him the support he needed to take greater risks. He wrote his own pieces instead of copying. He wrote longer pieces and shared his writing with the class. He started to collaborate on pieces with other students and stay engaged in activities for longer periods of time. He attempted to write a play. He continued to write about important events in his life (see Figure 21-6). Taking these risks

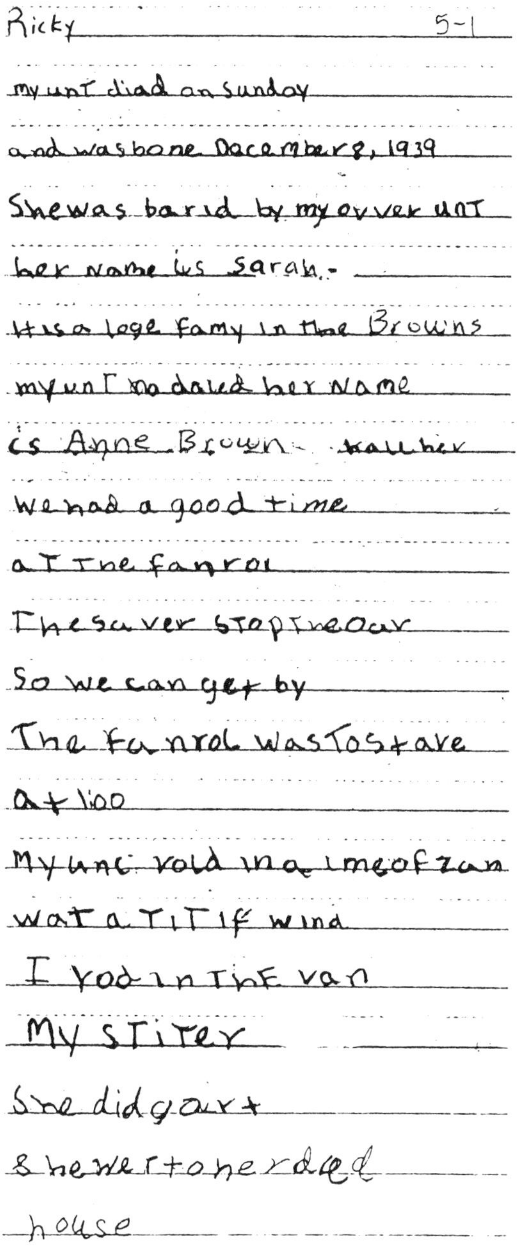

Ricky 5-1

my unT diad on sunday
and was bone December 8, 1939
Shewas barid by my ovver unT
her name is Sarah.-
It is a loge famy in the Browns
myunT ma daid her Name
is Anne Brown - kall her
We had a good time
aT The fanral
The saver stop The car
So we can get by
The fanrol was To stare
at 1:00
My unc rold in a lmeofzan
waT a TiTif wind
I rod in The van
My STiTer
She didgart
she werTtoherdad
house

My aunt died on Sunday
and was born December 8, 1939.
She was buried by my other aunt.
Her name is [Sarah].
It is a large family in the [Browns].
My aunt who died, her name
is [Ann Brown] we call her.
We had a good time
at the funeral.
The supervisor stopped the cars
so we can get by.
The funeral was to start
at 1:00.
My uncle rode in a limousine
[?]
I rode in the van.
My sister,
she didn't go,
she went to her dad's
house.

FIG. 21-6 *"My Aunt Died on Sunday"*

created some tension for him. It was easily seen in the way he printed. When he was trying new forms he returned to using tense, small letters, many times scrunching all the print on the left side of the page.

Over the course of the school year we saw Ricky change from a distant, wary child to a child who hugged his teacher in the morning. By the end of the year he excitedly shared his discoveries and obviously felt more confident about himself. He had taken some big risks; the biggest was daring to trust us. We didn't let him down. Our community of learners had expected and at times demanded that he be a contributing and successful member. We offered the support to make it possible for Ricky to be a success and drew him into the community. Books became the door through his wall of distrust.

Edwin Markham, in his poem *Outwitted*, expresses so well what happened in our classroom with Ricky:

He drew a circle that shut me out—
Heretic, rebel, a thing to flout.
But Love and I had the wit to win:
We drew a circle that took him in.

TWENTY-TWO

A Loving Child

Ricky in Third Grade at Walnut Street School

with Teachers Susan Willis and Judy Smith

"I think I be a reader when I grow up"

Ricky grew to love books in Barbara's class, a love that he resumed immediately upon entering Susan's third-grade classroom. Well versed in the routines of reading workshop, he chose *Amelia Bedelia* (Parish, 1963) the first day, carefully marking his place at the end of the workshop. The next day he finished the book. This was the child who had flitted from book to book for so long the previous year. Later in the week he read *Harold and the Purple Crayon* (Johnson, 1958), which Barbara had given him to keep at the end of second grade. This gift must have been important to Ricky; he not only kept it through the summer but brought it to school to share. After he reread this old favorite he recommended it to Susan—good books are for sharing.

These first few days of school established a pattern for Ricky that was to continue throughout the year. He read constantly. He asked to go to the library more than any child in the class, and his desk often overflowed with books. "He seemed to hoard them," Judy noted. "When the librarian recalled missing books from our room at the end of the year, we found most of them in Ricky's desk!" During a parent-teacher conference his mom remarked that he was "always reading" at home, books from the class and school libraries. Ricky's reading interests were diverse, including a great deal of nonfiction, especially biographies (often about prominent African Americans). He recommended several books to his first quarter pen pal, including *Miss Nelson Is Missing* (Allard, 1977), *The Best Sports Book in the Whole Wide World* (Kunnas, 1984), *The Whipping Boy* (Fleischman, 1986), *Arthur for the Very First Time* (MacLachlan, 1980), and his favorite, *Charlotte's Web* (White, 1952), which he read along from a library copy when Susan read it to the class. He was quick to request books recommended by Susan, JoBeth, and his classmates. As Ricky wrote on his questionnaire, "I like to read about *inething*."

Although neither teacher was able to write this chapter, both contributed through observational notes, writing samples, weekly data analysis sessions, and feedback on drafts of the chapters. JoBeth is the author of the chapter.

Books seemed to help Ricky overcome his shyness, serving as a kind of intermediary gift to others, as if he were saying, "I don't know if you would be interested in me, but let's talk about this book that I know you will like." When Susan returned to the classroom in January, after a frightening illness, weeks of absence, and a series of substitutes, the class seemed to heave a collective sigh of relief and to demonstrate a sense of security. A week after she returned, Susan wrote, "Ricky and Kim came up front to demonstrate a puppet play (impromptu). He shared his book and really spoke loud and told about several things. He asked for and answered all the questions." Ricky had shared infrequently earlier in the year, and not at all during Susan's absence. The next day Susan noted, "Ricky read a dinosaur book. He wanted to be the first to share about his book. Someone asked a question. He couldn't answer, but it didn't bother him at all. Ricky has come a long way." A week later Ricky shared during both reading and writing workshop for the first time, sharing a picture and text he had written about John Kennedy, as well as sharing the actual biography. This time he answered questions confidently, easily locating specific pictures, showing the assassin and the car where JFK was shot.

Ricky was a capable reader. Unlike some of the other children we studied, who read books over and over as a kind of self-sponsored practice, Ricky read widely, coming back to a favorite only occasionally. Although his reading of sight word lists at the beginning of the year showed 80 percent on the 1.2 list and 24 percent on the 2.1 list, on September 1 he read "My Dinosaur's Day at the Park" from the 3.1 reader with 93 percent word recognition and accurate comprehension. He often self-corrected for meaning when he read. When he read aloud to an adult he occasionally commented on his reading strategies. On September 26 when he came to "still" in his book he said, "Look, st . . . ill, that [ill] is our spelling word. Still." In January, he told Susan he remembered "stampede" from a basal story the class had read together when he came to it in another book. Later that month, he showed Susan the word "commercials" in his book and told her he had figured out how to say it "by spelling it out."

Near the end of school he chose *Commander Toad and the Space Pirates* (Yolen, 1986) to read to JoBeth. It was very difficult but he stuck with it, asking JoBeth to pronounce words like "galaxies," "alien," "copilot," "lieutenant," and "salamander." He read "reserve" for "reverse," and "energy" for "engine," although he read it correctly the next time. He had nineteen such miscues and teacher-pronounced words on the first twenty-four pages, an acceptable although surely confusing word recognition rate; yet he summarized the story accurately and showed his appreciation of the humor at several points.

Security and risk taking

Ricky's teachers discussed what they perceived as his need for security and worked to provide him with a dependable routine and trustworthy, caring adults. With this security he was willing to take risks, academic risks as well as interpersonal ones. In the "Something About Me" questionnaire Ricky provided some clues to his need for security. In several responses he wrote about liking to play outdoors (e.g., "I'd like school better *if we can go outdoors in the moning.*") Then in another response he wrote, "I wish my parents *will let me go out doors win I get home*." A classmate who lived near Ricky said she couldn't go out either because her mother said it was dangerous. Ricky told about a man dying at his apartment a long time ago. In another response he wrote, "I worry about *averthing*." He lived in a very rough neighborhood, one that was often in the papers for drug arrests, drug-related shootings and stabbings, and domestic violence.

In *There Are No Children Here*, Alex Kotlowitz (1991) described a young man who reminded us very much of Ricky. His name was Pharoah Rivers and he lived in a violent, drug-gang dominated housing project in Chicago. He was sensitive, eager to please his teachers and his mother, and he longed for a safe, secure place to be. Kotlowitz observed that " . . . Pharoah talked and moved freely at school because he felt protected there. With a sense of security comes comfort, and Pharoah, who in the streets often seemed withdrawn and flighty, livened up at school" (p. 68). "Pharoah loved school. Unlike the streets, where his stammer [which dogged his speech since the day he was caught in a crossfire of bullets] and small size made him the object of ridicule, he stood tall in school" (p. 61). The day he stood the tallest was when he conquered his fear and stuttering to take second place to his friend in the all-school spelling bee, a contest in which his words had frozen the year before. Ricky also seemed to have decided that school was a safe place, with people he could trust. He showed Pharoah's kind of school confidence when he read and talked or wrote about books.

Writing about books was, in fact, Ricky's favorite topic. Throughout the year he wrote for a variety of purposes, including establishing and maintaining relationships with adults, recording events in his life, and creating stories, but the most consistent topic was the books he read. Books served a similar role in his writing to the role they served in his oral communication: they were a tried and true medium, always interesting to himself and others, always available when other topics might be elusive. As Susan noted in November, "Ricky was so excited about the book he checked out yesterday. He wanted to read it quickly so he could write about it." Sometimes he wrote about a topic he was reading about; sometimes he wrote a new version of a book he had enjoyed, as he did in November with *The Jolly Postman* (Ahlberg, 1986), incorporating their social studies theme of contrasting city and country living. But most often he wrote summaries, as he did with Aladdin.

The children had not written in well over a month when Susan returned in January and reinstated the daily routine. Ricky had been reading *Aladdin and the Magic Lamp* (Daniels, 1980) and wrote brief notes on it (see Figure 22–1). Susan had a conference with him, told him it sounded like a wonderful story, and said she would like to hear more. The next day Ricky wrote the summary in Figure 22–2.

Aladdin and the wonderful lamp

Long ago a little boy named Aladdin, he lived far away. Aladdin was a lazy boy. A stranger came. He said, "I am your uncle now," he said to Aladdin. He took Aladdin for a walk. He showed him some magic for Aladdin. Aladdin said to his false uncle, "My mother and dad died when I was born. I cried when my mother died, and dad. It was a rock, he made a rock move. His fake uncle said, "Go down there." Aladdin went down there. Aladdin's treasures is down there. Aladdin find a wonderful lamp in there. Aladdin could not get up there. The rock begin to move. Aladdin rub the lamp. "What is your wish," the magic lamp said. Aladdin said, "Will you get me out

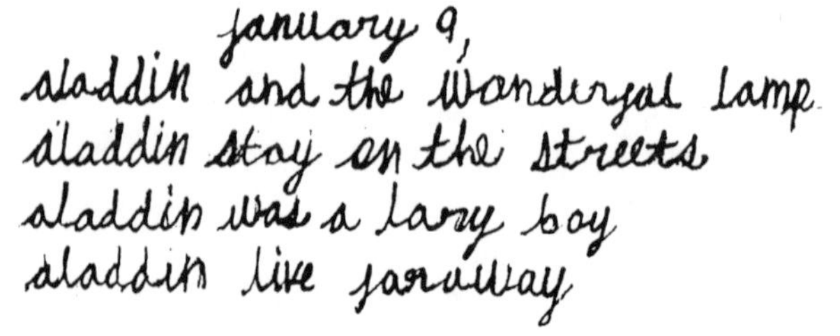

january 9,
aladdin and the wonderyal lamp
aladdin stay on the streets
aladdin was a lazy boy
aladdin live faraway

FIG. 22-1 *Notes on Aladdin*

of here now?" he said. The lamp let him out of the cave. Aladdin went home. He let his mother see it. His mother fainted. His false uncle came back.

Ricky was back on track as a writer, supported by an interested teacher and his beloved books.

Ricky was one of the most active members of the reading community in third grade. He frequently recommended books for Susan and Judy to read themselves and to read aloud to the class. During the spring Judy told her class about watching "*The Shell Seekers*" (based on a book by the same name; Pilcher, 1987), and how much better the book was than the TV version. She showed them the thick, dog-eared paperback that she had immersed herself in for days and nights. As the other children began to read after this mini-lesson, Ricky pulled gently on Judy's sleeve. "Could I borrow that book, Ms. Smith?" he asked eagerly. When JoBeth had asked him several months earlier, "What kinds of things will you need or want to read when you're grown up?" Ricky had replied, "A big old book. I probably be a reader when I grow up."

Ricky's trust/risk taking often showed in the physical aspects of his writing. His writing actually *looked* fearful during unsettled times, such as when he was adjusting to new relationships, or when he tried a different focus with his writing (see Graves' discussion of levels of concern, 1983). Although he developed a fine cursive hand, during stressful periods he often reverted to manuscript, as when he wrote Susan at her home, "I wash I cold spen ChrisMiss with you Miss Wilis." Ricky was also aware of what he didn't know, and on the questionnaire wrote, "I don't know how *to spell other people name*" and "I wish someone would help me *spell people name*."

As Ricky became more secure with Susan and the rest of the class his writing covered the whole page, left to right and often top to bottom, as it had by the end of the previous year. Susan asked him several times if he would like to share his writing with the group, but he consistently declined until the end of October. Although he again shook his head no when Susan gave him the opportunity (in a private conference) to share, he said she could read his story. She agreed, if he would stand beside her and "help me out if I have trouble with a word." With this supported risk taking, he slowly exhibited more confidence in his writing. He began to share it spontaneously with Susan, although still not with the whole class.

ame

Thursday jan 11,

aladdin and the wonderful lamp

long ago a little boy name aladdin
he live fair a way. aladdin was a
lazy boy. a stranger came he seid
i am your uncle now he sied to aladdin,
he tock aladdin for a wake. he show
him some ^shant coner^ magic for aladdin. alddin
side to his false uncle my mother and
dad dide whin i was bone. i cry
whin my mother dide and dad
it was a rock he made a rock
move. has fale uncle sied go downe
there. alddin went down there
alddin treasures is downe there.
alddin find a a wonderful lamp in
there. alddin cade not get up
there the rock bgein to move
alddin rub the lamp wete is your
waesh the magec lamp sied. alddin
sied will you get me out of here
now he sied the lamp let him out
of the cave alddin went home.
he let hass mother see it has mother
fant it has fased uncel came
black,

FIG. 22–2 *Revision of Aladdin and the Wonderful Lamp*

Finally, on January 18 he shared his piece on JFK at the end of writing workshop. "Bernard called on him," Susan noted, "and he went without hesitation."

Ricky had also become a risk taker with people, especially teachers. The child who had not allowed anyone to touch him much of last year was described by several adults as "a loving child." He asked JoBeth if he could read to her every week when she visited. He always had something to share with an adult and frequently hugged his teachers and others. He hugged his fall quarter pen pal Leslie on first meeting, after moving from "From Ricky" in his first two letters to "Love Ricky" in the rest. After writing back and forth about their mutual love of *Charlotte's Web* for two weeks, on October 25 Ricky wrote:

> Dear Leslie
>
> I like your letter. I will let your havv my Charlotte's Web Book. Have you red Arthur For The Very First Time. It is A Good Stroy. do you wont Charlottes Wed I holp [hope] thit you want it I am ten year old. I got a lot of frid [friends] in one is besid me her namen Barbra Ann and the other one name Laquita. My Taecher Name Mis Wilis and her husbin namen Mr. Wilis. I am goin to geve it to you Charlottes Web is a good book. I am goin to give Charlotte Web. to you plas send it bcik nex week
>
> Love
>
> Ricky

In an analysis of their meeting at the end of the quarter Leslie wrote, "The first thing he wanted to do was read the books I had brought with me. . . . He wanted to give me . . . his copy of *Charlotte's Web*. He . . . told me . . . that he had [my picture, sent on request] on his wall at home."

Ricky and Susan also became very close. He often imitated her teaching role by sitting on her high stool and pretending he was reading to the class during buddy reading (rather than choosing a partner to read with). On his questionnaire he wrote, "I want to be *a school teacher*." He wrote a story for Susan on her birthday in November, and sent her several letters when she was home sick. He even had a kind word for one of the substitutes:

> 12/6 Dear Mis Wilis Mis Adams is nice. everbody ben bad in the class room and Lee and Laquita got in a fight. how did you get sike. Santa woke shop [At Santa's workshop] I got Tanya a ring Lee and Laquita went to the ofices. Love Ricky I love you Miss Wilis

This was in sharp contrast to the hard time most of the children had with—and gave—the substitutes. Kim wrote, "Ms. Willis got sick, something wrong with her blood—we had a sub—and then another—I think if I see another sub I'm going to scream."

By the time Judy became the permanent teacher in February, the loss of Susan seemed to drain Ricky's sense of security. Judy noted that he was often off task, "piddling around," lacking in confidence, and unwilling to share. Once again, his writing was scrunched up on the left side of the paper for a few weeks. He began to give up on tasks, like math tests, whereas earlier in the year Susan had remarked on the pride Ricky took in the careful completion even of the occasional worksheet. When Judy read *Freckle Juice* (Blume, 1971) to the class and then had a Freckle Juice party, all the children told what they would change about themselves if the magic potion really worked. "I would be a ghost," Ricky said softly, "so no one could see me." He seemed to be literally closing up, pulling the cloak of isolation and safe choices tightly around himself again.

He reacted similarly when he got a new pen pal in April, writing in very small print a letter which he didn't even finish:

> Dear Lynn
> last time i had a pen pale name Lieies She was a good pen pale. i love to see you what colir [are you][no signature]

He mentioned Leslie again in his next letter (and asked again if Lynn was black or white). He never did warm up to this pen pal, but by the end of the school year he and Judy had become friends. He recommended books to her, chose books for her to read to the class like *Stringbean's Trip to the Shining Sea*, and hugged her several times. But it was a rough transition and we worried about what would happen next year when he had a new teacher. We didn't find out until the end of the school year how truly confidence shaking the transition would be.

Community . . .

One of the goals of many teachers, and a goal explicitly stated by many whole language teachers, is to make the school community as much like a supportive home environment as possible. Elementary teachers read to and with their children, engage with them in purposeful writing, and encourage them to learn with their friends, as most children do outside of school settings. But often we don't know a great deal about children's actual home environments and whether we are establishing congruent structures and events at school, or are teaching new ways of learning. If children haven't engaged in parent-child storybook reading, written communication, or collaborative learning, our approach may be different and our explanations more explicit. We didn't know a lot about Ricky's home life. What we did learn provided us with a picture of a home where reading was encouraged, as well as one where solitude was the norm.

As he had done in second grade, Ricky brought a book from home on several occasions. One time he brought a small Bible, with excerpts that he said he had gotten from church. He asked Susan to read a particular page, saying it was his favorite. Taking his writing home was very important to him, so important that many things disappeared permanently from his folder. At a parent-teacher conference his mother said that he read all the time at home. Although mostly silent behind dark glasses, when she saw Ricky's report card of Excellents, Goods, and Satisfactories, she smiled and said, "He's really doing good."

There were also some troubling signs from home. He was absent several days at the end of school because he missed the school bus; on the questionnaire he wrote, "I don't understand why *my mother wont get up*." There were many instances throughout the year when Ricky laid his head on the desk, seeming tired, once even sleeping. Whereas last year he had been a very tidy dresser, this year he was not. Various teachers described Ricky's older brother (fifth grade) as "vicious." We got the impression that his mother was not home (or awake when he was) very often, perhaps because of her demanding work schedule.

Yet Ricky did not seem like a child who was totally on his own, either. As previously noted, his mother was concerned about his welfare in their rough neighborhood and did not let him play outdoors. On Valentine's Day, Ricky brought a bag of candy from home to share with his classmates. And one of Ricky's "fictional" stories (1/23) seems to provide us with the picture of a mother who both disciplines and loves her son:

> **The Bully**
>
> Once there was Bully, he like to pick on pepol. One day his mother sind him up for school. on the first day he was good. he was bad yesterday. he call his frind name. The Boy he was picking at he tod on himm The Bully got a not home. his mother gave him a spanking. One day he did not go to school. his mother was look for him, but she did not find him. She went out the house she saw him. yesterday he came bake. his mother hug him. then the next day he went to school he was good The End

Ricky did not become an outgoing socializer in third, but neither was he withdrawn and reclusive as he had been for much of second grade, nor violent as he had been in kindergarten and first. Now the "circle that drew him in" was more casual about it, and accepting of Ricky's frequent choice to read and write alone. Ricky rarely chose to read with anyone during buddy reading; one exception was in November when he and Lawrence were both reading *Charlotte's Web* and Ricky asked to read with him. They read silently, side by side, the entire period.

On several occasions Susan facilitated Ricky's interaction with his peers, providing him with just the support he seemed to need. Early in September she had the children share their books with a partner before whole group share, so that everyone had a chance to share and everyone got a little practice thinking about how to share a book. She put Ricky with LaShay, who had not spoken at all in class since school started. Yet with Ricky she talked freely, and he with her. In November a group of children made a play out of *Chocolate Fever* (Smith, 1978), which Susan had read to the class. They needed someone to be the doctor, but Ricky shook his head when asked. Susan pointed out that he could play this role without talking and that she had a toy stethoscope at home to help with his costume. He finally agreed and the play was a great success. "This was a big step!" Susan noted. Another intervention was also related to a classroom drama project, but it was not directed specifically at Ricky. Susan merely provided the materials for the children to construct a puppet stage. Ricky and some others presented their original puppet play, and for the first time he spoke loudly and with confidence in front of the whole class—but behind the protection of the curtain. As Ricky said in his October 26 interview, "I'm learning to share, but it's hard if you be shy."

Beginning in January JoBeth recorded something new, something that had not appeared in her notes the previous year and a half. Ricky began laughing and joking with the children around him. He asked to be moved by Kenneth, another very solid worker, and they became friends. He was moved by Bernard near the end of the year ("as a calming influence"), and the two talked often, even too much at times. "It almost became a problem," said Judy, "but it was so good for Ricky that I didn't move him. By the end of the year, when we went on our field trip to Memorial Park Zoo and to swim at the YWCO pool, he was a well-accepted and integral part of the group, laughing softly, enjoying the events and the people." He had come out from under the desk and joined the community.

. . . and chaos

But it was not enough. Ricky passed the reading test but failed the math portion of the state-mandated Criterion Referenced Test (CRT) in March. Ricky had hurried through the whole test, Judy noted, and subtraction was really the big problem. The school provided some tutoring for all the third graders who failed, and they took the test again in May. By this time Ricky's anxiety was very high. His promotion to fourth grade depended on this test. Again he failed, coming within a few points.

Judy told the kids who didn't pass one at a time, on the last day of school. She put her arm around Ricky and explained that he could take the math part again next year, "and when you pass you go right on to the fourth grade." The three children who failed reacted differently. Reggie was mad. Benton cried. "Ricky was so sad when I told him. He withdrew from everyone, just closed up," Judy explained sadly.

Walnut Street School had worked very hard in recent years to considerably reduce its retention rate. Even though the state required all third graders to pass both reading and math sections of the CRT, the school provided tutoring and kept administering the test until most children passed. Children sometimes began the year spending some time in both third- and fourth-grade classrooms, becoming full-time fourth graders as soon as they passed the test. But such an option was not to be available to Ricky because he also got caught in the chaos of redrawing district boundaries. He was transferred to Poplar Grove Elementary, where retention was viewed more favorably than at Walnut Street. Dual class membership was not an option.

Ricky was hopeful about the coming year when JoBeth interviewed him at the end of May, before he learned of his retention. He said several of his friends would be going there, and named Frances, Matthew, and Tanya. "I believe that's a good school," he told JoBeth. We hoped he would be right.

TWENTY-THREE

Ricky in Third Grade—Again

Poplar Street School

October

"Ricky is such a sweet boy! He's really cooperative and participates more than his early records show. He seems to be really happy, really cheerful. I don't see why he is in Behavioral Disorders. He's quiet, but not withdrawn. He shares his work and talks with me a lot. He automatically qualified for Chapter 1 for reading because he is a repeater [because he failed the math CRT, but there is no Chapter 1 math at this school]. He goes to Chapter 1 and BD every day—no wonder he never finishes tasks—and that's what he's in BD for! He goes to Chapter 1 from 8:00 to 8:45, reads with me for thirty minutes, then goes to BD at 9:15. They work on building self-esteem in there; he showed me a mood sticker he got for one of the activities.

"I talked with him and the other four who didn't pass the CRT and told them I enjoyed having them in third grade. They all passed the reading part of the CRT but failed the math. They are all in the same reading group, in *Journeys* (3.2 basal); Ricky is always eager to read. We're going slowly. He can call words; he reads fairly fluently. But I can tell from the skills pages that he doesn't always understand. When we talk about things he makes connections, like when we did word referents the other day he explained it perfectly. We haven't done much silent reading because they don't seem to understand. We also have a listening center, where they listen to short passages, follow along, and then discuss. Also, for two weeks in October and two weeks in the spring we have 'Drop Everything and Read' for the first fifteen minutes of the day—everybody in the school. He does this in Chapter 1.

"Ricky has been writing on his own, pretty often, really. Writing is one of their 'Quiet Time' choices, and everyone has a folder. I feel kind of bad that I haven't been doing any writing. He seems so proud when he shows me his [independent writing] folder. Sometimes I have them write something, like about going to the Harvest Festival. Then I have them get a partner and read what they wrote, share with their partner. The new English series does emphasize writing; we've done some clustering and webbing on the board—we even did that with our spelling words one week as an example of prewriting. When his group was reading 'The

---

As told to JoBeth in interviews with his teacher Ms. Gilcrest (pseudonym) in October, March, and June. The interviews have been edited for what we felt was pertinent, and for narrative flow. Ricky's teacher is the same as Jeremiah's.

Fastest Quitter in Town,' I asked them to predict what might happen next. Ricky said, 'We could write about his next game.'

"Ricky wrote a story, 'The New Boy at School,' that I thought was really good."

Ricky

September 21

The New Boy at School

Once ther was a frind of myen but he move/ away. I did not have no frind one day ther/ was a new frind in our school we had to be/ good to him. the techer indurst [introduced] him to our clas/ rome. We had to play a game me and him play a game/ theat game we play it called candy land./ me and him made frind we went to lunch at lunch/ we trade lunch we had chicking [writing too light to read] / then we left lunch We went out to play/ We had a good time outsied. We went/ over to [swing?] we stard to [?] he got stun [stung]/ By a Beey he feell down to the ground/ He starde to cry he went to the techer/ he go to the ofoinc [office] the ofoinc gave him som/ ahoolle [alcohol]. it hutter [hurted] him he call his mother/ his mother came and got him his mother/ took him home. So ther a nother Frind/ gon. the nex day he came to school He/ was stell my frind thay stell was frind the End

The class returned to the room from music. Ricky went over to JoBeth and began telling her about his writing. He then got *Charlotte's Web* (his own copy) from his desk. "Ms. Gilcrest is reading this to us after lunch every day. I read mine along while she reads to us."

Barbara sent Ricky a blank book and a letter (see Figure 23-1) on October 16. Ricky wrote back the next day (see Figure 23-2), asking Ms. Gilcrest to mail it, which she did.

March

"I started daily journals in February, and Ricky has done less writing in his folder since then—he mostly writes in his journal. Sometimes I give them a topic, but it's usually just their topics, thoughts of the day, that kind of thing.

"Ricky's not going to BD any more. He just stopped going, removed himself. I probably helped because I didn't understand why he was in. He was going out for Chapter 1 and BD, and he wasn't getting his work done; it was affecting his self-esteem. Ricky's goal seems to be to get work finished. He preferred to be in here, and worked quietly when he stayed here. So they rewrote his IEP.

"He's just a quiet, soft-spoken child, but he does interact. He has his group of friends and he always talks to me, shows me new things. Sometimes he volunteers in reading group. He does tend to be a follower, though, and I'm worried about that. He's getting to a macho age. I worry about him following Laneal's (from his class last year) lead. Laneal has trouble with unstructured time, and he doesn't read much. Ricky doesn't seem strong enough to decide on his own.

"He spent two weeks reading *Pecos Bill* (Kellogg, 1986) recently, then did a book report and shared the book with the class—he called him "Pesco Bill" the

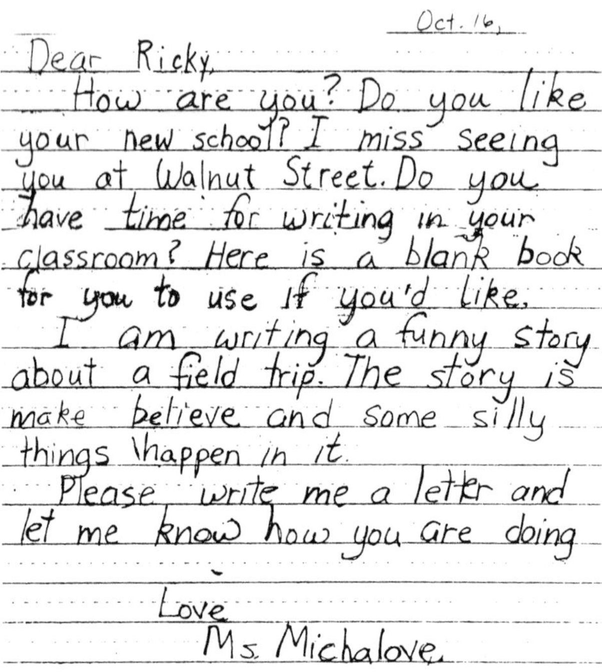

Oct. 16,

Dear Ricky,
How are you? Do you like your new school? I miss seeing you at Walnut Street. Do you have time for writing in your classroom? Here is a blank book for you to use if you'd like.
I am writing a funny story about a field trip. The story is make believe and some silly things happen in it.
Please write me a letter and let me know how you are doing.

Love
Ms Michalove

FIG. 23–1 *Barbara's Letter to Ricky*

whole time. He's reading longer books than at the first of the year. His group just finished the second magazine of *Journeys*. I'll test them this week. He was in this book last year and seems to have the best retention of the stories, especially at the literal level; he misses some inferences. He catches on quicker than the others in his group on decoding skills. His group is one magazine behind the top group. We usually read two to three paragraphs and discuss them for understanding. I do the skill pages with them too. We do guided practice together, but I just assign the skill practice because they can do that independently now.

"I'm really pleased with how Ricky's year has gone. He's really likable. Ricky gives it his all."

JoBeth interviewed Ricky (see Chapter 20, "Third Grade Repeated: March") and he read to her from Jackson's *How to Play Better Football* (his choice) and *Flights*, the fourth-grade basal. He had eight miscues (e.g., Try-Athlon, attention, except/expect) on a 300-word passage, and he seemed to enjoy retelling the story of the shy fourth grader in the story.

June

"Ricky's still not using capitalization and punctuation on first drafts, but he can go back and correct. One day he wrote a love letter for another boy to a girl! He

Dear ms michdlove oct 18,

how are you doing i murse
you when is you go to come
to see me my teacher name is
ms Gilcrest She is a nice teacher
Whit School do you teach do you
Stell teach Walnut Street What
Walnut look like i am writing
a Story about halloween
gost Story me and my teacher
have fun what do you do you do
at your School i love this School
how meny pepul in your classrome
thank you fewr that Book what
do you do in that Book we have
math Spelling ErlSh and writing

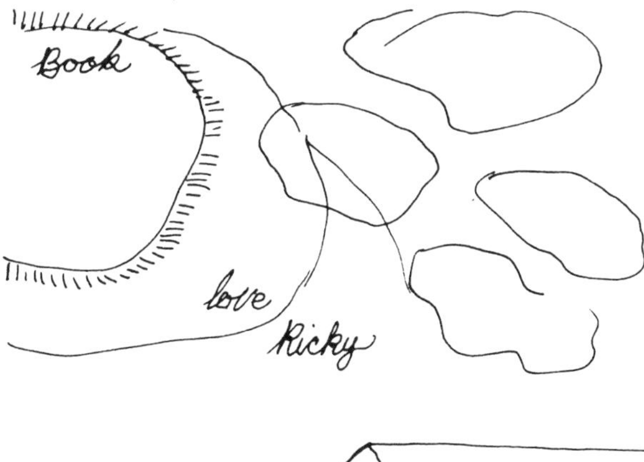

Book

love
Ricky

FIG. 23–2 *Ricky's Response to Barbara*

preferred to share his writing with one or two friends, never to the whole class, although he did share the books he read with the whole class.

"I didn't put his group in *Flights*; it would have been too hard. I did give it to him to read over the summer. He didn't show mastery on all his tests, like on unstressed syllables, but he could discuss the stories and support his answers. When we finished *Journeys* we did stories in an anthology. They made their own workbooks, with questions, vocabulary words, etc. He was really big on spontaneously using the glossary when he got to a word he didn't know.

"Ricky has been doing a really good job of completing his work, not talking with friends, like Laneal. They did reevaluate him for BD, and he's not. We thought maybe LD, because of the variance, but he's not. He had been so reluctant to go, just because he didn't like to leave the group. He seemed to feel very much a part of our class. I didn't push and neither did the BD teacher, so he didn't go much. Then he tested out.

"I met with his mother about the change and she seemed really happy. She came in for both conferences, and just dropped by two other times. She always asks how he's doing, says he's real happy, and that he talks with her about school most days when he gets home. She's real proud of him."

Continuing Worries

Ricky seemed to have had a good year. He made the transition from a whole language classroom in second, through a stormy series of instructional approaches in third, to a textbook-oriented classroom when he repeated third grade. He maintained his love of reading and continued to relate well, especially with his teacher. Ricky pushed the system to recognize his social growth; both Ms. Gilcrest and his BD teacher responded by reevaluating him and allowing him to stay with his class more of the day. He continued to write on his own and to use his writing to explore his own life, to extend his love of books, and to relate to people he cared about. He also, at least on one occasion, worked on a self-initiated revision; his later version of "The New Boy at School," which he dedicated and gave to Ms. Gilcrest, is shown in Figure 23-3.

Ricky's year presents an interesting contrast with Jeremiah's. Ricky worked hard and had a positive attitude. When he came up to Ms. Gilcrest, as he did frequently, it was to share information, his writing, or a book; Jeremiah had usually tattled or complained. Ricky's mom took an active interest; Jeremiah's did not, at least from the school's standpoint. Ricky was quiet but "he has his group of friends"; Jeremiah did not.

But these two boys share a devastating statistical classification: as African-American males who have been failed twice. There is only a one in ten chance that either will graduate from high school. They are in remedial reading tracks, Chapter 1 outside the classroom, and slow, low-level skills work within the classroom (Allington, 1983). They both risk low expectations from future teachers as double repeaters.

Ricky learned to trust "school" adults; have we been worthy of his trust? He has become a reader and a writer; have we implied to him that this is enough, that he will now be successful? If so, we have been unwittingly deceptive and are guilty of continuing a pattern of educational promises that never materialize in social and economic terms, especially for historically oppressed minorities (Ogbu, 1988).

We continue to worry about Ricky.

Ricky oct 15,
To my teacher Mis Gilcrest
my teacher frome me to you.
the new Boy at school
By Ricky
once there was a boy But the
next new Day he had to move away
the next Day I Was alllon By mysef.
the next day new there was a new boy at
School. his name was Bart. our teacher
endeont him to the class. he Was
my frind. we made up at lunch. we
Sat nex to Each other. aftter lunch
We went out Sied we had funy
out Sied. then we went Back to our
classrome. we had to do math. math
Was fun. the nex day we had fun
we play game We play condyland. it
was fun. we had to play a game in
math. We had fun it was time to
go to lunch we had chinke sunpaer
he did not went his chinke Sumper
So he ask me do I want it i Sied
yes. So we went Back out Sied
We had more fun. We play on the
Bired we jump on the Bright. we sumw on the
Suad. we had fun But we had to
go in. So we had to go home. my teach
er sied you was the Best one
in the classrome. and you to the
teacher Sied they got on the
Bus we talk in kind. i love you
the She Sied.
End
by
Ricky

I love you

FIG. 23–3 *"The New Boy at School"*

LEE

TWENTY-FOUR
Lee in His Own Voice

Second grade with Ms. Michalove, Walnut Street School

September

I'm learning how to read, like spelling, and read some books. My brother help me. When we get home, he bring some of his books and he let me read them—he's in third. I don't know what I'm going to learn next, but when I'm a grown-up, I read a magazine, like a newspaper. I think I be a poultry farmer, and he read so he can learn how to catch them when they get loose.

I'm learning how to write some books and some notes. My friends, Reggie and Nathan and David, they help me, like when you need a word, they'll tell you and spell it for you. I don't know what I'll learn next. When I'm a grown-up, I'll write some stories and write some books. I'll write some about a poultry farmer, like if they get lost you can go find it, write "chickens" and what street it was on.

December

I'm learning how to read books and how to read in your *Carousel* book and *Adventures* so you know how to read in newspapers. We supposed to read newspapers and listen to the news and you'll learn how to read. Sometime Van help, like every time when I don't know the word he tells me, and then we read and we tell what we like. I'm going to learn to read—when you get grown you can read to your children and read to the school children. You always got to try, and you get a bunch of books and read them. When I get grown up I read a newspaper and a magazine and some books, and when they say "STOP" on the highway, because if you go ahead, you probably have a wreck.

I'm learning how to do your [own] rap. If you don't know how to do your handwriting, somebody help you. Reggie helped me do some of my rap, Van and Drew help —Drew help me spell. I want to learn to write in cursive. Ms. Michalove help me, she teach me how to write in handwriting good. When I'm a grown-up, I'll write in cursive, and you can write stuff in newspapers and look in there and write down something you want and take it to the grocery—like a shopping list.

March

I'm learning how to read books. What I do, I look at the back and it has a pink part and I read it easy [gets Windmill set of pink books]. See, "The kitten grow [grew] into a cat. The puppy grow into a dog. . . . " Here, I can read this one too. "*Splish Splash* . . . " I know these words. I'm going to learn how to read a magazine, *TV*

Guide, if I go to school and learn. My teacher, my friends Reggie and David and Laneal help me. Sometimes I didn't know how to word it and Ricky helped me with some words. When I'm a grown-up, I'm going to read a magazine, and I can read newspaper and paperbacks, and those books with animals on it.

I'm learning to write stuff at home sometimes, and go home and find stuff to write at school, like when my dog jump over the fence. Sometime my friend Reggie and Ricky and Laneal help me. Sometime I ask them to spell a word and they spell it. Next I'm going to write about my cat—when he scratched my dog. My other dog got some puppies—I think ten. Because I know how to spell "cat," and sometimes I ask Ms. Michalove to help me. When I'm a grown-up I'll write what's on the news and people's phone number and stuff, and stuff for information, like when your child is sick, and fill in the application when you don't have a job.

June

We reading "The Little Red Hen" in Ms. Gibbons' [special education]. We finished, but we never got to this book [*Carousels*, the next basal after the one "The Little Red Hen" is in]. Sometime the teacher help me; she tell me, I don't know a word. I don't know what I'll learn next, but when I'm a grown-up, I read a newspaper and a magazine. I might have a job in a store, then I read the stuff on the cans.

I'm learning to spell all my words right—sometimes. Sometimes I write it back over; I look in a book or something. Reggie and Laneal and David and Kenton help, like when they read a story like the play, and I don't know a word, they tell me. Sometimes Nathan tell me. When I'm a grown-up I write a newspaper or a note; if somebody come and I ain't going to be here, just write a note on the door.

Third grade with Ms. Willis (August–February 6), Walnut Street School

I'm reading *Little Bear* [Minarik, 1957], and the Berenstain Bears, when they have a race and at the end the daddy wins, but at the beginning the little girl . . . [he continues with the rest of the story]. Sometime I skip some words. Sometime when I skip a word, Shannon come up and help me. I want to learn to go back and look at the first beginning letter and sound it out, just go back and look at the first letter, and then the second. When I'm grown up, I'll read magazines and newspapers like—I forgot what kind.

I'm writing long stories, like about my dog and my sister—my *brother* and my sister. Ms. Willis help me; if I have a word misspelled she tell me how to spell it. I'm going to write about Boys Club. Reggie and Benton can help me; sometimes they go there, and we can write about it. When I'm a grown-up, I'll write letters to peoples, like my uncle. And I'll fill out a application.

January

I learned to read some books with pink on the back in Ms. Gibbons'—one day can we go to her room and get a book? [We go to Ms. Gibbons' special education classroom and Lee selects several books; he reads *Ten Apples Up on Top* (Geisel, 1961) to JoBeth.] I learned how to read *Ten Apples Up on Top* because I practiced it and then when I start to know it, I start reading it. Bernard helped me some, he told me a word I didn't know. Next I want to read hard books. I'll sound the words out. Look at that, see, they got six apples here, then . . . [he explains the structure of the book]. No, I don't have no books at home.

I can write some stories. They helped, Reggie and Benton and them. We started talking about what we going to write, and then he write and I copy him and then they copy some too and then we get up and talk some like we did last time. I want to learn to write about something new, like how you get a job, and your phone number, and all that. I'll learn that by reading—read it and sign it and pay for it. When I'm grown up, I'll write in books, write a letter to the bank, or write a check. I might be a police, then we write any kind of papers you can sign.

Third grade with Ms. Smith (February 6–June), Walnut Street School

June

I'm learning to read books, like these kind [*Frog and Toad All Year* (Lobel, 1976)], and an informational book about animals. I read about the same as last year, but I read harder books this year. I'm learning by sounding words out, and put two words together and sound it out and put it all together. I want to learn to read the newspaper. My mama reads it, and reads magazines too. I don't know how I'll learn— you could ask your mama questions.

We ain't never wrote yet—we never write. I wrote a story about Teenage Mutant Ninja Turtles, and the two guinea pigs in Ms. Gibbons' room, they sister and brother. I did them by myself, we had to work by ourself. I don't know about next year, maybe I'll write books, like storybooks. Just use your brain, figuring—I don't know. When I grow up I'll read newspapers. I might be a policeman, like my uncle. He write a case and a wreck.

Fourth grade with Ms. Hales, Walnut Street School

November

I'm learning to read books, fun books. I like, I picked it at the library, Dr. Seuss, and I like H. A. Rey books—he got some good books. I like when Curious George got a rabbit for that boy. I'm sounding out the words; sometimes my student teacher helps. I want to read newspapers, but I don't know how I'm going to learn—maybe when I get a better listener; if I listen good I can read it back over. I'll read lots of stuff when I'm a grown-up. If you want a job you got to read a lot of questions; if you go to the hospital you got to fill stuff out.

I'm writing stories and poems. I wrote a song when we got our pen pal letters; I put it in my letter to my pen pal. Sometimes I copy my stories out of a book and change it back, make it different, like we did *The Giving Tree* [Silverstein, 1964]. We had four people, the boy, the tree, a dog, and the old man, and Stan wrote the boy and the old man and I wrote the tree and the dog part. Next, I don't know, I might write some books, little books like we got in the library. I'm going to get smarter and smarter. Me and Stan, he going to write the story and I'll write the pictures. And when I grow up I'm going to write books, storybooks about me and Stan, because we stay close together; he live close to me on the highway. We write *The Giving Tree*, we changed it. He wrote some funny parts and made everyone laugh when he said the little boy had a mustache; I told him to change it, but he didn't change the funny part. You want to read it?

February

I'm learning to read hard books, like a chapter book. Me and Stan were reading it. We going to write a story about the book. We going to write a poem, maybe jokes. We going to do like the [Fresh] Prince [of Belair] did, when they were cracking at each other. This book about the little mermaid; we were going to make it longer, but Stan said he didn't want to. I get my chapter books from Ms. Welty and Ms. Erdrich [special education teachers]. I got *Lady and the Tramp* at home. That's a good book, like when he ate the spaghetti. I read it by myself, but my brother Brandon like it too. I read the shorter pages, he read the long ones. He's smart; he always do his homework. I do mine at school.

Brandon always help me. When I don't know a word I used to know, he'll make up a sentence with it and I have to guess it. My mom, she ain't help this week, so I got my sister to pronounce the word out, and if I don't know it she'll say the word. If it don't make sense I go back and read it. I want to study magazines, like the *World Records*. I like *all* of them magazines. We just look at them, not read them. They come in the mail, I be the first one when they come. They're mostly about the ladies, like dresses—ain't no boys or men in them. I'll learn to read them by pronouncing the words out, or maybe have somebody read so you can read it back over.

When I'm a grown-up, I'll maybe read newspapers, your mail, the TV guide, magazines, books to your children, and when you make an appointment, read the information. And read the application for a job, and signs on the road, and the test so you can drive—my mom took one of those. She's been in the hospital, but she's coming home today. We stayed up to 1:15 watching TV—it was fun!

I don't write this year because whenever they do writing, I be gone. They be showing me some of their good stories. We write sometime in Ms. Welty's room. I got a story about a bunny. Sometimes we write what she say write, and sometimes we write what we want. She helps us; sometime when we ask what a word is, we write it in our spelling dictionary. I want to be a author. It's fun—you get an award, and you feel good, and you want to keep writing. Stan say *my* story good: "The Wish Washer Man." See, he going to a dance contest, and he was wish washing everyone, and twisting and dancing, and the announcer say, "The winner is the Wish Washer man!" Stan wrote it in cursive. I wrote it, and he wrote it back over in cursive. You got to go back over and check your writing, like Ms. Hales say. She'll mark it if it need correcting.

We wrote to Saudi Arabia, but we ain't got it back yet. I hope I get some money from him; Ronald did. They say the war be over soon. My daddy's son over there. My daddy didn't want him to go. When I'm a grown-up, I'm going to write peoples. Like when you taking a check to the bank, you write how much you put in or take out, or if you borrowing from the government, like my daddy borrowed some.

June

I'm reading more books, just reading books. I sound out words and skip them and go to the other words and come back and read it over. Once you get to the other word, you can come back and get what that word is. The teacher that was working with me, she help me a lot, Ms. Morrison. I want to learn how to read the fifth grade book, the harder one. I'll read magazines and newspapers when I grow up.

I'm writing a ballet thing in the classroom. I finished mine. We writing to these people somewhere, so we telling them how we do the ballet, what it all about. We had one Friday; I was the set designer. Ms. Hale start us off, and we looked at a movie of a ballet and we put one on: "How the Dachshund Got Its Long Body"—he got stuck in a tree hole. We write with Ms. Erdrich, we just making up stories, fairy tale stories. Sometime we look at the books and change them around, like the witch to a wizard or any kind of evil person, or the *four* bears, with two Goldilocks, two baby bears, one papa and the mother. I took it home because Thomas didn't want it. We did it together; he drew the pictures. One of the baby bears had a cat he found in a tree, the other baby bear just kept shaking the tree, and the two Goldilocks. . . . [He told the whole story.]

I want to write like a author, a book reporter. Maybe I'll write fairy tale books. We can have a little group teamed up together and we can write different kinds of books. When I'm grown up, I can send off letters to other countries. I be a police, and write some mysteries and stuff.

TWENTY-FIVE

"You Always Got to Try"

Lee in Second Grade at Walnut Street School

Lee's motto seemed to be what he told us in his December interview: "You always got to try!" It remains a mystery to me (Barbara) how Lee developed this positive attitude. Many people would have become defeated by the difficulties Lee faced.

Lee was a premature baby, weighing three pounds at birth. He lived with his alcoholic mother until he was two years old. He was removed from her home, along with his six siblings, for neglect. He was returned after a brief period, then taken away again. Lee lived with the Walkers, a gentle, caring older couple who have been foster parents for numerous children with severe problems. They struggled to make ends meet. Many times Lee came to school in clothes that were inappropriate for the weather; he did not have a winter coat. But he did have a parent at every teacher conference, as did the other children in the family.

At the time Lee was in my classroom the Walkers had six foster children, all between six and eight years old. Three of these children were staffed into special education programs at our school; two of the children were Lee's biological brothers. Earlier, an older brother was removed from the foster home for sexually molesting some of the younger children, including Lee's younger brother. Lee repeatedly told the story of watching the police shoot another teenage brother. His foster mother said it was never clarified if the death was a police shooting or suicide. Lee visited his natural mother briefly once or twice a month.

In spite of the numerous difficulties Lee experienced in his home life he was an open, loving little boy. He was generous and always willing to share whatever he had, many times giving away his possessions. If he brought a snack to school, he always shared it with a friend. When he came back to our classroom from his special education class with a sticker or piece of candy, he frequently gave it to one of his friends.

Lee moved to Walnut Street in first grade, after spending two years in kindergarten at another school. At this time he was staffed MIMH (mildly mentally handicapped) and spent two hours a day in a resource room. He continued this schedule in second grade.

When we began to identify the children we worried about the most, Lee was at the top of the list. His mentally handicapped status created some of the concern. He functioned several years below the majority of the students in reading and writing. Information from his first-grade teacher increased our questions about how a whole language classroom would affect Lee. Ms. Clifton described

FIG. 25-1 *Lee's First Attempt at Writing*

him as a very shy child. He wouldn't talk or participate in class activities in first grade; he couldn't write his name or recognize any letters of the alphabet; he didn't seem to understand anything about reading. She feared with his limited intelligence that he would never learn to read.

I was ambivalent about including Lee in our study. We had not discussed the possibility of studying mentally handicapped students, and I wasn't so sure it was a good idea. I had lots of questions. What if he didn't grow as a learner? How much progress was Lee actually capable of making, regardless of the type of instruction he received? What would it mean for me, as a whole language teacher, if he made little progress? I didn't know what to do about Lee. Since I had taught kindergarten previously, this was the first year I had children in my classroom who were staffed MIMH (Lee and Wendy). Lee didn't recognize many letters of the alphabet. In fact when I saw his first attempt at writing, shown in Figure 25-1, I wondered if he differentiated words and drawings.

I had observed other teachers using dittos to keep students like Lee busy and working on the skills they needed. Dittos didn't seem very exciting to me; I rarely used them with the other students and felt uncomfortable with this option. I had no experience to help me know what would be best for Lee. Although I had confidence that a whole language approach would benefit the other children in the classroom, I wasn't so sure about a mentally handicapped child.

Even though I wasn't sure it was the best decision, I decided to include Lee in our reading and writing workshops. I did not supplement with alphabet recognition activities. From the start of school I expected him to be a contributing member of our community. I had no idea if Lee would learn in this environment, or how much progress he was capable of making. However, I knew that he had not made a great deal of progress the previous year in the basal system. I wanted Lee to be included in our literate community, not excluded because of his limited abilities. I felt that even though he was labeled MIMH, he had unique ideas and knowledge to add to our classroom.

Lee received extra help with reading in his special education classroom. In fact his resource teacher was responsible for his instruction in the basal reader. It seemed like a type of insurance for me. Even if he didn't make progress in our program, he would be getting traditional reading instruction.

As we observed him over the first months of school we were amazed at the ease with which he became part of the community. We began to wonder if he was really retarded.

Lee as a member of the literate community

Lee's first writings shocked and concerned me. His drawings seemed to be immature and to demonstrate a lack of small muscle control (see Figure 25-1). He appeared to have no concept of print representing language. However, through the interviews we learned of Lee's knowledge of the wide variety of purposes for reading and writing as an adult. He told us he would "write some stories and some books, write a shopping list, write people's phone numbers and stuff for information, fill in applications to get a job and write some about if your chickens get lost, write 'chickens' and what street it was on."

He told us when he grew up he would "read a magazine and a newspaper. Read to his children. Read when they say STOP on the highway, because if you go ahead, you probably have a wreck. Read books and the TV guide." Lee knew there were real reasons to learn to read and write. Perhaps having these reasons helped him to keep trying. He never gave up.

"My friends help me write"

Because of Lee's limitations I had imagined that his role in collaborations would be limited. This was not the case. When composing a piece with Reggie in September Lee told him, "Write LL Cool J." Reggie wrote "Lli." Lee said "No, that's a 'i.'" Reggie replied "Okay, you write it." Lee wrote another "L," then said "Oh yea! Now 'cool.'" When Laneal joined our class in mid-October Lee assumed a teaching role to help him understand how we organized our writing folders. He told him, "Erase that, that's just for topics. You write your story on other paper."

Even though Lee's writing skills were immature he received support and encouragement from the other students. In September he wrote a book that was illustrated with little shutters opening for animal cages, like a book I had shared recently with the class. The letters he wrote had little relation to what he read when he shared it with the class. He read, "I can see some bears. I can see dog. I can see lion. I can see pig. Any questions?" David asked, "What you going to name your title?" Lee responded, "I don't know." He called on Sarah who said, "I know a title—I Can See." The children were accepting Lee's writing as it was, yet encouraging him to add more by their questions and suggestions.

By the middle of October we began to see that Lee was developing concepts about sound-symbol correspondence. He asked JoBeth how to spell "die," then told her, "I got the 'D.'" When she asked him what sound is next he replied, "E?" She encouraged him to say it slowly; he did, then said "I!" He read his story to her. "I had a dog. It died. Oh,'T.'" He added "T" to his spelling of died. He wrote "I ya a bog si dit."

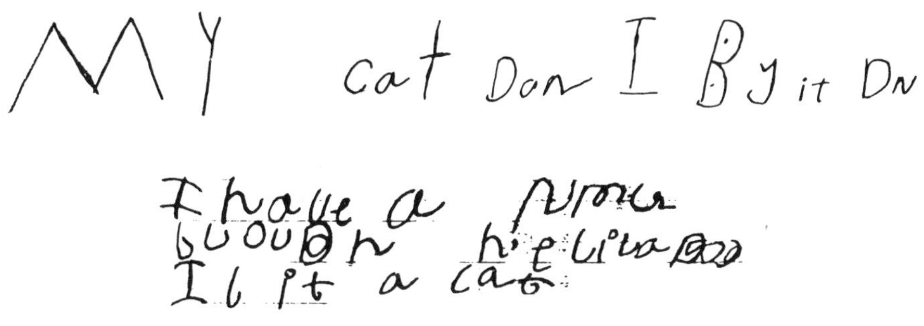

My cat died. I buried it. The End.

I have a new brother. He like a dog. I like a cat.

FIG. 25-2 *Lee's Progress*

When Wendy came over to ask how to spell Nikia, Lee readily told her "N." Later that same day he asked Vanessa how to spell Katherine. They wrote "Krn." As we observed Lee using the people resources in the community to get the help he needed, and supplying help to other students, we found that he was participating in our community of learners in the same way as the "regular" students, at times in the role of learner, at other times becoming a teacher.

Throughout the fall we saw Lee using his growing list of sight words and letter sounds in his writings. We observed him rereading as he wrote, erasing to edit, correcting the word sequence and trying to write in cursive. The results illustrated how far he had come in such a short time (see Figure 25-2).

Lee worked with other children all year long. Fredrick was one student he worked with frequently in reading and writing. They easily reversed roles in their work together. In April Fredrick asked Lee, "How do you spell animals?" Lee pointed to the bulletin board and said, "Up there." Lee continued his writing about lions. He wrote: "Wa BiT peirl and run Wa Will BiT Peirl I will sho the LioNs." (They bite people and run. They will bite people. I will shoot the lions.) When he read it aloud Fredrick reached over and added "t" to "sho."

Lee also became involved in various group attempts at writing. Reggie, Lee, and Laneal worked together often. They wrote about shared experiences at the Boys Club and wrote some plays. At the beginning of the year Lee participated in the verbal composing, then copied his friends' writing as best he could. As his writing skills improved he collaborated in the written products as well as the oral composing. By spring he began attempting to write his part for a play by himself. He wrote, "You stolt my child and my cot and my big fi T: it wht a tfi t v." (You stole my child and my car and my big (?), it was a (?) TV.) By the end of the school year he was able to write the following script on his own: "I cit the cops in the face and I blwow away Reggie hrad and they put me and the elaktrk chir. (I hit the cops in the face and I blowed away Reggie's head and they put me in the electric chair.)

By the beginning of May Lee had reached a new place with his writing (see Figure 25-3). Physically he had more control of his pencil. He also wanted the

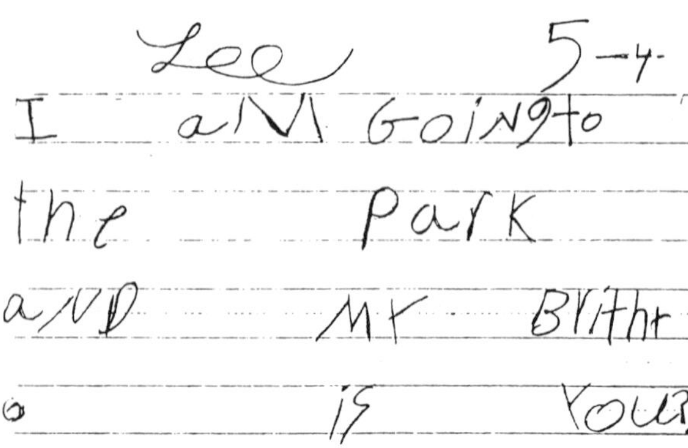

FIG. 25-3 *"I Am Going to the Park"*

words to be "right" and would get stumped when trying to write because he didn't know how to spell a word. He told us in the June interview, "I'm learning to spell all my words right, sometimes. Sometimes I write it back over. I look in a book or something."

Other children included Lee and listened to his responses during sharing time. He had a lot of good questions and ideas. He recalled seeing Kentucky Fried Chicken on a city map when someone asked how to spell Kentucky. When Drew and Norris struggled to perform Norris' play Lee told them, "Somebody else needs to be Santa, and Norris need to read it. Y'all need to practice, this don't make sense!" When they didn't respond he told them very directly, "Norris, you should read and Drew should be Santa."

Lee saw his friends as very important in learning how to write. He told us this in the interviews. He mentioned them each time and told how they helped him. He told us, "My friends help me when I don't know how to spell a word. They help me with my handwriting and help me do my rap. I write stuff at home sometimes, and I go home and find stuff to write at school."

"I'm going to learn to read"

Lee listened attentively when I read to the class. He liked books and hoarded them in his desk. You could always find a stack of books in there. The kids would search his desk when we were looking for missing books.

Lee's friends were also important to him as a reader. He told us this in the interviews and we observed him reading with various friends throughout the year. Although Lee was at a picture-governed stage of emergent reading (Sulzby, 1985) when he entered our classroom, he had not turned off as a reader or exhibited the kinds of defeat many struggling readers do after three unsuccessful years in school. He was interested in books and joined other children to listen to stories during reading workshop. He chose books that were interesting but much too hard for him. He would carefully study the pictures and tell a story about the pictures. At the end of September he showed a lot of interest in the book *Dear Zoo* (Campbell, 1982).

He took his book and sat next to Thomas, a competent reader. Thomas read the book while Lee listened attentively.

Lee began to choose some easy books to read with his friend Reggie. Reggie was able to help him on the words he didn't recognize. He became quite confident with a few of these books and even read one to the whole class. When someone asked him to read the last page, which was a summary with no picture clues, he did with the help of his classmates.

At the beginning of October Lee began to use the listening center. It was his favorite activity and he listened to favorite stories over and over. He liked sharing this activity with friends, and they helped him by being sure he had the correct tape for the story. Lee listened and listened and listened. He became very involved with the stories, often commenting aloud, warning a character that something was about to happen, joining in a song, or commenting loudly as he listened to *Stone Soup* (McGovern, 1986), "MMM-mmm, that soup sure smells good!"

Because this repeated storybook reading seemed so important I encouraged his intense engagement, even at times other than reading workshop. Initially, Lee was not following along in the texts; listening was pure enjoyment. I showed him how to turn the tape over so the beeps would let him know when to turn the page. He continued to spend a lot of time at the listening center, eventually following along in the texts.

Although by mid-October we had observed Lee using letter sounds correctly in his writing, it was the end of November before he began to apply this skill to his reading. He had chosen *Perfect, the Pig* (Jeschke, 1980) to read. It was a hard book, and he struggled to read it to JoBeth, using sounds of first letters, the story line, and the pictures for help. He sometimes looked at the pictures to invent appropriate text, then tried to match print. His eyes went back and forth between pictures and print. He read familiar words correctly and monitored himself saying, "I don't know this word, is this 'house' or 'home'?" and "What's that word? It looks like Kent's name."

Lee read the book for twenty-five minutes. At the end of the period he turned to his neighbor to tell about the story. He said, "It's about a pig. He got wings and he can fly away. That man, where that part? See, this that man that stole the pig. The pig tried to get away. He finally got loose." Vanessa, a competent reader, said, "I love that story, but I don't like to read it because it's too hard."

I rarely heard Lee say, "It's too hard." He seemed to believe that if he kept trying he would learn. He never gave up or got frustrated with himself. In the December interview he told JoBeth, "I'm going to learn to read. You always got to try. You get a bunch of books and read them." Lee kept on trying. As he became a more capable reader his interest in reading increased. One day in December on the way to recess he asked me, "Ms. Michalove, when we come back in are we going to be able to read our books?"

As Lee became a reader his role with his classmates changed from just listening to them read to reading along with them. In March we observed him reading with Reggie. Lee corrected Reggie several times on mispronounced words. He now joined groups of children reading multiple copies of books together. When he read with a friend he read as much as he listened. He read *Little Bear* with Vanessa; she helped him on one or two words per page. Once she just pointed to a word he missed that confused him. He read twenty-one pages with very little help. She quietly listened and read a word when he paused long enough or asked for help.

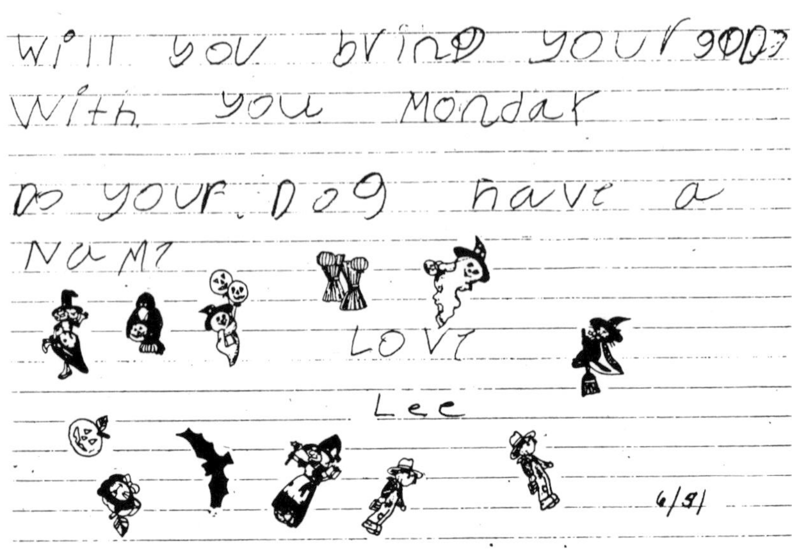

"will you bring you god [dog] with you Monday Do your Dog have a nam?"

FIG. 25–4 *October Letter to Pen Pal*

He also began to be a leader within a small group. He read a book that had a recipe and directions for making "kooky clay." He asked me if they could make it. I told him as long as they brought the ingredients it would be okay. He organized a few children, made sure they had everything they needed, then followed the recipe in the book. Pretty good for a mentally handicapped boy who his teachers feared would never learn to read!

In fact it was so good we began to wonder if someone with limited mental abilities could really make this much progress in nine months. We began to wonder if Lee was really mentally handicapped. This was quite a lot of progress, from poorly controlled drawings to the letter to his pen pal in Figure 25–4.

"Can I read to your class?"

Here was a child who barely talked all of first grade, yet from the very first day of second grade dared to stand up in front of the class and share his writing. He composed without hesitation during writing workshop. I wasn't sure he was really aware of how different his writings were from the other students. However, when Lee was the only child in the class who didn't want a pen pal I realized that he was not oblivious to how different his writing looked from the other children. When we asked him why he didn't want a pen pal he told us it was because he couldn't write. But when the letters arrived he took a letter addressed to Robert, crossed out Robert's name, and wrote his own.

I can see a cat.
I can see a dog.
I can see a h...

FIG. 25-5 *October Story*

Once again he took the risk of attempting to do something that he knew would not be easy. It wasn't. His pen pal had a very difficult time understanding his letters. He did not use letter form and to her seemed to be writing random letters for words; actually, his pen-pal letter is similar to his written stories around this time (see Figure 25-5).

By the fifth letter she began to be able to read Lee's writing. He had begun to imitate her letters. He asked her questions and told her a little about himself. He used question marks correctly in some of the letters. He was really trying to communicate. She wrote to him about Thanksgiving, telling him that her grandmother came to her house. He responded, "Dea Lea I like Piz Do you yes r no I hm go o ym Grandma Love Lee." (Dear Lea I like pizza. Do you? yes or no I am going over my grandma Love Lee.)

The pen pal letters were different from the other writing we did in our classroom. All the other times that the children communicated with writing they were right there with the audience to clarify things for the reader. With the pen pal letters they had to accomplish this totally with print. This was a challenge for all of the students, and especially for Lee. He stuck with it and chose to have a new pen pal the following quarter. She was able to decipher his letters from the start. His first four letters were written in the same form. They contained a statement and a question. Twice he answered the questions himself. In the other letters he wrote "yes or no" with little boxes next to the words so his pen pal could respond.

On one letter Lee included colons between each of the words. I had noticed that he did this in his other writing at this time. When I asked him why he put these marks between words he said, "So there's room between the words. That

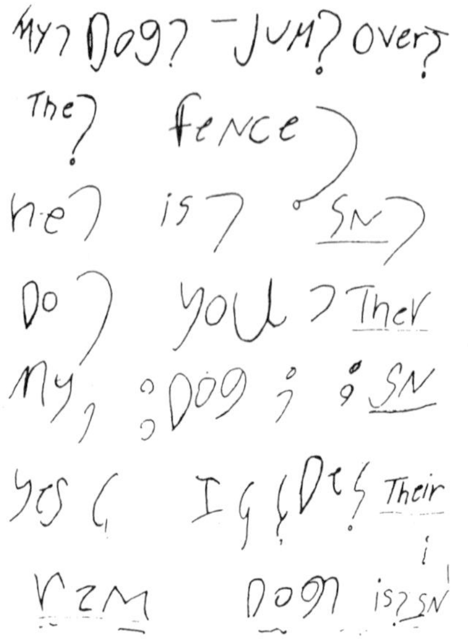

My dog jumped over the fence. He is superman. Do you think my dog is superman? Yes, I does. Their ? dog is superman.

[The underlined words are words that Lee underlined himself after I directed the class to underline words they thought were misspelled; someone had already helped him correct "their."]

FIG. 25–6 *March Writing*

goes between the words." He also chose a piece of writing to publish in March that included punctuation marks between each word (see Figure 25–6).

When his pen pal helped him edit his writing she asked him why one question mark was after each word. He told her, "Those aren't question marks, they're things. That is so I know where my words are and I won't be lost." When she copied his story for him, at his request, she asked him if she should include the marks. He said, "No, I don't want you to, just move your hand over." Lee understood the concept of spacing and was on the edge of understanding the convention.

During winter quarter we took a field trip to the university to visit with our pen pals. JoBeth and I scheduled the time so that the kids and their pen pals had an hour to explore campus and an hour to read a book together; the pen pals were also to help the children revise and edit one of their writing pieces for publication. We were studying about different jobs in the community so the kids, with their pen pals' help, interviewed at least one worker as they explored the campus. It was a wonderful field trip, especially for Lee.

Lee and his pen pal Missie waited for the bus. When the bus arrived it was very crowded so Lee asked a campus police officer, who had stopped behind the bus, if he would give them a ride. He agreed to give them a ride, and even turned on his siren and lights for them. This would have been exciting for any second grader; for Lee it had a special meaning.

His concept of the police included his belief that a police officer shot his older brother. In fact he asked the campus police officer if he had ever shot anybody. (He hadn't.) He also asked him the interview questions to find out what he did in his job. Not only did Lee have an exciting ride in a police car, he widened his ideas about police in general.

Dear Missie I like the police man
when he turned on the siren

FIG. 25–7 *March Pen-Pal Letter*

When we wrote to our pen pals next, Lee produced his neatest writing to tell Missie something he liked about the field trip. It had been important for him and his writing reflected this feeling. The letter was the greatest effort I had seen him make with his writing. I was delighted with how far his drawing and writing had come (see Figure 25–7) since the beginning of school.

Lee had been so unsure of his writing ability at the beginning of our pen pal correspondence that he hadn't even wanted one. Even though he had made so much progress, he continued to feel like he wasn't good at writing. He told his new pen pal in April, "I don't write too good." He also told her he loved having pen pals. Lee's pen pal was surprised when she received his first letter. She wondered "how he could be in second grade, because she had so much trouble reading his writing." I knew the whole story and wondered, once again, how a retarded child could make this much progress since September. He began all of his letters with "Dear Sharon." He told her things about himself and his family. He left space between each word. He spelled the majority of the words correctly. He closed with "From Lee" or "Love Lee." Without Lee's willingness to take risks and his "you always got to try" attitude I doubt he would have come so far.

This optimism and perseverence served him well in learning to read also. While at the beginning of the year he mostly listened to other children read and looked at books, Lee discovered, through his repeated story sessions at the tape player, that by reading a book numerous times he could read it independently. He chose these well-learned books when he first began to read with friends, rather than just listen to them read. He read these familiar books with friends, accepting help when he needed it.

He branched out and began practicing other books, working on one book for weeks at a time until he could read it fluently. One of his favorites was *Little Bear*. After practicing it for weeks he asked if he could read it to his former first-grade teacher's class. Lee wrote Ms. Clifton a letter to arrange an appointment, chose a part of the book he thought the younger kids would enjoy, and practiced with me for several days. He received a reply and then remembered to go when I was not there to remind him. Ms. Clifton reported, with tears in her eyes, that this child who had not spoken in front of the class one time last year and who she feared would never learn to read or write had read the book confidently to her whole class.

TWENTY-SIX

"I Bet You Need a Hug"

Lee in Third Grade at Walnut Street School

with Teachers Susan Willis and Judy Smith

On the first day of school Lee was at a court hearing until 10:30. He walked in, saw that everyone was reading, and immediately chose a book. He sat down by Ricky and began reading aloud—well. He was again an important member of the literate community, learning with and from his friends. The stability of this structure, including the assumptions that he was responsible for his own learning within it and was a full member of the classroom, seemed to give Lee the support he needed. Although initially he had trouble thinking of three possible topics on that first day, he wrote down "movies," "camping," and "summer" after conferring with Susan. Four school days later he had fourteen topics on his list, and Susan used it in her minilesson on topic lists. He wrote about his life (see Figure 26–1), especially about his dogs and cats (see Figure 26–2); he worked hard at editing his writing.

At the end of the year Susan and Judy agreed that "Lee was always accepted as a member of the group. Other kids seemed to recognize that some things were difficult for him, and they encouraged his efforts." Lee himself wrote, "My classmates are *good to me*" on the questionnaire ("Something about Me").

A scene from the January 23 reading workshop demonstrates two of Lee's intersecting strengths: (1) he learned a great deal from his peers, and (2) he was a hard worker, so he did not become dependent on others to read or write for him. For example, one day Lee chose a book about a boy's birthday. Karen insisted on helping him read it. She read many words for him when he paused to figure them out, words that he might have gotten, given more time. She also put her finger over words to get him to focus on beginning sounds, a technique she may have learned in some other class. Lee remained unperturbed and persistent in his reading. He did not become dependent on her "reader's welfare" system but tried every word himself. Finally he did ask for "trike," after which she tried to read the whole story for him. He patiently kept reading at his own slower pace. She eventually stopped reading and helped only when he paused. He accepted her help, even though he had not asked for it, and she accepted him as a reader, although a bit condescendingly. This interaction was typical of Lee's perseverance with books

---

Although neither teacher was able to write this chapter, both contributed through observational notes, writing samples, weekly data analysis sessions, and feedback on drafts of the chapters. JoBeth is the author.

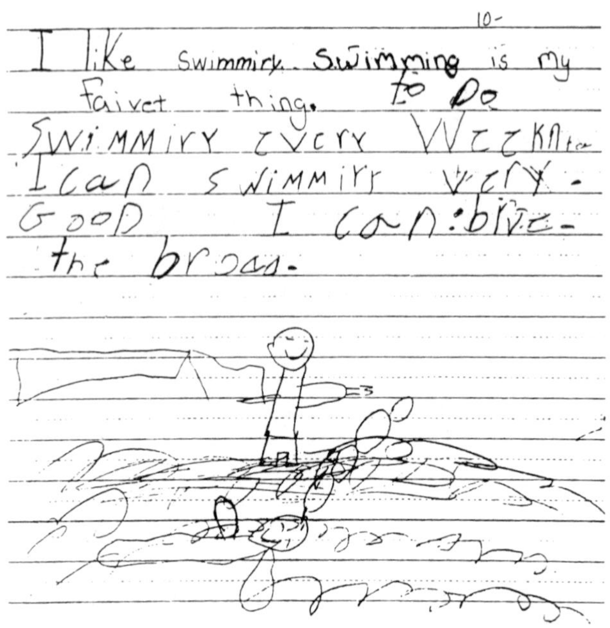

FIG. 26–1 *Swimming Story*

DOG is BiG.
therr: Get petoel.
therr vun at.
cat.
I LiKe MY DOG.
MY DOG is BiG
black and white.
Be a GOOD DOG
said Lee.

FIG. 26–2 *Dog Story*

that were very difficult for him but that he was interested in and insisted on reading. He learned to read several books in which, on initial reading, he knew barely half the words.

"I learned how to read . . . because I practiced it"

Lee's perseverance was especially effective in his becoming a real reader. He continued the pattern he had developed in second grade of repeated readings, a pattern he seemed to have internalized from listening to endless replayings of read-along tapes. We speculated that one reason he was willing to work so hard to read was that he loved stories. When we interviewed most of the children about what they were learning as readers, they told us about various aspects of the process. Lee always told us about the books, often recounting in detail the story line, aspects about individual characters, and his favorite parts, especially humorous ones. He often chose the group he would read with based on the book they were reading rather than who was in the group; we didn't notice this with any other focal children.

Both Susan and Judy noted how much Lee loved to be read to. Susan added, "If he wasn't doing something else, Lee always enjoyed getting a familiar book out." He often read in Ms. Gibbons' special education class and brought books from her room to his own, as he did mid-September with *Frog and Toad*. It was a favorite from last year and he wanted Susan to read it (she did, after "practicing it" at home). Even when he was experiencing real difficulty in the classroom after Judy became the teacher, and they both came to value the time he spent with Ms. Gibbons, he asked to stay and listen to another chapter of *The Boxcar Children*.

Perhaps because "the story" was so important to Lee, he often monitored his reading. Several times when he chose a book that was much too difficult for him, he exchanged it for one he could understand. Throughout the year, many of his miscues allowed him to keep the meaning, and frequently the structure, of the text. He self-corrected more as the year went on, especially on words that affected the meaning of the story. His interview responses (see Chapter 24) show Lee's awareness of his own strategies. In November he talked about skipping words but wanting to be able to go back and figure them out. In January he explained, "I practiced it and then when I start to know it, I start reading it." While he saw decoding as a letter-by-letter process in November, he was talking about putting words together by June. In interviews up to this time he had talked about selecting easy books; now he knew he was reading harder books.

One such book was *Anna Banana and Me* by Lenore Blegvad (1985). For several weeks in March and April he read the book daily. He read it to Judy (who was the teacher by then), he read it to Ms. Gibbons, he read it to JoBeth; he even begged to read it to Susan one day when she visited her old classroom. She was—we all were—impressed. On April 3 he chose (what else!) *Anna Banana* to read during his quarterly reading/interview session. He was, after all these weeks, still excited about the book. He read for over twenty minutes without seeming to tire. He still had numerous miscues, but self-corrected about one in four (e.g., "shouts" to "calls," "get" to "grabs," "hold his" to "hear her"). Uncorrected miscues included words like "underneath" (under), "comes" (came), and "playground" (park) that maintained the general meaning. There were several uncorrected miscues that did not make sense (such as "reaches" for "where" and "see" for "shall"), but on several of these he looked quizzically at JoBeth. At one point he skipped a page, began the next one, then realized he had missed something and read the page he had missed. At the end, he gave an excellent summation of the story.

The first week of school, when Susan had the children read to her individually and read lists of sight words, Lee had read only seventeen out of forty words from

My Dinosaur's Day at the Park

by Elizabeth Winthrop

My pet dinosaur got in trouble
When we went for a walk in the park.
I took off his leash and let him run free.
He didn't come back until dark.

He ate up the new row of oak trees
(The gardener was fit to be tied).
Then he stopped in the playground and bent down his head
And the kids used his neck for a slide.

He knocked down the fence by the boat pond
With a swing of his twenty-foot tail;
When he stopped to explain he was sorry,
His legs blocked the bicycle trail.

When the sun set, my dino got worried;
He's always been scared of the dark.
He sat down on the ground and started to cry.
His tears flooded out, the whole park.

A friend of mine rowed his boat over
When he heard my pet dino's sad roar.
He showed him the way home to my house
And helped him unlock the front door.

He's a loveable, lumbering fellow
But after my pet had his spree,
They put up a sign in the park and it reads,
NO DINOS ALLOWED TO RUN FREE.

FIG. 26-3 *First Week of School Reading*

the first two preprimer lists. He attempted five lines of the 3.1 "Dinosaur" passage, with 50 percent word recognition; in April, on the same passage, he read the entire poem with 68 percent word recognition and a thorough gist of the story (see Figures 26-3 and 26-4).

My Dinosaur's Day at the Park

by Elizabeth Winthrop

My pet dinosaur got in trouble
When we went for a walk in the park.
I took off his leash and let him run free.
He didn't come back until dark.

He ate up the new row of oak trees
(The gardener was fit to be tied).
Then he stopped in the playground and bent down his head
And the kids used his neck for a slide.

He knocked down the fence by the boat pond
With a swing of his twenty-foot tail;
When he stopped to explain he was sorry,
His legs blocked the bicycle trail.

When the sun set, my dino got worried;
He's always been scared of the dark.
He sat down on the ground and started to cry.
His tears flooded out the whole park.

A friend of mine rowed his boat over
When he heard my pet dino's sad roar.
He showed him the way home to my house
And helped him unlock the front door.

He's a loveable, lumbering fellow
But after my pet had his spree,
They put up a sign in the park and it reads,
NO DINOS ALLOWED TO RUN FREE.

FIG. 26–4 *April Reading*

"You always got to try"

We wondered how Lee developed the perseverance to read a difficult book for weeks until he learned it, to write his pen pal regularly, to read and write with peers who were more advanced. As was true of the other children (except Jeremiah), he seemed to take more risks when he felt more competent. He liked to read to the class during sharing, but never did so until he had practiced the section to near fluency. When he had a story or other work of which he was particularly proud, he often posted it on the bulletin board. When he wrote to his pen pal he took special pains to get someone to help him with the spelling and other editing concerns, as he did in this midyear letter to Susie (see Figure 26–5).

We marveled at how Lee became a risk taker through circumstances that most people would find totally defeating. We learned from his caseworker that his father had committed suicide; that the brother Lee thought had been shot by the police had actually shot himself when the police tried to arrest him, rather than return to prison; that several family members had been incarcerated for sex offenses; and that his birth mother was only allowed to visit the children once a month for two hours.

Lee didn't talk about his birth family. Mama and Daddy were his foster parents, the Walkers, and the children in that household were his brothers and sisters. The Walkers may have been a big part of why Lee was both loving and risk taking. They had taken in children for years and provided a loving home for them as long as they were needed, often until the children were on their own. They came to every conference for every child in their home. They took the children to Sandy Creek Nature Center for their spring break workshops and to day camp every summer. Lee did not miss one day of school. During the fall parent-teacher conference, Mr. Walker talked about how Lee had really settled down. "When he and [his brother] first came to us, they were really wild. I took him to the doctor—he's a little bit off, his mind wanders off," he volunteered, with obvious love and acceptance. Lee also spoke lovingly of his mama and daddy, noting in his interviews that his mama read the newspaper and magazines, and she could help him learn to read them, too. Once, when he had taken home a good behavior report from Judy, he returned the next day with a big grin. "My mama was real proud of me."

"I don't know how I'll learn"

But Lee seemed to need stability, as well as a feeling of competence, to take risks. The first day of Susan's first long-term absence, Lee gave the substitute a very hard time and ended up in timeout the next day. Ms. Gibbons noticed increased behavior problems and lack of engagement the whole time Susan was home sick, but told her on January 9 that he was doing better since she was back, and not only in his behavior. His reading seemed to have made another move forward. A month later Judy became the teacher and saw both behavior and academic problems.

"Lee seemed to regress almost back to the beginning. He didn't write a word the first day I taught. Then I would get maybe one sentence from him during writing workshop. He often missed writing because of Ms. Gibbons' class; when he came back in the middle of it, he would often just read quietly, rather than start writing something. When I made a point to work with him individually, then he wrote. I spent more time with him than any other student because he worked so much better one-on-one. By the end of the year he seemed to be writing again."

The situation deteriorated. After eight days of teaching Judy said in frustration, "I've lost all control of Lee. He has such an awful mouth—every other word out of his mouth today was 'nigger.' He's been really aggressive with everyone; he

Dear: Susie
Did You bave
a good vacation?
I DiD have a good
time.
Me and MY BoYG twenD
out. I read a good
book abor Go Dog

FIG. 26-5 *Lee's Letter to Susie*

even got into a fistfight with Ricky in PE (a new teacher in there, too). He was sent to Ms. Gibbons for the rest of the day."

February 13 was a typical day for this time period, although totally atypical for the previous year and a half. By 10:09 Lee's clothespin was already on red (in Judy's new discipline system red indicated sitting out for five minutes of recess). Judy divided the children into three groups to do rotating tasks: math pages from that morning, figuring out word meanings from context clues, and working with a partner scouring the newspaper to find ten describing words, action words, compound words, and a sentence with three commas. Lee's group was assigned to the newspaper. He yelled at Portia, "Get out of my chair!" as he kicked the empty chair next to his. He and Marcus began looking at the newspaper and laughed over a lingerie ad. "That's a ugly woman," Lee commented, drawing on several of the pictures. He wrote down the phone number on the lingerie ad. "I'm going to call her," he boasted, then tore the number up, saying, "She ain't got (?)" Some children were reading the paper; others were searching for words and writing them down. Lee and Marcus were writing words for their adjectives (big, score, rose), when Lee yelled at Lynn, who was trying to look at his paper, "*Put* my paper down —I'll tear this paper up—you stupid!" Marcus warned, "Teacher going to get you." He and Lee pretended to fight. Marcus read, "Lakers." Lee spelled, "L-a- " and then drew a big line across his paper. "We need one more," he said, pulling Marcus's hair. He quickly copied "her" and shouted, "We finished!" Judy came over to help his group. When she realized that they were not writing describing words, she had the whole class stop and asked his group to fold their newspapers. Lee laughed and threw his paper on the table. Judy asked him again, and he folded it carelessly.

Judy told his group to move to the math worksheets. He and Marcus crawled under a table; a female voice wailed, "Ow, Lee!" Lee copied answers off Marcus's paper, until they got into an argument about Lee cheating. "Go get the second sheet," Marcus commanded. "God, nigger, get this junk up. Take this chalkboard, I don't need it!" Lee retorted, throwing the chalkboard down.

It was time to move to the third group. Lee got into an argument with Tanya during the switch. Judy helped Lee and Marcus read the first two sentences, then moved on. "I read all down here, nigger, you better read . . . " at which point they burst into a wrestling match. Again Judy helped them read, providing pronunciations for words like "disregarded" and "illusion." "Quit kicking me, Lee," Tammy complained. Lee and Marcus continued reading, alternating sentences, with Lee missing about a third of the words but trying each one. Miraculously, he figured out all seven of the word meanings anyway, including "eagerly" and "astonish." Judy had been sitting with them; she left to help another group. Tabitha walked by and Lee threatened, "Girl, I knock you down, you keep stepping on my stuff." Judy called for the class to clean up. Lee growled at Lynn, "Get your stuff out of my way, I knock your head off." He kicked at Tammy.

It was the first time in fourteen months of observation that we had seen this angry, aggressive behavior and language. As the weeks wore slowly on for all concerned, JoBeth noticed that Lee became more physically affectionate with her. Many of the kids hugged her each week when she visited; Lee had been only an occasional hugger. The moments of affection became more frequent throughout March. Toward the end of April they met by surprise in the hall, and Lee wrapped his arms around her. "I bet you need a hug!" he predicted. We suspect he hadn't been getting a lot of hugs himself recently, at least at school.

"Lee really does have a loving streak," Judy pointed out. "He really misses Susan. He seems to live for the time he can leave the room and go to Ms. Gibbons'." As a child staffed for special education, Lee could be sent to Ms. Gibbons at any time. Many of the substitutes chose this option of dealing with him, as did Judy on several occasions when he was disrupting the whole class. Ms. Gibbons was the most stable aspect of Lee's school life. They had worked together for three years. They were even together during the summers because Ms. Gibbons made special arrangements for Lee to attend the nature camp where she worked. She loved Lee, and Lee loved Ms. Gibbons. Being sent to her room when things were not going well for him in some other part of the school was not a punishment, but a safe haven. Lee seemed to push people as far as he needed to get sent to her room.

Another safe haven was Barbara's room. When she learned of Lee's difficulties with the succession of substitutes in December, she left word that Lee was welcome in her room anytime. The grateful substitutes sent him earlier and earlier in the day, with a note such as, "Lee has worked really well today and has earned the rest of the day in your room." Barbara really liked having him there. He was never a behavior problem, he knew the routines and participated fully, and he fit in well academically. The school had just created "families" of teachers and students to provide more stability for the students (see Chapter 3 for further explanation); in this case, Lee's extended family worked out an alternative that benefitted everyone.

An additional upheaval in the children's schedule during this period was the preparation for and taking of the state-mandated Criterion Referenced Test (CRT). Judy and Ms. Gibbons both spent two to three weeks helping the children prepare for the test, translating daily activities and competence into test language and protocols. Lee did not have to pass the CRT because of his Individualized Education Plan, but he had to practice for it and take it. He and Ricky, along with several other children receiving special services, took the test in Ms. Burns' special education trailer.

Lee was reading *Little Red Riding Hood* aloud as the testing began, but finally put it away and began the test. It was a reading section of paragraphs and questions. He began reading silently, but soon switched to soft oral reading, pointing to each word. His strategy soon moved to reading only the questions. The paragraph was about getting milk from various animals, including a llama. Lee misread most of the content words but kept trying. After finishing the section he began reading his book again. Ms. Burns quietly returned it to her shelf and encouraged him to go on to the next section. He attempted the next three sections with decreasing concentration. He began reading another book, and was asked to put it away until their break. Finally, on a math section, he closed his eyes, circled above the paper with his pencil, landed, and with open eyes marked the response nearest his pencil. Lee did not pass the CRT.

It took over a month of Judy's attention and support before Lee's behavior improved much. Judy looked for ways he could help her and for ways he could gain positive attention. Lee was excellent at handsprings, Judy knew from PE, but handsprings were not allowed on the playground. So Judy had Handspring Day, holding the event the last hour before school was out. Lee was perfect all day. Eventually, Lee must have decided she was a person to be trusted and that she was going to stay. "Help me stay on green (a reference to Judy's discipline system)," he requested of Judy in the middle of March. She asked his advice. "I'll do better if you move me," he suggested, and he moved his desk away from his group. During times when group work was encouraged, he slid the desk back. Whether this was something another teacher had tried in earlier years, something Lee had observed in other classrooms, or his own idea, he did indeed "stay on green" (or at least yellow) more often for the next few weeks. This was also the time period of his intensive reading of *Anna Banana*. On April 26 he quietly moved to a recently vacated desk within his group and remained there the rest of the year. It was surprising to us that a child who had learned so much from his peers the previous year would make this choice, and perhaps from our viewpoint it wasn't his best choice; but he *did* take responsibility for his own behavior.

The paradox of special education

In her first observational notes of the year JoBeth wrote, "Where's Lee?" It was a question that became increasingly telling as Lee attended two segments of special education daily, was sent to various rooms, got time outs in the office, etc.

Lee was always responsible for getting to Ms. Gibbons' each morning and afternoon; as previously noted, he really like going. But he was also aware that he missed things in the classroom when he was gone. In mid-September he showed Susan a book about gardening when she began their study of plants. "You can read this during science—it's about food," he suggested. She agreed and said she

FIG. 26–6 *Writing in Ms. Gibbons' Room*

would read it that afternoon. "But I might be gone," he reminded her. "You'll be here for part of it," she promised.

On October 3 Lee was engrossed in reading workshop. Susan had something to share that day, a letter from her husband Scott, who had visited the previous week to talk about being a lawyer. Lee had been fascinated and had written to the judge Scott worked for with several questions. At 11:56 Lee remembered his 11:00 class. He went down to explain to Ms. Gibbons, who was pleased he'd had such an interesting morning. Several times throughout the fall, Lee went to Ms. Gibbons' room to ask if he could stay in the classroom for something that was particularly interesting; she was always happy for him to do so. Ms. Gibbons was encouraged when the children got so engaged in their classroom community that they didn't want to leave it.

She also encouraged interaction between the two settings, invited Lee to take books from her room to his, and even let him take her guinea pigs to his homeroom trailer for a visit. Lee loved animals; there were several dogs and cats at home, the guinea pigs in Ms. Gibbons' class, and the cat he found on the way to school in February that Judy let him bring into the trailer. He chose to write about these animals more than any other topic. He also read many books about dogs, snakes, Frog and Toad, Rose the Horse, and Curious George, often choosing to read *Zoobook* magazine in Ms. Gibbons' room after he finished his work. He truly loved all animals (even a caterpillar he kept on his desk for several days), and freedom to choose what he read and wrote about allowed him to pursue this major interest. Ms. Gibbons' room was a place with a caring teacher he had known for several years and two real live animals (the guinea pigs), which he often fed and stroked. No wonder he loved her room.

Still, Lee missed out on certain things. He missed much of writing workshop, especially the last four months. During his June interview he said, "We ain't never wrote yet—we never write." Even on days when he had time to write he often had to miss sharing, a time when positive attention could be focused on him. He wrote occasionally in Ms. Gibbons' room, where she helped him with spelling and punctuation (see Figure 26–6).

Then, in the middle of March Lee was retested, as mandated every three years by special education procedures. He tested out of special education. He was no longer officially "mildly mentally handicapped." He was "cured"!

Our elation was short-lived. Lee had made tremendous progress as a reader, and some progress as a writer, but he could not be expected to meet district standards for promotion, which were based on progress in the basal testing system. He was covered for third because of his IEP, but what about fourth? And what about his relationship with Ms. Gibbons? Who would be his "safety valve" in fourth grade? Ms. Gibbons left the school at the end of the year to teach at Oak Street School, but before she left she voiced her concern: "He has really come to rely on the support he gets in here. Did this hold him back, or did it help him feel comfortable, develop the confidence to take risks? Now we are just dumping him off on his own, from two segments a day to none. I worry about him."

TWENTY-SEVEN

"I'm Going to Get Smarter and Smarter"

Lee in Fourth Grade

with Kay Hales

For Lee the system seemed to be working. Walnut Street School's commitment to creating a stable and supportive environment for its children succeeded: Lee was not transferred to a new school, his teacher (Kay) was within the same extended family Lee had been in previously, and Kay was interested in studying the impact of whole language instruction on a child teachers continued to worry about. Further, Lee had tested out of special education; he seemed, indeed, to be getting "smarter and smarter" (see Chapter 24, fourth-grade interview, November). It promised to be a good year.

By the third day of class everyone in the room seemed comfortable in the routines of Kay's room. *Everyone* wrote during writing workshop, and *everyone* read during reading workshop (pullout programs had not started yet). Children who had been in rooms with these structures in previous years quickly initiated those who had not. Lee wrote about lowriders, a hot topic among speed enthusiasts in the room; Kay selected one of his sentences from the previous day for her lesson on telling and asking sentences. During reading workshop several children chose books Kay thought were too difficult for them. "It seems important to them to have a long, chapter book, now that they are in fourth grade." Others chose familiar favorites from previous years, like *Stone Soup* (McGovern, 1986)and *Where the Wild Things Are* (Sendak, 1963). Lee leafed through a soccer book, put it back, and selected *The Ghost in Dobbs Diner* (Alley, 1981). He read a few lines softly to himself, then leafed slowly through the whole book. He returned to the beginning and began reading softly to himself, struggling with about a third of the words. He read for twenty minutes, looking at each picture on pages where they were present before he read. Four children shared their books, and then Kay got out the read-aloud book they had begun the first day, *Christina's Ghost* (Wright, 1985). "Alright!" Lee cheered.

Kay wrote her observations of Lee throughout the year, met with JoBeth for monthly analysis sessions, and responded to JoBeth's drafts of this chapter.

Stability becomes an issue: The special education paradox revisited

Yet by September 3 Kay worried aloud, "He's doomed. He's just doomed to fail fourth grade." According to the record of basal testing Lee was in *Carousels*, the first-grade reader. The county required all fourth graders to pass the testing through *Journeys*, the 3.2 basal. Lee would have to complete the 1, 2.1, 2.2, 3.1, and 3.2 basals to be promoted, unless . . . "I am going to try another SST (support service team), see if we can get him some extra support. I'd like to have him tested for a learning disability or a behavior disorder. We've *got* to get him into special ed or he will fail. We've got to find a way to help him."

Lee had spent two segments a day for the past three years with Ms. Gibbons. This year he went to Chapter 1, along with half of his class, in a new arrangement between Kay and the Chapter 1 teacher, Ms. Piercy. They divided the class in half (nearly half qualified for Chapter 1 services) and taught an hour-long reading workshop at the same time, but in different rooms. They felt that everyone benefitted in this arrangement: No one missed instruction from leaving the classroom, no instructional sequences were interrupted, and all the children had more teacher attention and could confer and share more frequently.

Still, Kay worried that Lee needed more instruction at his working level. He began to go to the third grade next door for math. Ms. Morrison, a teacher's aide, began tutoring him in reading for half an hour every day. With Chapter 1 and the daily "specials" of art/music/PE/library, Lee was in and out of the classroom a great deal, as we can see from his schedule on October 1:

- 7:45 Lee arrived at school, put his things away, and went to third grade for math
- 8:15 tornado drill
- 9:37 Lee returned to Kay's room, about half an hour later than usual because of the tornado drill; the class was doing a combined social studies/language assignment; Kay went over his personal spelling list with him and he wrote his words, then began reading *Barkley*, by Sid Hoff
- 9:47 recess
- 10:00 math; Lee continued reading *Barkley*, remarking to JoBeth that he had also read *Danny and the Dinosaur*, by Sid Hoff, and that he had read this book to the class last week; he read aloud to JoBeth, missing about one word every two pages
- 10:25 Betsy and Lee told each other about their books
- 10:38 art
- 10:45 Lee got sent to the office for misbehaving in art
- 11:35 Lee was still waiting in the office, pink slip in hand, for Ms. Naylor; this was Lee's time to meet with Ms. Morrison, so JoBeth brought her to the office
- 11:40 Ms. Morrison had Lee read to her from *Danny and the Dinosaur*, helping with each word he had trouble with by helping him sound it out, discussing the meaning if the word seemed unfamiliar; Lee read for 32 minutes without stopping, noting "I like *Barkley* better than *Danny*"
- 12:12 Ms. Morrison returned to her classroom
- 12:26 Ms. Naylor returned to her office and gently guided Lee through the door; at her request, he explained the "severe disruption—Immediate action by the principal" and "noncompliance with teacher request" comments on the pink slip by telling how he and Brandy had been calling names, making people laugh, but Brandy had not been sent to the office; Ms. Naylor

pointed out that he was the object of discussion, that he had been in her office three times already, and that he needed to take responsibility: "You aren't doing your job, and you're keeping other people from doing their job. . . . All boys and girls read and write differently, but they can all behave the same. You're a good-looking boy . . . somebody's looking after you, now *you* have got to look after you . . . You're getting a lot of help, more than most of the children, you have got to do your part. . . . I want to see something you're *proud* of before the day's over." After eliciting a promise and a plan of action, Ms. Naylor sent Lee on his way with a pat on the arm.

12:43 Lee apologized to the art teacher, went to the bathroom, and then to Ms. Piercy's room; he never mentioned lunch, which his class had eaten at 12:00

12:47 Ms. Piercy was doing a mini-lesson on painting as a response to the books they had been reading; she compared it with other options of writing a response on the computer or making a clay model

12:53 Lee got another favorite book, *The Biggest Bear* (Ward), and began listening to the read-along tape while he looked at the book; Ms. Piercy checked to see if he was reading along, then began conferring with various children on the content of their books

1:08 the children talked as a group about their books; Lee asked to take his home, promising Ms. Piercy he'd return it; the group returned to Kay's room, where the rest of the class was finishing sharing

1:21 fire drill

1:38 Kay read from *Amelia Bedelia* (Parish), with frequent discussions of homophones

1:48 time to write; Kay checked her conference schedule and called the first writer; the others began writing; Lee asked Kay if he could take the story he has just finished to show Ms. Naylor; she suggested 2:00

1:51 a report of an overflowing toilet drew several children to the bathroom, including Lee

1:55 Kay called Lee for a conference on his plans for his next piece; he was tracing the cover of the bear book, and told her he planned to take it home to read; he summarized the whole story for Kay, read a page (missing only "orchard"), and showed her that it had won an award (Caldicott); he said he was just going to copy the cover, but write his own story

2:15 clean up

2:20 home (or in Lee's case, Boys Club)

With both fire and tornado drills, this was not a typical day—or was it? Doesn't there always seem to be something of "importance" interrupting teaching and learning? Lee did, as Ms. Naylor pointed out, get more extra help than most of the children, so he went out of the classroom more often; but eighteen of the twenty-two children in Kay's class left the room at some time each day for special education, gifted class, or Chapter 1.

There were two major schedule changes in the next month: Ms. Piercy didn't feel she was making enough progress with Lee, so she moved him to another teacher who worked with third graders; and Kay shifted his schedule so he could be in class for science and social studies, since he seemed to be so interested in these subjects. By the end of November Lee had been staffed as Emotionally Disturbed. The social worker who had interviewed Lee noted that he had many fears, including a fear of his biological mother. She was only allowed two hours a month with her children, so apparently others feared for her time with them also. Nevertheless, Kay felt this was a move in the right direction. She believed Lee would benefit from the smaller groups in the resource room and from those teachers' expertise. Also, Lee would not have to meet district promotion guidelines now. "He just wouldn't understand failing," she observed. "He thinks he's doing great."

He began a new schedule of going to Ms. Welty (special education) for language arts from 8:15 to 9:45 (along with three classmates and two children from another class), to Ms. Morrison (instructional aide) for math tutoring (they only did a little reading now, since Lee no longer went to the third-grade class for math) from 11:30 to 12:00, and to Ms. Erdrich (special education) from 1:30 until school was out for social skills development.

Ms. Welty incorporated elements of reading and writing workshop in her hour and a half session. "We take stories out of three of the alternative basals, stories related to whatever content we are studying as much as possible, plus I run off copies of legends, like next week we are studying Eskimos. No one is 'in' any one book; we all read from these sources as a group, then they choose other books sometimes too. Next we do spelling, which I try to tie into my other language instruction, like studying plurals; sometimes our words come from whatever content we are studying. I do their language study as a mini-lesson for writing workshop sometimes. Writing—that's what they love. We usually try to share. . . . Lee has less general information than most of the others, although he reads as well as some. Like he didn't know who the Eskimos were. He doesn't seem to sound out words to spell. I asked if he wanted to do the same spelling list as the class, and he said, 'Yeah, and how about some of these,' pointing to the Dolch basic sightword list.

"Then Lee comes back in the afternoon for social skills, since he's *supposed* to be ED. [Ms. Erdrich] and I usually do that together; we do projects, work on problem solving, friendships, how to share. We do a lot of modeling, role playing, and videotaping. Lee is wonderful in there; he likes to talk and role play."

"He's so much happier since he started going to [Ms. Welty]," Kay observed. "He has really settled down in the classroom. Fourth-grade work was just too difficult for him. He really likes working in a small group."

Our number one question when we began studying Lee was: Is he really retarded, and if so, what does that mean? We were still asking. The tests now said he wasn't, but if he was not "a little off," as his stepfather put it, why was he having so much trouble with classroom work? Did the miracle of Lee's learning to read and write pale now in light of expectations for more advanced work? Was the extra help helping or hurting? How *was* Lee doing?

"I read more books, just read books"

"The main thing I noticed about Lee from our notes all year was that he really expanded his reading," Kay said during a summer research analysis session. "He expanded the kinds of things he read, as well as reading things that were more difficult. At the beginning of the year he was reading books like Dr. Seuss; he would look at chapter books and magazines, but often I don't think he was reading them. Through the year he really did read chapter books, as well as poems and even entries in the *Guinness Book of World Records*. From his interviews he showed that he realized how important reading and writing are to everyday life—reading newspapers, *TV Guide*, job applications, reading to his own children. I think that was why he was so adamant about going to Ms. Morrison; he would go *find* her if she didn't come for him. He was going to be a successful reader; he knew how important reading and writing were to his life."

Lee did spend a lot of the year reading. He still liked to read books over and over until he could read them fluently. "He loved for me to read aloud," Kay noted; "he was always right by me every day when I read. And the listening center was a favorite all year. I had about a dozen books and tapes, and he listened over and over. Repetition was an important strategy for him." He liked to read aloud, and often had that opportunity. While he was in Chapter 1 he read to two first graders for half an hour every week, a book that he had selected for them and practiced until he could read it well.

Lee talked about books and authors. In addition to the authors he mentioned in the interviews, Lee often recommended another book by an author he or someone else was reading. He loved to discover a new author and, like many kids his age, was fond of serialized books. His class read many of the James Howe series (*Bunnicula*, *The Celery Stalks at Midnight*, etc.) as read alouds, whole-class books, and individual choices. Although these were too difficult for Lee to read independently, he listened and discussed with great interest. When JoBeth brought in a batch of "Vic the Vampire" paperbacks in December, Lee immediately appropriated them. When his friend said, "Ms. Hales wants to see those," Lee responded, "Uh-huh, and so do I." Later, he took the whole stack to Ms. Welty's room and displayed them on the table.

Often when children shared the books they'd been reading Lee commented, as he did on February 5:

Tammy: This book is a mystery (showing cover).
Lee: That ghost scared everybody!
Kay: You read that book, didn't you.

Kathie: (reading section of *Trolly Car Family*, by E. Clymer)
Lee: That's a good book. . . .
Lee: (reading a poem from *Light in the Attic*) Shel Silverstein wrote this. He also wrote *Where the Sidewalk Ends*.

Yet first readings remained difficult. In the three basals Ms. Welty took stories from, Lee sight-read passages at 86 percent word recognition (2.1 reader), 75 percent (2.2 reader), and 81 percent (3.2 reader) by the middle of February (see Figure 27-1, from the 3.2 reader). However, both teachers reported that he did much better if he was familiar with the material. As Lee said on several occasions, "If I listen good, I can read it back over." In fourth grade he developed other helpful strategies too. While in his November interview he pointed to sounding words out and listening as ways he was learning to read, at the end of May he explained that "once you get to the other word, you can come back and get what that word is"—a fourth- grade definition of using context. We also noted that for Lee, as is true for most readers (Bussis, Chittendon, Aramel, & Klausner, 1985), the farther into the story he got, the more momentum he developed. Still, he could not pick up an unfamiliar text and read with understanding, and as a fourth grader (and increasingly from then on), this was what he needed to be able to do.

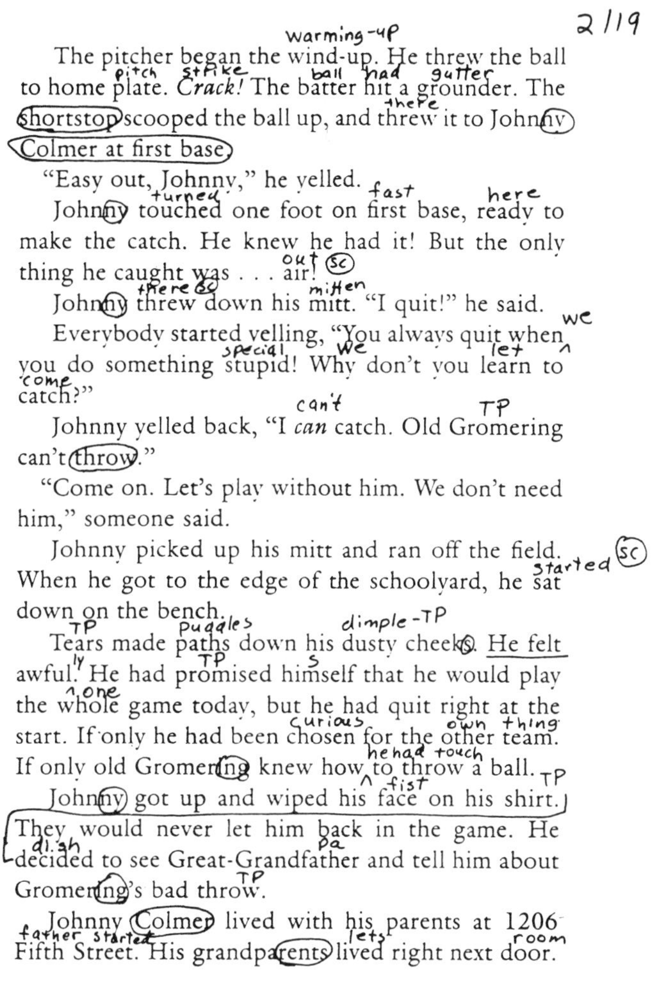

The pitcher began the wind-up. He threw the ball to home plate. *Crack!* The batter hit a grounder. The shortstop scooped the ball up, and threw it to Johnny Colmer at first base.

"Easy out, Johnny," he yelled.

Johnny touched one foot on first base, ready to make the catch. He knew he had it! But the only thing he caught was . . . air!

Johnny threw down his mitt. "I quit!" he said.

Everybody started yelling, "You always quit when you do something stupid! Why don't you learn to catch?"

Johnny yelled back, "I *can* catch. Old Gromering can't throw."

"Come on. Let's play without him. We don't need him," someone said.

Johnny picked up his mitt and ran off the field. When he got to the edge of the schoolyard, he sat down on the bench.

Tears made paths down his dusty cheeks. He felt awful. He had promised himself that he would play the whole game today, but he had quit right at the start. If only he had been chosen for the other team. If only old Gromering knew how to throw a ball.

Johnny got up and wiped his face on his shirt. They would never let him back in the game. He decided to see Great-Grandfather and tell him about Gromering's bad throw.

Johnny Colmer lived with his parents at 1206 Fifth Street. His grandparents lived right next door.

FIG. 27–1 *Sight-reading from the 3.2 Reader*

"Whenever they do writing, I be gone"

Lee and his friend Stan shared the first chapter of what they promised the class was going to be a twelve-chapter book on September 24. It was similar to *The Giving Tree*, a book that was to be one of Lee's favorites that year. They had named the boy "Roy" and the tree "Joe"; Lee read and Stan prompted once when he paused at a word. Eventually, as he explained in the November interview, they added two other characters, a dog and an old man. Lee liked to start with a familiar story in his writing, often tracing a picture or title, then making the story his own.

However, there were two issues affecting Lee's writing development. One was that he was often out of the room when the class wrote, as he had been the previous year. As he said, "I don't write this year, because whenever they do writing, I be gone. They be showing me all their good stories. We write sometime in Ms.

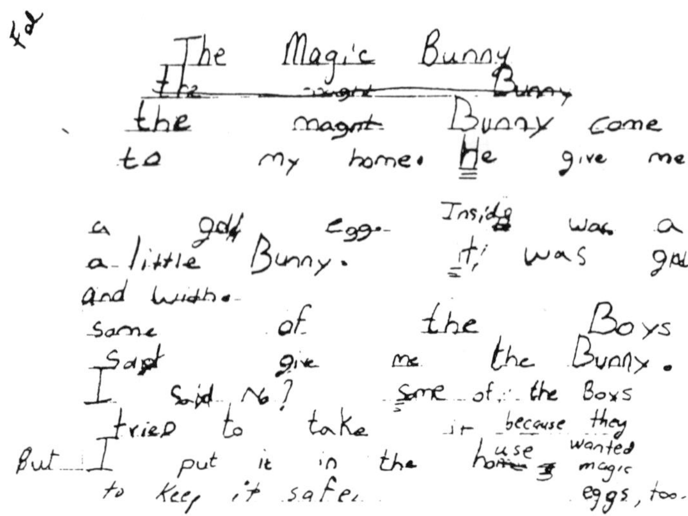

FIG. 27–2 *Conference Draft*

Welty's room. . . . Sometimes we write what she say write, and sometimes we write what we want." The choice of topics was the second issue: the children were writing more content-related pieces as fourth graders. Ms. Welty, in her attempts to have an integrated hour and a half, often had the children write something related to what they were studying (e.g., a legend, a report on an animal, etc.). She conferred regularly with the children, and several times during the year she worked with them on revising and editing to final form. One of these was Lee's magic bunny story, where once again his love of animals shines through (see Figures 27–2 and 27–3, the conference draft and final draft).

The children also did content-related writing in the classroom. During the spring, all the fourth grades in the school worked with the New York City ballet program to study ballet and write and produce their own. "Lee participated in the ballet, especially the movement workshop and the videos," Kay noted. "He got very involved with making scenery and costumes—he was the costume designer. He loved the local ballet we went to. But he didn't get into the writing part of it much." We can only speculate on why we didn't see as much writing development in Lee as we had hoped. There were very few products to analyze; Kay was not really sure what happened to Lee's writing, nor did he seem to know. "Stan say my story good," Lee told us one day, "but the next morning it was gone." We suspect that traveling between the various rooms and not having a set writing time throughout the year contributed to Lee's difficulties and ours in seeing steady writing progress.

Both Kay and Ms. Welty pointed out Lee's continuing difficulties with spelling. "He's not a phonetic speller," Kay said. "I had trouble reading his writing, and so did he at times. I think he had good ideas in his head, but had trouble getting them down." In a story he wrote in Ms. Welty's room in February he spelled "blowed" b-l-o-g, "big" b-g-i-n-g, and "honey" h-o-g-g-y. His writing was much

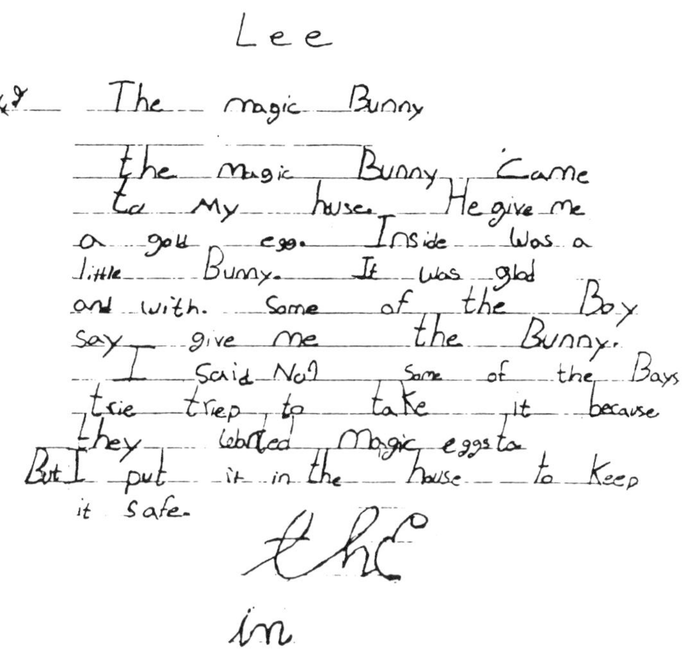

FIG. 27-3 *Final Draft*

more legible (see Figure 27-3) than it had been the previous year, and he even worked at writing in cursive on occasion, as in the following letter to his pen pal in November (shown in figure 27-4).

Overall, there was scant evidence of sustained writing development, but there were certainly impressive comparisons to Lee's writing in second grade, and even to the limited writing he did in third. He still wrote communicatively to his pen pal (he only had one for two months), he wrote collaboratively, and he saw literature as a springboard for his own writing. His writing had become more legible with letter formation improvement, spacing, and periods, which he could put in accurately in conference although not yet spontaneously. "I do hope," Kay said after studying Lee's comments about himself as a writer, "that Lee won't have to miss writing time in fifth grade."

Lee as a member of the community

"Lee was a behavior problem at times," Kay reflected. "I think a lot of it was his way of being accepted. I think he is starting to realize his limitations, not being quite up to fourth-grade work. For example, the ITBS was a complete disaster. He literally cut the test into pieces—he fixed us! I don't blame him, he couldn't read the passages, and it was really frustrating. That was a whole week wasted in that child's life.

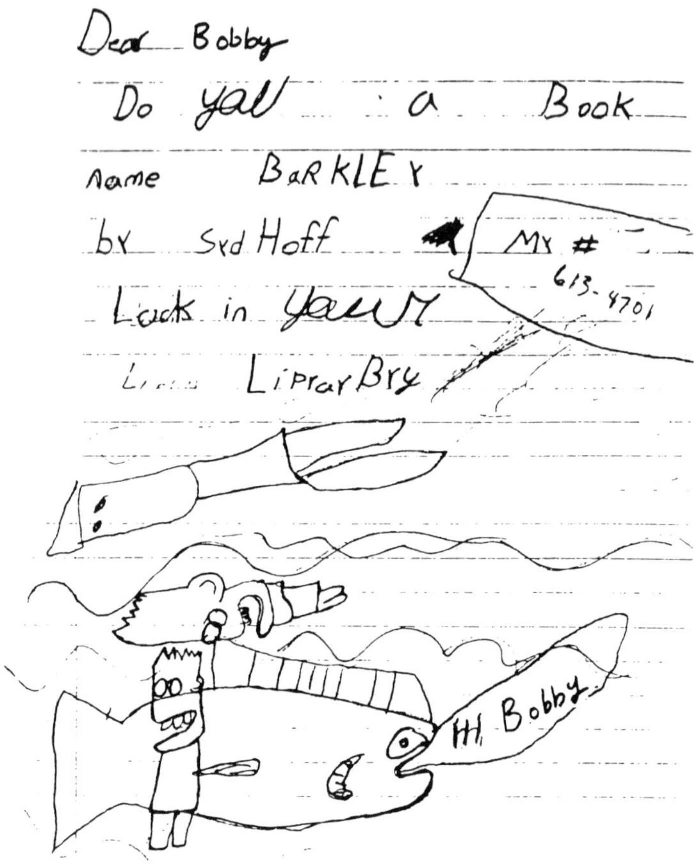

FIG. 27-4 *November Pen-pal Letter*

"He wanted to be able to fit in, and I think some of his fighting, cussing, and telling people off was his way of saying, 'I *am* a fourth grader.' Luckily he is very athletic, so he really can compete that way, especially through football. He's not mean. There wasn't really any aggressive, out-of-control behavior. He did give Makita a hard time from the day she joined our class. She was cute and new and smart, and he just didn't know how to deal with her. He went to her for help, just like nearly everyone else in the class, but he also picked on her."

In November Kay asked everyone in the class to write down, in a private note to her, two people they would like to work with so that she could form new groups. No one wrote Lee's name down. One reason could be that he was often distracting to the other students. Another could be that several times during the year Lee's desk was separated from his group because they complained or Kay felt he wasn't working well. The day they wrote down names, Lee's desk was separate. Another reason could be that Lee was out of the room so often, his classmates may not have seen him as an integral member of the community. Regardless of the reason or reasons, Lee did not seem to be as valued in the classroom as he was on the playground or the football field.

We did not have a lot of clues from Lee about how he was perceiving himself; during his interviews he was always very enthusiastic, especially about himself as a reader. There were, however, two incidents that bothered us. In March Lee went to court, along with his older brother who lived in another home. They had been part of a group that broke into a house. Lee told Kay when he got back from juvenile court, "I'm not in trouble, but I'm about to be if I'm not careful." The second incident was late in May. He was talking with a group of other kids about some school-related event (perhaps promotion?) and said, "It don't matter anyway. I'm going to quit school when I'm sixteen. I can get a good job when I'm sixteen."

What happened to "You always got to try"? Was the most characteristic aspect of Lee as a learner changing? We saw his determination in reading throughout the year, but less and less in other areas, including writing. "He realizes he's behind," Kay reflected at the end of the year. "I worry about him realizing that he doesn't fit into the academic setting. Social studies and science will be so hard for him next year, even though he's really interested in those areas, because he can't read the texts. Sometimes he surprises us, and himself, when he really focuses. He explained the concept of weather changes and the North and South poles to the class last week, and I didn't even think he had been paying attention. But he's been having more behavior problems, and he is so distractable. What will happen to him in middle school? He needs to be in a class where there are a lot of projects, and reading and writing workshop. Then he can really contribute. And he needs to work one-on-one with someone. The most progress he made all year was when he was reading every day with Ms. Morrison. It was remarkable, really."

Cynthia Rylant (1985) wrote about a young man who reminded us a great deal of Lee. In fact his name was Leo.

> Leo was ten years old. . . . He hadn't many friends because he was slower than the rest. That was the way his father said it: "Slower than the rest." Leo was slow in reading, slow in numbers, slow in understanding nearly everything that passed before him in a classroom. As a result, in fourth grade Leo had been separated from the rest of his classmates and placed in a room with other children who were as slow as he. (p. 2)

Was our Lee "slower than the rest"? We were back to the intriguing question of three years ago, the question that prompted us to study Lee, the question that made us so glad we had. We knew Lee wasn't retarded one day and of "normal" intelligence the next, that he wasn't emotionally stable one day and disturbed the next. We also knew that he had trouble maintaining a stable spelling even for words he had been writing for three years, that he had read words hundreds of times in context that he could not pronounce out of context, and that his friends were starting to notice.

What we don't know is what is best for Lee. This is a problem that many of the special education and grade-level teachers at Walnut Street struggle with for the many children there who qualify for special services. In a study of second, third, and fourth graders with learning disabilities, emotional/behavioral problems, and mild retardation, a team of researchers ended up with the same dilemma. They concluded that these children "get short-changed in mainstream classes, but that simply placing them in special education classes does not necessarily provide them with more opportunities to learn" (O'Sullivan, Ysseldyke, Christenson, & Thurlow, 1990, p. 131). They recommended, as Kay did, more opportunities for meaningful engagement within the mainstream classroom.

Continuing Worries

Lee and his teachers last year pointed to Ms. Morrison, the patient and caring aide who listened to him read, as the person who helped him the most. He made progress, but not enough that he could continue to learn at a similar rate in his classrooms. What could the schools do that would help him the most, both for his last year of elementary school and for the critical years of middle school: a stable fifth-grade classroom with "projects and reading and writing workshop" where he stayed all day, all year? A continuation of a range of special services? A self-contained special education classroom like Leo was in? ("Leo thought he would never get over it. He saw no way to be happy after that.")

We will continue to follow the life and learning of Lee, as well as of Joseph, Jeremiah, Shannon, Reggie, and Ricky. We will continue to ask questions, love the children, feel frustrated for them, feel empathy for their teachers, and investigate the systemic risk makers as well as those beyond education's control. We feel more strongly than ever that literacy around whole texts, literate models, real purposes for reading and writing, supported risk taking, responsibility, time, and belonging to the classroom community leads to successful literacy learning (Allen, Michalove, Shockley, and West, 1991). We also know that our original question was simplistic. Each child's world was a complex macrocosm, as we will see in the final chapter, and we were naive to think that (1) we could provide stability in the school setting that would guarantee both a consistent whole language curriculum and a nurturing extended educational family, and (2) that this stability would change children's lives. What would this mean, ultimately, for a child like Lee, a child who is "slower than the rest"?

ENGAGEMENT, COMMUNITY, AND STABILITY

TWENTY-EIGHT

Engaging Children, Teachers, and School Systems in Successful Literacy Learning

We became engaged by these children, as we hope you have, as they became engaged with reading, writing, and learning. In addition to learning from the individual children we began to see important themes across their lives. Early on and throughout the study we were struck by two overriding themes: *engagement* and *community*. Not becoming engaged by literacy opportunities was something that worried us initially about most of the children we chose to study; likewise, not seeming to belong in the classroom community of learners concerned us. As these children became engaged in literacy and as they found their places as legitimate members of literate communities, we saw their risks reduced and their chances to succeed increased. In the second year of the study, the theme of *stability* bombarded us. It became an issue for each child by the end of that year, and may have been an issue long before that.

A macrostructure lens (Bronfenbrenner, 1979) magnifies and clarifies each of these themes. Viewing the children within multiple, interacting environments, we are trying to see elements of the larger society as well as the more easily-recorded classroom society. We have read, discussed, and sought the input of others on issues such as institutional racism, cultural norms and expectations affecting teacher attitudes, and gender disparities. We have identified systemic risk makers that cross all three themes, sometimes separating children from their communities, sometimes making literacy engagement undesirable or impossible, and often creating instability in learners' lives.

In this final chapter we first look at decisions that teachers made and decisions that students made that increased community, engagement, and stability. Next, we examine those systemic risk makers and how they affected our six children. Finally, we make recommendations to our primary audience—educators.

Part of this chapter was published in a slightly different form in "I'm really worried about Joseph," by JoBeth Allen, Barbara Michalove, Betty Shockley, and Marsha West in the March, 1991 *Reading Teacher*, and is reprinted here by permission. The article was recognized in the "Learned Article" category by Education Press.

Decisions that increased engagement, community, and stability

The children that worried us the most at the beginning of the study were often those who were either not engaging with literacy events or who had nonproductive roles within the literate community. Many of the decisions teachers made increased students' engagement with literate activity: interacting with characters, authors, language, and ideas as they read and wrote. Engagement and community certainly overlapped, for in several instances engagement with literacy came about through membership in the classroom community, and the community led some children to literacy. But community was more important than a road to literacy, having to do with the "living well" as much as reading and writing well (Calkins, 1991). We illustrate these themes with several specific decisions we made, decisions based on the *beliefs about language learning* detailed in Chapter 1 and on our specific attention to increasing success for the children we were worried about the most.

Engagement

Decisions Betty and Barbara made that seemed to increase genuine engagement with literacy were based on our beliefs that (1) children need whole texts initially, (2) children need adult models of literacy, (3) children need real reasons for reading and writing, (4) children need time to read and write, and (5) children need support for their risk taking. (However, initially these professional beliefs had to be negotiated in the dominant basal culture.)

Betty and Barbara made the decision from day one to involve children in a whole language curriculum. They read to the children frequently and provided reading and writing workshop times daily. From these *wholes*, they discussed language *parts* to help children become skilled analyzers as well as users of language. This emphasis on whole texts seemed important to all the emergent readers, but it may have been most crucial to Lee. Because listening to read-along tapes seemed so important, Barbara allowed this engagement even beyond reading workshop times. Lee discovered that by reading a book numerous times he became competent. He branched out and began practicing other books for weeks at a time until he could read them fluently. Reading whole books made Lee a real reader.

One of the most enjoyable aspects of exploring whole language philosophy was rediscovering our own literacy (Graves, 1990). All of us love to read. Now, however, Betty and Barbara began seeing their pleasure reading as an integral part of their roles as teachers of reading. They told our kids about the books they were reading. They occasionally used their own books in mini-lessons, as when Betty read the opening lines of *Beloved* to begin a discussion of how children start their own stories. They also developed a strong sense of how their enjoyment of both adult and kid books—their models of "joyous literacy"—affected their students as readers.

But they were modeling more than the joy of reading; they were modeling many processes of reading. They self-corrected, phrased for meaning, talked about unfamiliar words, reread old favorites, sought other books by favorite authors, and occasionally abandoned a book they didn't like. For Joseph, Lee, and Reggie, those who were at the earliest stages of emergent reading (Sulzby, 1985), these models seemed especially important. The books they read to the class were quite often ones the children chose to read. Since there was always a clamor for the read alouds, Betty and Barbara often gave the book to the children who needed that kind of supported reading experience most, with the suggestion to others to "read with Joseph," or "ask Lee if you can read it after he finishes." They were not only inviting children into the "literacy club" (Smith, 1988a), they were providing successful initiation experiences.

There were many opportunities for real reasons for reading and writing, reasons that were important to the children that we had not anticipated. Bateson (1989) writes of women who are "composing a life." In many ways we saw our students composing their lives, working out problems, exploring their identities. Shannon wrote about "the girl with the black and white face," who eventually falls into a volcano. The piece could be a parable of her life and fears. The first personal writing Ricky produced, ten weeks into the school year, was "Me and my mom wet to see my dad. He sed woh [who] are you/ I am [Ricky]." The students included these struggles not only in their workshop writing but in transactional writing to peers and teachers.

Even when kids have compelling reasons to read and write, they probably won't unless they have dependable, structured time to do so (Graves, 1983; Hansen, 1987). We have become adamant about the importance of this dependable time, *especially* for the students we worry about. In fact, designated time is often not enough, as we saw with Lee's engagement with the read-along tapes. Shannon's writing was so important to her that her mother reported, "She writes *all* the time" at home. Reggie would become so engaged with writing that he would continue writing with one hand during sharing, the other in the air to ask the author a question or request the next turn. The loss of that dependable time to write was a noticeable, and articulated, problem for many of the children during the second and/or third year of the study.

Time was also a major issue for Jeremiah, but for a different reason. Jeremiah rarely wrote during writing workshop in first grade, and initially in second grade. He "created" first—book covers, puppet characters, props, and so on; he also interacted extensively with other writers (usually not very productively). Betty and Barbara had different approaches. Betty allowed Jeremiah to continue writing, through sharing and other parts of the day. Barbara, in second grade, structured his time for him, placing him in a group of writers at a table where she provided extra support and supervision. Both strategies produced more writing. When there was no expectation of regular writing, and no specified writing time in his third-grade class, he produced very little writing.

For some students, interaction with books and creating texts are successful, rewarding experiences from the beginning. This was not true of many of the students we studied. Simply creating a literate environment was not enough; supporting them in their risk taking was essential. As we looked back over our data two things became clear: (1) the fact that we were actively studying these children led us to important decisions of how and when to support them, and (2) this active, intentional support seems to be crucial for increasing the success of students we worry about. When Reggie had built his confidence with simple storybooks, but seemed unable or unwilling to try other literature, Barbara suggested he choose a new book, showing him interesting choices. He insisted that he couldn't read them, a signal that he needed more direct support. Barbara helped him find a book she thought he would enjoy and alternated reading pages with him until Reggie saw that he could indeed read the book. It was a turning point for Reggie as a reader.

Both Barbara and Betty have given paperback books to children on occasions, for example, when we visited in their homes. We are well aware that many of the children we teach do not have their own books. We were not prepared for what an impact actually owning a book would have. *The Doorbell Rang* (Hutchins, 1986) became the only book Shannon read with confidence the first year. With it, Shannon was able to read at home, as she had been writing at home. When we interviewed her in June of her first grade year, she told us she was learning to "read new words and read *The Doorbell Rang* . . . because Ms. Shockley gave me the book." She was still referring to this book as how she learned to read in her third-grade interviews.

Of course it is not just whole language teachers who support children as risk takers. Shannon's fourth-grade teacher worked with her in the summer, on her own time, to help her catch up in reading. Reggie's teacher read with him one-on-one so he would not be embarrassed in his reading group. Joseph's teacher bought him a book at the school book fair and read it with him in class. Ricky's teachers, both classroom and special education, supported his decision to take himself out of a special education setting that actually kept him from engaging in the reading and writing that were so important to him. Good teachers make good decisions about individual children all the time, decisions that make the children feel special, important, smart, capable. There are many accounts in our data of such "little" decisions as helping a child read a new book, suggesting that a withdrawn child read with a partner, helping a child move beyond copying a text to modifying the story, and other decisions that supported risk taking; there were also some "big" decisions, discussed in subsequent sections.

Community

Decisions Betty and Barbara made that seemed to increase effective membership in the literate community were based on our beliefs that (1) children need real reasons for reading and writing, (2) children need support for their risk taking, (3) children need to be responsible for their own learning, and (4) children need to feel that they belong in a literate community.

Writing to pen pals was an important reason for all of the children to write. Several times we heard children explain, as they sought help, that they had to write so their pen pals could read it. Legibility was not always a requirement of in-class writing that was not published, but we saw children push themselves in new ways through this genuine correspondence. Reading to other classes was another way children made their literacy public, and they read passages over and over to gain fluency, phrasing, and story intonation before reading to others. In these instances the community extended outside the classroom, creating new opportunities.

Supporting risk taking led not only to increased engagement but to new and beneficial roles within the community. When Barbara had Jeremiah work in a reading group and a writing group, his usual pouting and squabbling diminished greatly. As one of the more competent readers and writers in these two groups, he began to be viewed as a helpful resource rather than nuisance by the other kids.

Teachers were not the only ones to support risk taking. Over and over, in every classroom, the children encouraged, taught, challenged, and supported each other. The insistence of Ricky's classmates that he read with them created a new role for him, from isolate to community member.

Being a part of a whole language classroom means taking responsibility for your own learning (Atwell, 1987; Hansen, 1987). Having real choices to make leads to real responsibility, not just learning to do what one is told (Shockley & Allen, 1990). Choices that affect literacy development the most seem to be the choice of reading and writing partners or groups. Reggie learned how to choose classmates who could really help him read. Lee learned to write initially by copying what his friends wrote; eventually, he became a genuine collaborator, first in the oral composing of the story, and then in the physical writing.

By the end of the first year, we were beginning to see that choice was important not only to literacy learning but to development in an area that puts many students at risk: behavior. Membership in an active community of learners made use of Reggie's primary skill: social interaction, a skill that had often relegated him to isolation in classrooms that were not structured for his constant verbal involvement. And for Joseph, making his own choices and taking charge of his literacy development allowed him to remain the "boss" without being the classroom bully.

Belonging has been identified in countless studies as a critical condition for school success (Berrueta-Clement, Schwienhart, Barnett, Epstein, & Weikart, 1984; Finn, 1989). As the routines and expectations for interaction in these classrooms became internalized, these children developed their roles as teachers, learners, and collaborators in their literate communities. We feel that our inclusion of all children, from the very first day, in reading and writing workshops increased the successes of students who had already experienced a great deal of failure. Betty and Barbara worked on schedules with special education teachers to make sure our students who received academic and behavior services could participate in workshops.

Everyone started off and remained on equal ground with other members of the community during the first year. They chose from the same books, struggled with the same general concerns, and their contributions were valued during sharing in the same ways. When Reggie and Lee shared "LL Cool J" their peers initially wondered what it meant, but readily accepted their explanation—and them as writers. This piece, like many others, allowed the boys to bring their interests and home community to their school community. "LL Cool J" and other raps and language play become sanctioned by the school through writing, and appreciated by peers through sharing. This is one way teachers of any cultural background can support what Irvine (1990) calls a "Black verbal communication style" of "ribbing, jiving, woofing, signifying, playing the dozens, capping, joning, styling, profiling" (p. 27). They, and their language, belonged.

Belonging also meant belonging in the classroom. By the end of first grade, Joseph decided he belonged in the classroom most of the time, and he stopped going to his special education class. In third grade at Poplar Street, Ricky quietly made the same decision. Lee often chose not to leave during reading or writing times. Shannon tried several times to stay with her classroom community, sometimes successfully and sometimes unsuccessfully. In most of these cases, both resource and homeroom teachers supported students in their desire to be integral parts of their homeroom community of learners.

This study has helped us answer the question our colleague Helen raised at the beginning of the study: "How will we know that what we're doing is actually any better than what we've always done?" We have learned from these children that whole language instruction leads to increased literacy engagement and to a supportive and interactive community of learners, and that these in turn lead to increased success. However, being literate may not be enough.

Stability

In the middle of the second year of the study, when the stability we had tried to establish for these children began to degenerate into chaos, we became more aware that the children operated within a complex and dynamic macrostructure. Children always have to deal with the degree of congruity between their school lives and their beyond-school lives; now the third graders had to contend with the disintegration of their school lives. They adjusted, for better or for worse, to a succession of substitutes. Two failed the CRT and were retained. Four of our six were transferred to new schools.

Bronfenbrenner (1979) describes four levels of our ecological macrostructure. The first level is the child's primary setting or settings (e.g., home and school). The second level is the interaction of primary settings, the fit or lack thereof. The third level involves setting factors that affect the child more indirectly, such as parents' jobs. And the fourth level includes those factors that create subcultures, such as war or economic recession.

Bronfenbrenner postulated that it is when children move from one primary setting to another that they have the greatest potential for both growth and alienation. Changing grade levels, changing schools, changing teachers, all present children with a challenge that may be growth producing with the proper support. This is dependent on two things. The first is the "fit" between primary settings; how much adjustment will be necessary? The second is the extent to which the new "domains are open or closed to the developing person" (Bronfenbrenner, 1979, p. 288). In other words, is the new teacher able and willing to adjust to the new child, or must all the adapting be done by the child? Thus the school's role for the many transitions it entails is to examine the fit between settings, challenge children realistically to grow in each new setting, and support them academically, socially, and emotionally during difficult transitional periods.

What did teachers in our study do that created stability and support during transitions? There were several important decisions. Perhaps the most radical was Betty's decision, supported by the other concerned members of the staff, to graduate Shannon to third grade rather than second at the end of the year. The move by itself might actually have created more instability than a perfunctory move to second, but Betty believed after studying Shannon for a year that it would actually counter earlier destabilization caused by two retentions. Shannon had outgrown her peer group both physically and emotionally. She needed a better chance to beat the dropout odds.

Support for this move involved several factors. Betty talked with Shannon's mother and she was delighted, promising to support the move at home. Betty worked closely with Susan Willis in third grade to determine what specific learning Shannon might need before entering third. Betty also had Shannon tested to see if her unusual learning pattern involved a learning disability, which it did. As discussed earlier, this LD placement resulted in contradictory learning conditions, promoting Shannon with her new age mates at the end of third, separating her from them for daily resource room instruction. However, with continuing support from Betty, and active personal and academic support from her third- and fourth-grade teachers, Shannon is currently a successful (As and Bs) fifth grader.

Another decision to create stability was allowing children more time to engage with sustained and genuine reading and writing by redefining their special education services and schedules. That was initially a *child* decision. However, when Betty and Joseph's resource teacher, Ms. Gibbons, met to discuss his increasing reluctance to leave his home classroom, they honored his decision. Both teachers took him seriously, discussing his current needs as opposed to his needs at the last IEP staffing. "He just doesn't belong here any more," Ms. Gibbons agreed. They decided on two periods a week rather than two periods daily. A similar conference between Ricky's homeroom and resource teachers resulted in discontinuation of services for a behavior disorder that he no longer seemed to have. In both cases the daily lives of these children became significantly more stable.

Initially, this study was designed for maximum stability for children. Walnut School created nuclear families and extended families so that children would have a smaller group of peers and teachers to get to know. The idea of the study was to have our focal children in classrooms each year where teachers shared the whole language beliefs detailed in the first chapter—beliefs about time, choice, support, and belonging. The faculty had worked hard on creating this supportive environment. However, five of our six children ended up in other schools.

Barbara and Betty did several things to support children through transition. When Reggie, Lee, and Ricky moved to Susan's third grade, Barbara sent several books they liked and could read to Susan for the first few weeks. Before Jeremiah, Joseph, and six of their classmates moved to her second grade, Barbara spent time talking to Betty and even observed once in her classroom to learn how Betty taught and what her classroom was like. Finally, we talked to each other during research team meetings. We reflected on our observations of how the children were developing and on teaching practices. During summer data analysis sessions Betty and Barbara each focused on the children they had taught, but also learned something of the children they would have.

In many ways, some subtle and taken for granted, some radical and carefully negotiated, teachers can work to make school a more stable place and can support children in the inevitable transitions. However, we don't want to make it sound as if we are solely responsible for the progress these children made. For one thing, we learned from the interviews that every child had someone at home who read and/or encouraged the child to read, even though this information was unsolicited (Michalove & Allen, 1990). If you reread the child in his or her own voice at the beginning of each section, you will notice how the children see literacy being valued and supported in their homes.

We did not study the children in their homes, but we did study them in our classrooms and talk with their other teachers. We have been continually amazed at how resilient their spirits are. In many cases the children made decisions that brought them or someone else to more active community membership, deeper engagement, and a more stable learning environment. These decisions were highly effective when the student's right to make them was honored. Joseph and Ricky made choices about which communities they would learn with, Reggie chose peers who could help him learn to read, Shannon chose Betty as her advocate and anchor during difficult transitions, and Lee taught himself to read by repeated readings of books that were "too hard." Conversely, some decisions that were not honored created more problems for the child, as when Joseph refused to write in third grade because he no longer had authority over his writing. In too many schools children do not have real choices.

Systemic risk makers

In our study many individual teachers, homeroom and resource room, whole language and textbook oriented, European American and African American, cared about these children and taught them to the best of their abilities. Some went out of their way, and beyond school time, to try to make a difference in a child's life. But most of the children got caught by the very system that purports to educate them. Ricky, Reggie, and Jeremiah were all retained for the *second* time during our study, in spite of overwhelming evidence of the damaging effects (Holmes & Matthews, 1984; Shepard & Smith, 1989). In Jeremiah's case his teacher said, "I can't say that I feel bad. He just wasn't convinced he needed to do the work"; she seemed to believe he did not deserve to be promoted. In the other cases, however, it was against the teacher's beliefs about what was best for the child but was mandated by the state. Ricky was caught by a system that was supposed to support him; failing the state third-grade math test not only created a second year of failure, it placed him in a remedial *reading* program!

Why are decisions made for so many children that do not seem in their best interest? Why does the educational system adhere to policies that may actually be injurious when long-term effects are considered? Because we are European American and the six children in our study are African American, we turned to African-American educators and researchers for their perspectives.

Institutional racism

It was not by design that all of the children we studied were African American and that five of six are male, nor is it really a coincidence. As Wright (1991) pointed out in her study of 61 fourth- and fifth-grade African-American males, " . . . the educational vulnerability of African-American males begins early and is evident from grade school to graduate school" (p. 102). It is well documented in the disproportionate placement in low ability groups and classes; high suspension, expulsion, and dropout rates; and increasingly lower college completion rates of African-American males.

Some have argued that this high failure rate is a pervasive institutional racism. African-American educator Kunjufu (1984), in *Countering the Conspiracy to Destroy Black Boys*, points to overt racism (both historic and present) as well as passive racism: "parents, educators, and white liberals who deny being racist, but through their silence allow institutional racism to continue" (p. 1). Clark (1983) explained further: "Especially with ethnic minority groups and the poor, our schools have served as institutions that select, sort, and control; that is, the schools have tended to take most incoming ethnic students and teach them just enough to enter occupational positions that parallel the status positions of their parents. Irvine (1990) agreed, arguing that "schools have a sociopolitical purpose of maintaining the status quo by acting as an agent of social control . . . schools preserve their historical purpose—maintaining the existing social order, in which low- income and minority persons are 'educated' for less skilled, routine jobs and conditioned by schools for obedience, the acceptance of authority, and external control" (p. 2).

Many of the systemic risk makers for the children we studied serve a sorting purpose. Retention, ability grouping, compensatory classes, and state testing in theory are to provide a more appropriate eduction to each individual; in fact, they are disproportionately injurious to African-American children, males in particular. Recently, one of us visited three classrooms in an elementary school that is evenly divided racially. In each class, one to three children had their desks removed from the group, their faces to the walls. All were African-American males. In the front hallway of the school hung the pictures of twenty past recipients of the annual Outstanding Student award. One was an African-American male.

Teacher attitudes and expectations

Are some schools racist? Are some teachers? Are the teachers in our study, including us? Or, as Kunjufu argued, are we simply silent (or unaware) in the face of these systemic risk makers? We discussed institutions in the previous section; here we address individuals and what happens, or doesn't happen, in the classroom.

There is a large body of research pointing to teacher differences in attitudes and expectations. According to Dusek (1985), teachers prefer attractive, white, middle-class, obedient, and attentive children with common names. Rist (1973) found similar preferences of black teachers in an all-black school. In a study by Kedar-Voivoda (1983), teachers were asked to identify and describe students they were attached to, rejected, were indifferent to, or were concerned about. They tended to be attached to bright and obedient students, to reject those who were "defiant and aggressive," to be indifferent to those who were unattractive and introverted, and to be concerned about those who had learning problems but behaved. More non-white girls than white were in the "indifferent" category; more non-white boys than white were "rejected."

Race, gender, and age differences were also clear in Irvine's (1990) classroom interaction study. For African-American females her research found "an active, interacting, and initiating profile in the early grades" (p. 74), although they were more likely than other groups to be ignored by teachers and to be rebuffed by them when seeking attention. In the upper grades, they "received significantly less total teacher feedback, less positive feedback and fewer public response opportunities" than any other race or gender (p. 74). We think about Shannon as fitting the profile of an initiator, of actively seeking attention. She got this attention from each of her teachers, and it seemed critical to her increased school success. Interestingly, it was usually on a one-to-one basis, often beyond school time with Betty, Susan, Judy, and Ms. Hurston. We wonder now, was she interacted with less in class?

Black males in lower elementary, Irvine found, were less likely to interact with the teacher, more likely to have nonacademic interactions with peers, more likely to use a cooperative learning style, more likely to receive controlling statements and qualified praise, more likely to be labeled deviant and described negatively, less likely to receive positive feedback. In upper elementary, they were more likely to be in the lowest academic track (including special education), isolated socially and academically from white students, and judged inaccurately by teachers (Irvine, 1990, pp. 77–78).

Reading each year's report of Joseph, Jeremiah, Reggie, Ricky, and Lee, one can see evidence at one time or another of many of Irvine's findings. The perception of all the boys as mild to severe discipline problems by one or more of their teachers often overshadowed academic strengths as well as needs. These perceptions can, and perhaps for some of our children did, have lasting negative effects. As Irvine noted, based on her study on the stability of teacher expectations in relation to standardized test data, "teachers form stable, unchanging, and often inaccurate achievement expectations, in particular about black males. . . . It may be that teachers' expectations for black males' achievement are more influenced by their stereotypes of black males as potential disruptors than by their academic ability" (p. 77).

As a lens for our own data, we have considered institutional racism and teacher attitudes and expectations in general terms rather than specific because it was never the intent of this research to analyze teachers; rather, we have focused on the children. However, we cannot ignore the probability that these factors affected our children. Neither can we determine if they were active or passive, intentional or unrecognized, in ourselves or in others. What we can do, as educators, is raise the issues, to look at the effects of policy on African-American children, to examine our own attitudes and expectations. We can also examine our educational practice in light of research and theory on how African-American children learn most effectively, as we do in the next section.

Recommended educational practice

There is a growing body of research on educating, as opposed to training (Kunjufu, 1984) African-American children. While African-American educators are not always in agreement on specifics, there is strong consensus on several foundations of learning.

Some African-American educators are calling for an Afrocentric curriculum. Jacqueline Irvine (1990) points to Janice Hale-Benson, A. Wade Boykin, the National Alliance of Black School Educators, David Houlton, Godfrey L. Brandt, and Wilma S. Longstreet as educators who adopt this perspective (her book has an excellent review of research on effective strategies). Hale-Benson (1986) suggests strategies such as storytelling, frequent hugging, frequent physical movement in both play and learning activities, group rather than individual learning, and specific elements of African-American cultures. Boykin's (1986) recommendations for cultural learning styles include stimulating, sensory activities involving physical movement and a "noisy" classroom. The NABSE (1984) advocates the teaching of critical thinking, creativity, and problem solving. These abilities are rarely emphasized in an isolated skills curriculum, in low reading groups (Allington, 1983), or in remedial classes (McGill-Franzen & Allington, 1990).

Brandt (1986) recommends the elimination of didactic and individual approaches to instruction in favor of collaborative, group-centered learning, and that teachers directly address racism in classrooms. Further support for socially interactive classes is offered by Houlton (1986): Give children many opportunities to talk freely, to learn collaboratively, and to incorporate their out-of-school experiences into the classroom. We believe our whole language philosophy provided such opportunities.

This valuing of *community* is espoused by many leaders of the African-American community. Maulana Karenga in *The Theory of Kawaide* (cited in Kunjufu, 1986) outlines the principles honored during Kwanzaa. The emphasis on children working together and learning from each other, delineated by so many African-American educators, corresponds to two of these principles. They are *Umoja* (Unity: "To strive for and maintain unity in the family, community, nation, and race. Community means staying together"), and *Ujima* (Collective Work and Responsibility: "To build and maintain our community together and make our sisters' and brothers' problems our problems, and to solve them together. Ujima means working together and helping each other" (Porter, 1991, p. 54).

When we examine the current study in light of these recommendations, we find both congruence and discord. Hale-Benson makes a strong and detailed argument for an African-American cultural and historical base for curriculum and, ideally, for teachers who "share the culture of the children" (p. 167). Only two teachers in our study were African American. One, Shannon's fourth-grade teacher, included elements of an Afrocentric curriculum in her study of famous African Americans; children often memorized their poems and sayings.

The main curricular component in our own classrooms that was specific to the needs of African-American children was our emphasis on African-American authors and illustrators in classroom libraries and read-aloud selections. We did not provide an Afrocentric curriculum. However, in discussing model teaching strategies, Hale-Benson (1986) and others recommended two commonly accepted whole language principles that were integral to our classrooms:

1. "Equal talking time" for children, where they talk "conversationally, in recitation, and creatively" (Hale-Benson, 1986, p. 165). In our classrooms children talked about their writing, read it, talked about books and read them to peers, and discussed various aspects of curriculum throughout each and every day.
2. "Group learning" that includes heterogeneous groups ("family style") that rotate frequently. Our classrooms were not ability grouped for instruction, consisting rather of many student-formed and occasional teacher-formed dyads and groups.

While we believe in these principles and have learned each year more effective ways of insuring them, they did not seem to be beliefs held by some of the children's other teachers. Interviews with subsequent teachers alluded to ability grouping for reading instruction, to "doing your own work," and to valuing quiet over conversation.

Irvine (1990) makes overall recommendations based on her scholarly review:

> In summary, strategies for improving the school achievement of black students should involve interventions directed at (1) decreasing the cultural discontinuity by attending to students' learning styles, their values, language, and history, as well as the many resources in the home and the community; (2) increasing teacher expectations by effective instruction in schools administered by effective school leaders and eliminating rigid and inflexible ability groups and tracks; and (3) helping parents and relatives to assist and reinforce school learning. (1990, p. 114)

The literature on education for African-American children converges on important points (ones we would argue are essential elements for most children) of social interaction and learning through active involvement. Yet Goodlad's (1984) *A Place Called School* documents that passive routine predominates—children were expected to be doing seatwork or listening to the teacher most of the time; students rarely moved around or interacted with peers or the teacher. Irvine (1990) speculates, and Kozol (1991) corroborates, that "if this scenario is descriptive of the majority of our schools, then it seems fair to speculate that this dismal situation is intensified in schools that serve black children. In these schools, the overwhelming preoccupation seems to be with control—particularly controlling the physical movement and anticipated and perceived aggression of black male children" (p. 91).

Educational philosophies may vary by grade level. As we talked with teachers in the intermediate grades, we began to hear concern about preparing students for middle school, and an increased emphasis on learning from texts (e.g., science or social studies). In examining instruction across grades, Morgan (1980) found:

> When Blacks enter first grade, the stories they create express positive feelings about themselves in the schooling situation, but by the fifth grade, the overall feeling expressed by students is that of criticism. . . . Primary grades presented a more nurturing environment than intermediate or upper grades. In early childhood education, much of the activity is child-teacher centered with a great deal of interaction between children. The classroom environment in the upper grades is transformed from a socially interactive style to competitive individualistic and minimally socially interactive style of learning.

If the educational community is aware of these repeated, converging recommendations for African-American children, why haven't they been implemented? According to Irvine (1990) "School personnel have not been willing to pilot these strategies, preferring instead basic instructional technique of drill and practice, mastery learning, and the performance-based curriculum" (p. 90). The grassroots whole language teaching movement has grown in reaction to these same stunting practices. Whole language educators are rejecting packaged curriculum and decontextualized language exercises in favor of a dynamic curriculum based on student interests and needs.

However, Irvine goes on to say, "Black parents have in the past been reluctant to endorse innovative curricula and instead have preferred conservative and traditional schools" (p. 90). Delpit (1988) points out that this is often the preference of African-American teachers, as well. Delpit (1991) believes that the key factor is making the code of "the culture of power" explicit to African-American children, who are often not a part of that culture. "It is vital that everyone develop a sense of personal literacy—using literacy for entertainment, to further one's own thinking, to clarify one's emotions, to share with intimates. . . . But power code literacy gives you access to the world outside of yourself. . . . I believe teachers must create learning environments that promote both" (p. 543).

In the current study, we found empirical support for the social interaction and strong sense of community recommended by African-American educators. We also believe, with Delpit, that teacher support in terms of explicit instruction is critical, *especially* for the children teachers worry about the most.

Recommendations for educators

All of our recommendations in this final section are data based, although in different ways. In some cases we have documented the positive effects of certain actions, and recommend them on that basis. In others we have documented the deleterious effects of certain actions/systems, and recommend alternatives that we postulate would be more positive.

1. *Make clear your beliefs.* Routman (1989) emphasizs the importance of individual teachers knowing themselves through a process of defining beliefs and goals. Ideally, a whole school can work together through a series of meetings, sharing readings, debating principles, and formulating a Beliefs Statement. The ongoing process is as important as the product. The statement itself will be strongest if it is (1) grounded in the best available theory and classroom-based research, (2) a dynamic document that is revised regularly, and (3) a touchstone for decision making.
2. *Learn from children.* Listen to them talk about their literacy learning, perhaps through regularly scheduled interviews. Observe them in various settings, including independent and group, your classroom and others they may go to. Examine both processes and products over time, preferably with other educators. *Record* (write down or tape record) and compare responses, observations, and products over time to learn about your own teaching as well as students' insights and growth.
3. *Learn together.* Form a team, with as few as two or as many as can work together effectively. Figure out a time to meet regularly. We often got together outside of school time (often for meals, something we really looked forward to), but we also held regular school time meetings, making use of planning times and a substitute. Agree on individual responsibilities for each meeting, e.g., sharing a teaching journal entry, interviewing students, or reviewing a pertinent article.

   Engage in a school self-study (see Mitchell, 1989, for an example). As teachers talk together about reducing risks, they often discover solutions to dilemmas that seem hopeless to an individual. When we make the commitment to take on the "others," people or policies that seem to be dictating risk-making decisions, teachers make changes. In some places teachers have increased stability by keeping the same children for more than one year, increased the likelihood of literary engagement by spending basal workbook money on classroom libraries, and increased their own efficacy by self-governance. Maybe even a situation that seems out of our control, such as a child moving from school to school, could be solved creatively.
4. *Include all children in the literate community.* Start the first day of school, and protect the time your community has together. Resource teachers and homeroom classroom teachers can work together to determine what is in the child's best interest in terms of where help will be offered, how much time is needed, and how schedules can be arranged. Think in terms of diminishing services as the child makes progress, and involve the student in this decision-making process. Teach children who are not yet integral

community members how to be both contributing and accepting, both teachers and learners.

5. *Establish time and choice as inalienable rights* (Hansen, 1987). For meaningful choice of reading materials (and models of fine writing), we are continuously building extensive classroom libraries of *quality, multicultural children's literature*. Work closely with media specialists to make the school media center an extension of the classroom, readily accessible to all students. If we have to cut something in the day (and we always do!), it isn't the children's time to read books of their own choice, our time to read to them, or their time to write on topics and in modes of their own choosing.

   Time and choice are also vital to teaching faculties. The current strength of teachers' voices in shared decision making goes hand in hand with the kinds of decisions that increase engagement, community, and stability. Teachers need regular times within their work days to talk with each other about students, to plan curriculum, and to implement change.[7] Their professional choices must be honored at building, district, state, and national levels.
6. *Match high student input with high teacher input* (Calkins, 1986; Delpit, 1986). Nowhere is the need for skilled, insightful teaching greater than in whole language classrooms. This teaching demands a professional orchestration of knowledge about each individual student and strategies (Routman, 1991) that empower the learner. Teachers have a responsibility to make the code of power explicit (Delpit, 1991). We grow every teaching day in our understanding of how writers and readers develop on many planes, how language works, and how to help children develop these understandings. This professional development occurs through reading what other teachers are doing, studying children, talking with peers, attending conferences, and engaging in and examining our own literacy (Graves, 1990).
7. *Expect meaningful development from each student.* This has nothing to do with standardized norms, but rather with individual human potential. We are still learning how to work together with students in recording and evaluating their growth, using written observations, interviews, running records, writing samples, etc. The memory we hope each reader takes away from *Engaging Children* is of individual children who engaged in literacy in ways some thought beyond their abilities, an image of Lee reading—really reading—to his first-grade teacher, or Jeremiah learning to write plays with his friends, or Shannon writing her life.

---

7. Some schools have done this by scheduling teacher planning periods so that certain groups (e.g., grade levels, cross-grade teams) have the same time available; one or more days a week are then spent in group planning. At our school, a group of six teachers developed a rotational plan where two teachers dispersed their students for two hours to the remaining four for *planned* cross-grade learning activities, allowing the two teachers extended planning time. We have also hired substitutes for half- or full-day planning team meetings.

More research is needed for all of these recommendations that yields child-centered, specific information in various grades and subject areas, in various cultural and community settings. No single recommendation is likely to be sufficient for success; as we have shown, educational systems are amazingly complex, where even two "good" actions can clash (e.g., a school district's commitment to racially balanced schools versus children's need for stability). Maybe one teacher can't make all the difference. But teachers *can* make a difference, a lasting difference, for the children we worry about the most.

APPENDIX A

Data Collection and Analysis Procedures

Data Collection

JoBeth observed one day a week in each collaborative research classroom; her usual observations were during reading and writing workshop times. Betty and Barbara kept teaching journals in which they recorded information about the children we were studying. The whole research team read *Ways of Studying Children*, by Almy and Genishi (1979), and tried to apply their guidelines of observing, asking children about themselves, studying children in their groups, studying children through others, and assessing development.

From our discussions of these initial observations we decided on several other valuable sources of data. Almy and Genishi stress getting the child's own perspective; we did not feel our observations were providing enough of the children's reflection on their learning processes. Individual teachers constructed questionnaires or conducted informal interviews throughout the year. After talking with Jane Hansen, JoBeth adapted the questions Hansen and Graves were using in their evaluation study (see Hansen, 1989), and we *interviewed* the children four times during the year about what they were learning as readers and writers. Our adapted questions (with usual prompts) were the following:

- What are you learning to do in reading?
- How are you learning it? (who is helping you?)
- What would you like to learn to do next as a reader?
- How do you think you will learn it? (will anyone help you?)
- What kinds of things will you need to read or want to read when you are a grown-up? (for your job?)

The questions were repeated for writing.

Teachers saved as much as possible of the *written work* children produced (with some children some years this proved to be very difficult). Each child had a writing folder, and there were many other opportunities for written products.

Reading records included notes on books the children read and, beginning the second year, tapes of each child reading a basal selection and/or a passage from a trade book and telling about the passage. These readings were analyzed for miscue patterns and for comprehension through a retelling and discussion between the child and JoBeth.

Informal interviews were also conducted with other members of the child's world. Betty and JoBeth made home visits with the three focal children during spring parent-teacher conferences the first year. Barbara talked with the director of the Boys Club. We talked with teachers who had these students in art, music, PE, and library. JoBeth attended special/remedial classes with each child receiving services and discussed the child with the Chapter 1 or special education teacher.

Perhaps the most serendipitous data source was the *pen pal letters*. JoBeth's undergraduate classes each quarter corresponded with a child from each research classroom. All letters were saved, along with the analyses written by the preparatory teachers. Their analyses were based on one or two visits with the child (usually in the format of a reading and/or writing conference) and on the form and content of the letters.

In an attempt to provide a more complete context for readers, we also recorded and reflected on our evolving whole language teaching practices. Betty and Barbara consulted their lesson plans. JoBeth recorded "*a day in the life of*" each classroom. For these days, her observations focused on the teacher in interaction with the children, rather than on the focal children in interaction with everyone else. The teachers used these notes, in combination with their teaching journals and JoBeth's weekly field notes, to write descriptions of their teaching journeys (Chapters 2 and 3).

A final data source was the *research journal* JoBeth kept, which served as a record of decision points (Alvermann, 1988) about the research.

Data Analysis

There were three overlapping phases of data analysis. First, each collaborative team (Shockley/Allen and Michalove/Allen) met from thirty to sixty minutes weekly to discuss teaching journals, observational notes, and other data sources. During these weekly conferences, which JoBeth recorded in her field notes, many issues for individual children became evident.

Second, the research team as a whole met at least once, and often twice, a month during the first year. Our early meetings focused on data collection strategies. At times we brought our data with us and spent the two-hour session reading, making analytic notes, and sharing these observations. Other sessions, we shared research narratives in either written or oral form.

Third, we worked together for three weeks each summer. Before meeting together we studied case study analysis and read exemplary cases. We studied data analysis procedures, especially those for multiple case studies, recommended by other qualitative researchers (Goetz & LeCompte, 1984; Patton, 1980; Strauss, 1987; Yin, 1984). We read interesting cases of other teachers and learners by Allen and Carr (1989), Avery (1987) Bissex and Bullock (1987), Hansen (1989), Kirby (1985), Paley (1981), Perl and Wilson (1986), and Safter (1983). The research consultant for the project, Judith Preissle Goetz, met with us early the first summer to respond to the many questions generated from these readings. She suggested the following sequence of data analysis:

1. Initial reading: read transcripts and other data sources straight through for each child [Michelle Garrett, our research assistant, had color coded all transcripts by child]; write down notes, issues, possible themes, and categories.
2. Focused reading: re-read to develop themes.

3. Focused reading: re-read in context of theoretical frame developed by research team.
4. Focused reading: re-read for disconfirmation and negative cases.

We heeded Judith Green's (personal consultation, 1989) advice in thinking about each child, as a member of his/her classroom, in terms of norms and expectations, roles and relationships, and rights and obligations. We felt these were particularly important descriptors since such issues as teacher expectations for students, student roles in peer groups, and student rights and obligations are considerably different in many whole language classrooms than in many textbook-driven classrooms (Edelsky, Draper, & Smith, 1983).

It is difficult in qualitative data analysis to decide what is important. If we had just looked across the data at common themes, or at predetermined themes, we might have lost the children as individuals. We wanted, like Robert Coles in *The Call of Stories* (1989), to tell each child's story in a true and insightful manner. We wanted each child, through the data, to speak for himself or herself. Alexander (1990) identifies this as a "personological stance . . . with the intent of understanding as much as one could about the way in which another human being experienced the world" (p. 7). He identified nine "principal identifiers of salience," several of which we used (although we did not read his work until the final phase of our analysis):

- Primacy—what is the first thing a child says about him/herself, or the first thing others say about him/her, such as Ricky's teachers referring first to him as a sweet/loving child.
- Frequency—what is said or observed most often, such as the constant reference to Jeremiah as pouting and whining.
- Uniqueness—a key event that seems to be a point of departure or change, like when Ricky's friends "forced" him to read with them.
- Emphasis—a point a child or teacher accents in interviews, such as "Shannon is *such* a hard worker."
- Omission—what is missing, either in what is said about a child or what is observed, as when Jeremiah never talked or wrote about his family.
- Error or Distortion—a discrepency, intentional or unintentional, between data sources, as in Ms. Gilcrest's estimation of Ricky's reading ability and his actual oral reading.

Some of the transcript readings were done independently; some were done as collaborative teams using parallel sets of transcripts and other data. Simultaneously, we were analyzing through writing. Based on Patton's (1980) recommendation, each teacher wrote a case record of each focal child that was a narrative, chronological "story" of that child's year as we knew it, but without analytic or editorial comment.

During the second summer we were joined by the two teachers who taught four of our six children in third-grade: first Susan Willis, then Judy Smith. We did not go back to the first year's analysis; rather we analyzed for each child individually in terms of major issues for Year 2. Then during the final intensive analysis during the third summer, we used the following strategy:

1. We examined major issues identified for each child in Year 1.
2. We compared the major issues identified in Year 2, categorizing our findings as
   a. major issues reconfirmed
   b. shifting issues
   c. new issues
3. Using these categories as working hypotheses, we reanalyzed the data for both confirming and disconfirming evidence.
4. We organized the text to include the basic elements of a case study report, according to Lincoln & Guba (1985).

For the third year, the data were limited and we treated them in a very different way. Since we were not in the classrooms of Jeremiah, Shannon, Reggie, or Ricky at all, and were only in Joseph's briefly, we created a monologue of what each child's teacher had to say about him or her based on periodic teacher interviews. JoBeth conducted most of these interviews after school hours in the teachers' classrooms; others were conducted informally by phone calls with Betty, Barbara, or JoBeth. One teacher (Ms. Gilcrest) allowed end-of-school student interviews for Ricky and Jeremiah. Kay Hales and Margie Weiderhold wanted to collaborate in studying the effects of whole language instruction on the children we had been studying. Lee was interviewed three times and observed by JoBeth for a full day every four to six weeks.

We did not feel it was appropriate to analyze information from teachers at other schools, since these teachers were not collaborators in the study (although each was invited to participate to whatever degree desired) and since we had very limited contextual information. Therefore, we wrote a first-person reflection from each teacher's words; we took out our own questions and responses from the dialogue, moved related statements together, and revised conversational dialogue to create a cohesive narrative. (This process was subjective, as are all research processes, and we recognize that our biases influenced what we chose to include from the interviews and how we chose to arrange it, although we tried very hard to represent the teachers' intent.)

Perhaps the deepest levels of analysis have come during the process of writing and revising. We have met numerous times to read and comment on drafts of each other's work. Creating the profiles that begin each section (e.g., "Joseph in His Own Voice") provided tremendous insights (Michalove & Allen, 1990). Readers should know that we have *created* a narrative from these interviews, taking out our questions and making sentences out of what were often fragmented responses (our method of interviewing is discussed more fully under "Data Collection" at the beginning of this appendix).

APPENDIX B

Teacher and Writer Flow Chart

	Year 1	**Year 2**	**Year 3**
Original 1st Graders			
Joseph	**T**: Shockley	**T**: Michalove	**T**: Wiederhold, Bradley* (unknown) Weiderhold
	W: Shockley	**W**: Michalove	**W**: Allen
Jeremiah	**T**: Shockley	**T**: Michalove	**T**: Gilcrest*
	W: Shockley	**W**: Michalove	**W**: Allen
Shannon	**T**: Shockley	**T**: Willis/Smith*	**T**: Hurston*
	W: Shockley	**W**: Allen	**W**: Allen
Original 2nd Graders			
Ricky	**T**: Michalove	**T**: Willis/Smith	**T**: Gilcrest*
	W: Michalove	**W**: Allen	**W**: Allen
Reggie	**T**: Michalove	**T**: Willis/Smith	**T**: Walker*
	W: Michalove	**W**: Allen	**W**: Allen
Lee	**T**: Michalove	**T**: Willis/Smith	**T**: Hales
	W: Michalove	**W**: Allen	**W**: Allen

*Teachers who chose to use pseudonyms
T (teacher)
W (writer)

REFERENCES

Alexander, I. (1990). *Personology*. Durham, NC: Duke University Press.

Allen, J. (1989). Risk makers, risk takers, risk breakers. In J. Allen & J. Mason (Eds.), *Risk makers, risk takers, risk breakers*. Portsmouth, NH: Heinemann.

Allen, J., & Carr, E. (1989). Collaborative learning among kindergarten writers: James learns how to learn at school. In J. Allen & J. Mason (Eds.), *Risk makers, risk takers, risk breakers*. Portsmouth, NH: Heinemann.

Allen, J., Combs, J., Hendricks, M., Nash, P., & Wilson, S. (1988). Studying change: Teachers who become researchers. *Language Arts*, *65*(4), 379–387.

Allen, J., Michalove, B., Shockley, B., & West, M. (1991). "I'm really worried about Joseph": Reducing the risks of literacy learning. *The Reading Teacher*, *44*(7), 458–472.

Allen, L., & Glickman, C. (1992). School improvement: The elusive faces of shared governance. *NASSP Bulletin*, *76*(542), 80–87.

Allington, R. (1983). The reading instruction provided readers of differing ability. *Elementary School Journal*, *83*, 255–265.

Almy, M., & Genishi, C. (1979). *Ways of studying children*. New York: Teachers College Press.

Alvermann, D. (1988). *Data reduction and data display: Decisions facing the qualitative researcher*. Paper presented at Qualitative Research in Education Conference, Athens GA.

Atwell, N. (1987). *In the middle*. Portsmouth, NH: Heinemann.

Avery, C. (1987). Traci: A learning disabled child in a writing-process classroom. In G. Bissex & R. Bullock (Eds.), *Seeing for ourselves: Case-study research by teachers of writing*. Portsmouth, NH: Heinemann.

Bateson, M. C. (1989). *Composing a life*. New York: Penguin.

Berrueta-Clement, J. W, Schwienhart, L. H., Barnett, W. S., Epstein, A. S., & Weikart, D. P. (1984). *Changed lives: The effects of the Perry Preschool Program on youths through age 19*. Ypsilanti, MI: The High/Scope Educational Research Foundation.

Best, R. (1983). *We've all got scars: What boys and girls learn in elementary school*. Bloomington, IN: Indiana University Press.

Bissex, G. (1980). *Gyns at work*. Cambridge, MA: Harvard University Press.

Bissex, G., & Bullock, R. (1987). *Seeing for ourselves: Case-study research by teachers of writing*. Portsmouth, NH: Heinemann.

Bond, G. L., & Dykstra, R. (1967). The cooperative research program in first-grade reading instruction. *Reading Research Quarterly*, *II*(4), 5–142.

Boykin, A. W. (1986). The triple quandary and the schooling of Afro-American children. In U. Neisser (Ed.), *The school achievement of minority children* (pp. 57-92). Hillsdale, NJ: Lawrence Erlbaum.

Brandt, G. L. (1986). *The realization of anti-racist teaching*. London: Taylor & Francis.

Bronfenbrenner, U. (1979). *The ecology of human development*. Cambridge, MA: Harvard University Press.

Bussis, A., Chittendon, C., Amarel, M., & Klausner, E. (1985). *Inquiry into meaning*. Hillsdale, NJ: Lawrence Erlbaum.

Butler, A., & Turbill, J. (1984). *Towards a reading-writing classroom*. Portsmouth, NH: Heinemann.

Calkins, L. (1986). *The art of teaching writing*. Portsmouth, NH: Heinemann.

Calkins, L. (1991). *Living between the lines*. Portsmouth, NH: Heinemann.

Cambourne, B. (1988) *The whole story: Natural learning and the acquisition of literacy in the classroom*. New York: Scholastic.

Carr, E., & Allen, J. (1988). University/classroom teacher collaboration: Costs, benefits, and mutual respect. In J. Goetz & J. Allen (Eds.), *Qualitative Research in Education*. Athens, GA: University of Georgia, College of Education.

Carter, F. (1976). *The education of Little Tree*. New York: Delacorte.

Clark, R. (1983). *Family life and school achievement: Why poor black children succeed or fail*. Chicago: University of Chicago Press.

Clay, M. (1975). *What did I write?* Portsmouth, NH: Heinemann.

Clay, M. (1979, 1985). *The early detection of reading difficulties*. Portsmouth, NH: Heinemann.

Cleary, B. (1988). *A girl from Yamhill: A memoir*. New York: Morrow.

Coles, R. (1989). *The call of stories*. Boston: Houghton Mifflin

Delpit, L. (1986). Skills and other dilemmas of a progressive black educator. *Harvard Educational Review*, *56*, 379–385.

Delpit, L. (1988). The silenced dialogue: Power and pedagogy in educating other people's children. *Harvard Educational Review*, *58*, 280–298.

Delpit, L. (1991). A conversation with Lisa Delpit. *Language Arts*, *68*, 541–547.

Dusek, J.B. (ed), (1985). *Teacher expectancies*. Hillsdale, NJ: Lawrence Erlbaum.

Edelsky, C., Draper, K., & Smith, K. (1983). Hooken' 'em in at the start of school in a "whole language" classroom. *Anthropology and Education Quarterly*, *14*, 257–281.

Erickson, F. (1984). What makes school ethnography ethnographic? *Anthropology and Education Quarterly*, *15*, 51–66.

Fine, G. A., & Sandstrom, K. L. (1988). *Knowing children: Participant observation with minors*. Newbury Park, CA: Sage Publications.

Finn, J. (1989). Withdrawing from school. *Review of Educational Research*. *59*(2), 117–142.

Fueyo, J. (1989). One child moves into meaning—his way. *Language Arts*, *66*(2), 137–146.

Gibney, S. (1988). *An ethnographic case study of a school-based staff development process*. Unpublished doctoral dissertation, University of Georgia.

Goetz, J. P., & LeCompte, M. D. (1984). *Ethnographic and qualitative design in educational research*. San Diego, CA: Academic Press.

Goldenberg, C. (1989). Making success a more common occurrence for children at risk for failure: Lessons from Hispanic first graders learning to read. In J. Allen & J. Mason (Eds.), *Risk makers, risk takers, risk breakers*. Portsmouth, NH: Heinemann.

Goodlad, J. (1984). *A place called school*. New York: McGraw-Hill.

Goodman, Y. (1988). Evaluation of students. In K. Goodman, Y. Goodman, & W. Hood (Eds.), *The whole language evaluation book*. Portsmouth, NH: Heinemann.

Graves, D. (1983). *Writing: Teachers and children at work*. Portsmouth, NH: Heinemann.

Graves, D. (1990). *Discover your own literacy*. Portsmouth, NH: Heinemann.

Griffith-Roberts, C. (1991, September). The South in print. *Southern Living Magazine*, 137–138.

Hale-Benson, J. (1986). *Black children: Their roots, culture, and learning styles* (2nd ed.). Baltimore: Johns Hopkins University Press.

Hansen, J. (1987). *When writers read*. Portsmouth, NH: Heinemann.

Hansen, J. (1989). Anna evaluates herself. In J. Allen & J. Mason (Eds.), *Risk makers, risk takers, risk breakers*. Portsmouth, NH: Heinemann.

Hillocks, G. (1986). *Research on written composition*. Urbana, IL: National Council of Teachers of English.

Holdaway, D. (1979). *Foundations of literacy*. Portsmouth, NH: Heinemann.

Holdaway, D. (1984). *Stability and change in literacy learning*. Portsmouth, NH: Heinemann.

Holmes, C. T., & Matthews, K. M. (1984). The effects of nonpromotion on elementary and junior high school pupils: A meta-analysis. *Review of Educational Research*, *54*(2), 225–236.

Houlton, D. (1986). *Cultural diversity in the primary school*. London: BT Balsford.

Hurston, Z. N. (1937; 1978). *Their eyes were watching God*. Urbana, IL: University of Illinois Press.

Irvine, J. J. (1990). *Black students and school failure: Policies, practices, and prescriptions*. New York: Greenwood.

Jackson, R. (1988). *Adults with nonverbal learning disabilities and their roles in achieving independence: A qualitative study*. Unpublished doctoral dissertation, University of Georgia.

Kedar-Voivoda, G. (1983). The impact of elementary children's school roles and sex roles on teacher attitudes: An interactional analysis. *Review of Educational Research*, *53*, 415–437.

Kidder, T. (1989). *Among schoolchildren*. Boston: Houghton Mifflin.

Kirby, K. (1985). *Reading and writing processes of selected high-risk college freshmen*. Unpublished doctoral dissertation, University of Georgia.

Kozol, J. (1991). *Savage inequalities*. New York: Crown.

Kotlowitz, A. (1991). *There are no children here*. New York: Doubleday.

Kunjufu, J. (1984). *Countering the conspiracy to destroy black boys*. Chicago: Afro-Am Publishing.

Kunjufu, J. (1986). *Motivating and preparing black youth to work*. Chicago: African American Images.

Lightfoot, S.L. (1978). *Worlds apart: Relationships between families and schools*. New York: Basic Books.

Lightfoot, S. L. (1983). *The good high school: Portraits of character and culture*. New York: Basic Books.

Lincoln, Y., & Guba, E. (1985). *Naturalistic inquiry*. Beverly Hills, CA: Sage.

McGee, L., & Lomax, R. (1990). On combining apples and oranges: A response to Stahl and Miller. *Review of Educational Research*, *60*(1), 133–140.

McGill-Franzen, A., & Allington, R. (1990). Comprehension and coherence: Neglected elements of literacy instruction in remedial and resource room services. *Reading, Writing, and Learning Disabilities*, *6*, 149–181.

Michalove, B. & Allen, J. (1990, December) *Talking with the children we worry about: Lessons from interviewing children*. Paper presented at the National Reading Conference, Miami Beach: FL.

Mitchell, B. (1989). Emergent literacy and the transformation of schools, families, and communities: A policy agenda. In J. Allen & J. Mason (Eds.), *Risk makers, risk takers, risk breakers* (pp. 295–313). Portsmouth, NH: Heinemann.

Morgan, H. (1980, January–February). How schools fail black children. *Social Policy*, 49–54.

Morrison, T. (1984). *The bluest eye*. New York: New American Library.

National Alliance of Black School Educators, (1984). *Saving the African American child*. Washington, DC: NABSE.

Ogbu, J. (1988). Literacy and schooling in subordinate cultures: The case of black Americans. In B. Kintgen, B. Kroll, & M. Rose (Eds.), *Perspectives on literacy* (pp. 227–242). Carbondale, IL: Southern Illinois University Press.

O'Sullivan, P., Ysseldyke, J., Christenson, S., & Thurlow, M. (1990). Mildly handicapped elementary students' opportunity to learn during reading instruction in mainstream and special education settings. *Reading Research Quarterly, XXV* (2), 131–146.

Paley, V. G. (1990). *The boy who would be a helicopter*. Cambridge, MA: Harvard University Press.

Paley, V. G. (1981). *Wally's stories*. Cambridge, MA: Harvard University Press.

Patton, M. C. (1980). *Qualitative evaluation methods*. Newbury Park, CA: Sage Publications.

Perl, S., & Wilson, N. (1986). *Through teachers' eyes: Portraits of writing teachers at work*. Portsmouth, NH: Heinemann.

Pilcher, R. (1987) *The shell seekers*. New York: St. Martin Press.

Porter, A. P. (1991). *Kwanzaa*. Minneapolis, MN: Carolrhoda Books.

Reyes, M. de la Luz. (1991). A process approach to literacy using dialogue journals and literature logs with second language learners. *Research in the Teaching of English, 25*(3), 291–313.

Rist, R. (1973). *The urban school: A factory for failure*. Cambridge, MA: MIT Press.

Routman, R. (1989). *Transitions*. Portsmouth, NH: Heinemann.

Routman, R. (1991). *Invitations*. Portsmouth, NH: Heinemann.

Safter, H. (1983). *A phenomenological case study of highly gifted and creative adolescents*. Unpublished doctoral dissertation, University of Georgia.

Seidman, I. E. (1991). *Interviewing as qualitative research*. New York: Teachers College Press.

Shepard, L., & Smith, M. (1989). *Flunking grades: Research and policies on retention*. Philadelphia, PA: Falmer Press.

Shockley, B., & Allen, J. (1990). A classroom story: Texts and contexts for literacy connections. In T. Shanahan (Ed.), *Reading and writing together: New perspectives for the classroom*. Norwood, MA: Christopher-Gordon.

Smith, F. (1988a). *Joining the literacy club*. Portsmouth, NH: Heinemann.

Smith, F. (1988b) *Understanding Reading* (4th ed.). Hillsdale, NJ: Lawrence Erlbaum.

Smith, F. (1992). Learning to read: The never ending debate. *Phi Delta Kappan, 73* (6), 432–441.

Strauss, A. L. (1987). *Qualitative analysis for social scientists*. Cambridge, MA: Cambridge University Press.

Sulzby, E. (1985). Children's emergent reading of favorite storybooks: A developmental study. *Reading Research Quarterly, 20*(4), 458–481.

Temple, C., Nathan, R., Burris, N., & Temple, F. (1988). *The beginnings of writing* (2nd ed.). Newton, MA: Allyn & Bacon.

Walker, H., & Sylvester, R. (1991). Where is school along the path to prison? *Educational Leadership, 49* (1), 14–16.

Wright, L. (1991). *An investigation of psychosocial variables related to academic success achievement among fourth and fifth grade African American males*. Unpublished doctoral dissertation, Texas A & M.

Yin, R. (1984). *Case study research: Design and methods*. Newbury Park, CA: Sage Publications.

CHILDREN'S LITERATURE AND TEXTBOOKS

Ahlberg, J. (1986). *The jolly postman, or other people's letters*. Boston: Little, Brown.

Ahlberg, J., & Ahlberg, A. (1981). *Funnybones*. New York: Scholastic.

Ahlberg, J., & Ahlberg, A. (1978). *Each peach pear plum*. New York: Scholastic.

Allard, H. (1977). *Miss Nelson is missing!* Boston: Houghton Mifflin.

Alley, R. (1981). *The ghost in Dobbs Diner*. New York: Parents Magazine Press.

Bell, A. (1968). Adaptation of Hans Christian Andersen's *The little mermaid*. New York: Scholastic.

Bennett, J. (1989). *Teeny tiny*. Boston: Houghton Mifflin.

Blaine, M. (1982). *The terrible thing that happened at our house*. New York: Parents' Magazine Press.

Blake, O. (1979). *The mystery of the lost pearl.* Mahwah, NJ: Troll.

Blegvad, L. (1985). *Anna banana and me*. New York: Macmillan.

Blume, J. (1971). *Freckle juice*. New York: Four Winds.

Brown, M. (1980). *Arthur's valentine*. Boston: Little, Brown.

Brown, M. (1954). *Cinderella*. New York: Scribner.

Brown, M. W. (1947). *Goodnight moon*. New York: Harper.

Brown, M. W. (1946). *The little island*. Garden City, NY: Doubleday.

Byars, B. (1988). *The burning questions of Bingo Brown*. New York: Viking.

Cameron, A. (1981). *The stories Julian tells*. New York: Random House.

Campbell, R. (1982). *Dear Zoo*. New York: Four Winds.

Carbonali, J. L. (1986). *A day to forget (basal)*. Boston: Houghton Mifflin.

Cleary, B. (1975). Ramona the brave. New York: Morrow.

Clymer, E. (1987). *Trolley car family*. New York: Scholastic.

Cole, J. (1987). *The magic schoolbus: Inside the earth*. New York: Scholastic.

Collodi, C. (retold by J. Riordan, 1988) *Pinocchio*. Oxford University Press.

Crews, D. (1986). *Ten black dots*. New York: Greenwillow.

Daniels, P. (1980). *Aladdin and the magic lamp*. Milwaukee: Raintree.

Durr, W. (1986). Houghton Mifflin basal series, including *Adventures*, *Bells*, *Caravans*, *Carousels, Discoveries, Drums, Flights, Journeys, Parades, Trumpets.* Boston: Houghton Mifflin.

Faucher, E. (1989). *Honey I shrunk the kids*. New York: Scholastic.

Fleischman, S. (1986). *The whipping boy*. New York: Greenwillow.

Galdone, P. (1970). *The three little pigs*. New York: Seabury.

Geisel, T. S. (1961). *Ten apples up on top*. New York: Random House.

Greene, W. (1953). *Lady and the tramp*. New York: Simon & Schuster.

Harshman, T. W. (1988). *Porcupine's pajama party*. New York: Harper.

Hill, R. (1986). *Spot goes to the circus*. New York: Putnam.

Hoban, L. (1982). *Arthur's pen pal*. New York: Harper.

Hoff, S. (1975). *Barkley*. New York: Harper.

Hoff, S. (1958). *Danny and the dinosaur*. New York: Harper.

Hooker, Y. (1983). *Splish, splash!* New York: Putnam.

Howe, J. (1979). *Bunnicula: A rabbit tale of mystery*. New York: Atheneum.

Howe, J. (1983). *The celery stalks at midnight*. New York: Atheneum.

Hutchins, P. (1986). *The doorbell rang*. New York: Greenwillow.

Jeschke, S. (1980). *Perfect, the pig*. New York: Holt, Rinehart & Winston.

Jackson, P. (1972). *How to play better football*. New York: Crowell.

Johnson, C. (1958). *Harold and the purple crayon*. New York: Harper.

Keller, H. (1987). *Goodbye Max*. New York: Greenwillow.

Kellogg, S. (1986). *Pecos Bill: A tall tale*. New York: Morrow.

Kunnas, M. (1984). *The best sports book in the whole wide world*. New York: Crown.

Kuskin, K. (1986). *The Dallas Titans get ready for bed*. New York: Harper & Row.

L'Engle, M. (1984). *The twenty-four days before Christmas*. New York: Dell.

Leslie-Melville, B. (1987). *Daisy Rothschild*. New York: Doubleday.

Lionni, L. (1983). *Cornelius: A fable*. New York: Pantheon.

Littledale, F. (1986). *The magic fish*. New York: Scholastic.

Lobel, A. (1976). *Frog and toad all year*. New York: Harper.

Lobel, A. (1982). *Ming Lo moves the mountain*. New York: Greenwillow.

MacLachlan, P. (1980). *Arthur, for the very first time*. New York: Harper.

Marshall, J. (1972). *George & Martha*. Boston: Houghton Mifflin.

Martin, B. (1970). *The king of the mountain*. New York: Holt, Rinehart & Winston.

Martin, B., Jr. (1983). *Monday Monday, I like Monday*. New York: Holt, Rinehart & Winston.

Mathis, S. B. (1975). *The hundred penny box*. New York: Viking.

Mayer, M. (1984). *Sleeping beauty*. New York: Macmillan.

McFarlan, D. (1990–91). *Guinness book of world records*. New York: Bantam.

McGovern, A. (1986). *Stone soup*. New York: Scholastic.

McKissack, P. C. (1988). *Mirandy and brother wind*. New York: Random House.

Milne, A. A. (1961). *Winnie the pooh*. New York: Dutton.

Minarik, E. H. (1957). *Little bear*. New York: Harper.

Parish, P. (1963). *Amelia Bedelia*. New York: Harper.

Olson, H.K. (1986). The princess and the prime minister. In *Discoveries*. Boston: Houghton Mifflin.

Pearson, S. (1989). *Jack and the beanstalk*. New York: Simon & Schuster.

Plume, E. (1980). *The Brementown musicians*. New York: Doubleday.

Rey, H. A. (1941). *Curious George*. Boston: Houghton Mifflin.

Ruckman, I. (1984). *Night of the twisters*. New York: Crowell.

Rylant, C. (1985). Slower than the rest. In *Every living thing*. New York: Bradbury Press.

Sabin, F. (1982). *Wonders of the forest*. Mahwah, NJ: Troll.

Sachar, L. (1978). *Sideways stories from Wayside School*. New York: Avon.

Sendak, M. (1963). *Where the wild things are*. New York: Harper.

Sendak, M. (1986). *Chicken soup with rice*. New York: Scholastic.

Seuss, Dr. (1960). *Green eggs and ham.* New York: Random House.

Silverstein, S. (1964). *The giving tree*. New York: Harcourt Brace Jovanovich.

Silverstein, S. (1981). *Light in the attic*. New York: Harcourt Brace Jovanovich.

Silverstein, S. (1974). *Where the sidewalk ends*. New York: Harper.

Smith, R. K. (1978). *Chocolate fever*. New York: Dell.

Spier, P. (1961). *The fox went out on a chilly night*. New York: Doubleday.

Vaughan, M. (1986). *Where does the wind go*? United Kingdom: Multimedia International.

Ward, L. (1952). *The biggest bear*. Boston: Houghton Mifflin.

Warner, G. (1989). *The box car children*. Niles, IL: Whitman.

Westcott, N. (1987). *Peanut butter and jelly*. New York: Dutton.

White, E. B. (1952). *Charlotte's web*. New York: Harper.

Williams, V. B., & Williams, J. (1988). *Stringbean's trip to the shining sea*. New York: Greenwillow.

Wright, B. R. (1985). *Christina's ghost*. New York: Holiday.

Yolen, J. (1986). *Commander Toad and the space pirates*. New York: Putnam.

Zoobooks, San Diego, CA: Wildlife Education Ltd.